Preface Books

A series of scholarly and critical studies of major writers intended for those needing modern and authoritative guidance through the characteristic difficulties of their work to reach an intelligent understanding and enjoyment of it.

General Editor: MAURICE HUSSEY

Available now:

A Preface to Wordsworth	JOHN PURKIS
A Preface to Milton	LOIS POTTER
A Preface to Coleridge	ALLAN GRANT
A Preface to Jane Austen	CHRISTOPHER GILLIE
A Preface to Yeats	EDWARD MALINS
A Preface to Pope	I.R.F. GORDON
A Preface to Hardy	MERRYN WILLIAMS
A Preface to Dryden	DAVID WYKES
A Preface to Spenser	HELENA SHIRE
A Preface to James Joyce	SYDNEY BOLT
A Preface to Hopkins	GRAHAM STOREY
A Preface to Donne	JAMES WINNY

In preparation:

A Preface to Conrad	CEDRIC WATTS

The melancholy and pleasant humour were in him so contempered that each gave advantage to the other, and made his Company one of the delights of Mankind. (Walton)

A Preface to Donne

James Winny

REVISED EDITION

Longman   London and New York

LONGMAN GROUP LIMITED
Longman House
Burnt Mill, Harlow, Essex
Published in the United States of America by Longman Inc., New York

First published 1970
Revised edition 1981

Library of Congress Cataloging in Publication Data
Winny, James
  A preface to Donne—Revised ed.—(Preface books).
  1. Donne, John—Criticism and interpretation
  I. Title II. Series
  821'.3   PR2248   80-40184
  ISBN 0 582 35246 0

Set in 10/11pt Baskerville
by Pearl Island Filmsetters (HK) Ltd

Printed in Hong Kong by
Sheck Wah Tong Printing Press Ltd

JAMES WINNY, Professor of English Literature at Trent University, Peterborough, Ontario, Canada, formerly taught at the universities of Cambridge and Leicester. He has edited several works by Chaucer and Renaissance writers. In addition to two books on Shakespeare, Dr Winny has published *Chaucer's Dream Poems* (Chatto and Windus, 1973).

Contents

List of illustrations

Acknowledgements

We are grateful to the following for permission to reproduce photographs:
Bodleian Library, Oxford pages 42 and 124; British Museum, pages 44, 66 and 80; Chatto and Windus, page 121 (from *English Emblem Books* by Rosemary Freeman); Crown Copyright, pages 90 (photo: Science Museum, London) and 185 (photo: Commission on Ancient and Historical Monuments in Wales); Giraudon, cover (Musée Condé, Chantilly); John A Green, Ipswich, page 30 *below*; Heinemann, page 13 (from *Life and Letters of John Donne*, 1899); A F Kersting, London, page 23; Lord Salisbury, page 109 (photo: *Country Life*); Mansell Collection, page 39; Master of the Benches, Lincoln's Inn, page 187 (photo: Longman Photo Library); Most Hon The Marquess of Lothian, page ii (photo: National Portrait Gallery, London); National Portrait Gallery, London, page 32; Syndics of Cambridge University Library, page 69; Syndics of the Fitzwilliam Museum, Cambridge, page 30 *above*.

Whilst we have made every effort, we are unable to trace the copyright owners of the photographs reproduced on page 19, 27, 85 and 111 and would appreciate any information which would enable us to do so.

Foreword

Dr Winny's book is intended for those who are fresh to the poetry of Donne and realize that critical guidance is essential before this intricate verbal art can communicate to us today—and this in spite of the fact that Donne has been claimed as a modern ever since T. S. Eliot drew critical attention to him through his literary criticism and his own modernist poetry of the 1920s.

A number of intellectual, scientific, religious and artistic patterns are traced in the first four chapters. These may suggest to the reader that Donne is more medieval than modern, though the voice that emerges from the study and is present in the poems analysed in the fifth section is universal and compelling. We do not assume that the poetry is in any meaningful way *about* maps, mandrakes or compasses: nor are D. H. Lawrence's novels about the psychology of Freud. Donne and Lawrence, together with Shakespeare and Hardy, are pre-eminent in their definitions of the stages of love because of the sensitivity they show to the intellectual currents of their age as well as the power they possess of realizing emotional states.

Especially important in the present study, I believe, is the attempt to revise the common estimate of the poetry of the early seventeenth century, for years said to be the work of a 'school of Donne'. In Dr Winny's words: 'There could be no school of Donne, for his style was a uniquely personal instrument which could not serve the needs of other poets.' His philosophical ideas were largely familiar to educated people in 1590, but the attitudes taken up towards such inherited concepts are inimitably Donne's own. In order to equip the reader, who already has the sensibility, with the necessary information and then to blend both in his imaginative recreation of the poetry has been the guiding principle in the preparation of this book.

In preparing the revised edition a good deal of new material has been added and the layout has been slightly altered. The *Elegies* are poems frequently neglected, especially by those who know their Donne only through anthologies, and a discussion of some of them gives a more fully rounded analysis of the poetic output of a virtuoso writer. Since a great deal of Donne's adult life was spent in the service of the Church it is of particular value to the reader to consider the series of meditations *Devotions upon Emergent Occasions*, a record of a psychological breakdown, with which Part Two now ends. This substantial addition to the book will be welcomed especially by those who recollect that Donne's reputation among his contemporaries was established not as a love poet but as Dean.

MAURICE HUSSEY General Editor

For Maurice

Part One
The Poet and His Setting

Chronological table

	DONNE'S LIFE	HISTORICAL EVENTS
1570		Elizabeth I excommunicated and deposed by the Pope
1572	John Donne born, third child of John Donne, a London ironmonger, and his wife Elizabeth (formerly Heywood)	Massacre of St Bartholomew's Day
1574		Persecution of English papists begins
1575		English Anabaptists burnt at the stake
1576	Death of Donne's father. His mother remarries	Theatre playhouse built in London suburb. First recusant priests arrive secretly in England
1577		Drake's circumnavigation begins (1577–80)
1578		Lyly's *Euphues, the Anatomy of Wit* published
1579		Jesuit mission to England organized
1580		English recusants encouraged to regard assassination of the Queen as 'lawful and meritorious'
1581		Clandestine recusant press set up in Essex. Edmund Campion executed
1582		Plague in London

1583		Somerville's recusant plot exposed
1584	Donne and his brother Henry matriculate from Hart Hall, Oxford: probably at Oxford until 1588	
1585		Netherlands expedition under Leicester
1586		Death of Sidney. Following the battle of Zutphen. Trial of Mary Queen of Scots. Star Chamber decree requiring all published works to have ecclesiastical approval
1587		Execution of Mary Queen of Scots. Pope proclaims a crusade against England
1588	Death of Donne's stepfather	Defeat of the Spanish Armada
1589– 91	Donne probably travelling in Europe	
1591	Donne enters Thavies Inn as a law student. His mother married for the third time	Increasingly severe measures taken against recusants
1592	Donne admitted to Lincoln's Inn. Most productive period of poetic writing—*Songs and Sonets, Satires, Elegies*—probably begins about this date	
1592– 3		Plague in London; all playhouses closed
1593	Death of Henry Donne of jail-fever in Newgate prison	Penalties for recusancy increased. Death of Marlowe

1595		Robert Southwell executed. Deaths of Drake and Hawkins in West Indies
1596	Takes part in the expedition to Cadiz as gentleman adventurer	Essex storms Cadiz
1597	Sails with the Islands expedition, July–October	Failure of expedition to the Azores
1598	Enters service of Sir Thomas Egerton as secretary	
1599		Death of Spenser. Essex sent to Ireland; returns to England without permission and is imprisoned
1600		East India Company founded
1601	Elected MP for Brackley. Lives in the Savoy and in December marries Ann More	Rising and execution of Essex
1602	Marriage revealed to Sir George More. Donne briefly imprisoned, and dismissed from his secretarial post. Reunited with his wife after a lawsuit establishes the validity of his marriage	
1603	Living in Pyrford, Surrey, at the home of his wife's cousin	Conquest of Ireland completed. Death of Elizabeth I; accession of James I (1603–25)
1604– 7	Working with Thomas Morton, one of the King's chaplains, to convert recusants to Anglicanism	
1605		Gunpowder Plot exposed

1606	Moves to Mitcham with his family of three children. Friendship with Mrs Herbert may date from this time	Penal legislation against recusants
1607	Morton urges Donne to take holy orders	
1608	Countess of Bedford acts as godmother to Donne's second daughter, Lucy. Tries without success to obtain secretaryship in Ireland	Milton born. Separatists emigrate to Holland
1610	Publishes *Pseudo-Martyr*, arguing that recusants are sham martyrs. Receives honorary MA from Oxford	Commons' Petition of Right and Petition of Grievances
1611	Publishes *The First Anniversary*. In November, leaves England for Amiens, Paris and Germany with Sir Robert Drury, returning in September 1612	King James Bible published
1612	Moves to a house in Drury Lane with his family of seven children	Death of Prince Henry, the heir-apparent
1613	Seeks appointment as ambassador at Venice	
1614	Sits as MP for Taunton. Deaths of two of his children	Parliament dissolved after protesting against impositions
1615	Ordained deacon and priest at St Paul's cathedral, and appointed a royal chaplain. At the King's command, receives honorary DD from Cambridge	

1616	Granted livings in Huntingdonshire and Kent	Death of Shakespeare
1617	Ann Donne dies after giving birth to a stillborn child	Pocohontas presented at Court
1618		Ralegh executed
1619	Travels to Germany as chaplain with ambassadorial party: *A Hymn to Christ at the Author's last going into Germany*	Death of Queen Anne
1620	Returns to London	Voyage of the Mayflower to New England
1621	Installed as Dean of St Paul's	Andrew Marvell born
1622	Appointed JP for Kent and Bedfordshire; instituted as rector of Blunham in Bedfordshire	King restricts preaching
1623	Seriously ill in November–December. His daughter Constance marries Edward Alleyn, the actor	
1642	Publishes *Devotions upon Emergent Occasions*	
1625	Preaches first sermon to Charles I. Again falls ill. Goes to live in Chelsea to avoid the plague	Death of James I; accession of Charles I (1625–49). King marries Henrietta Maria of Spain. Recusancy laws suspended. Plague in London
1629		Death of Bacon. Parliament impeaches Buckingham, and declares poundage and tonnage illegal
1627	Deaths of his daughter Lucy, his close friend Sir	

	Henry Goodyer, the Countess of Bedford and the former Mrs Magdalen Herbert, all within six months	
1628	Death of his lifelong friend Christopher Brooke	Petition of Right becomes law. Buckingham assassinated. Bunyan born
1629		Laudian censorship of the press. Commons passes resolution against popery and Arminianism
1630	Falls seriously ill, makes his will	Great Migration to New England begins. George Herbert rector of Bemerton
1631	Death of his mother. Delivers his last sermon at Court on 26 February. Dies on 31 March	Laud enforces religious conformity
1632	Effigy placed in St Paul's, showing him in his shroud	
1633	Unauthorised publication of his poems, with further editions in 1635 and 1639	Laud appointed Archbishop. Death of Herbert
1640	*LXXX Sermons* published	

1   John Donne

Donne is not usually seen as a typical Elizabethan. Many of his readers, indeed, seem unready to associate him with the period of Elizabeth, and prefer to regard him primarily as a seventeenth-century poet, ignoring Ben Jonson's opinion that Donne wrote 'all his best pieces' before he was twenty-five, and thus before the end of the sixteenth century. It is not difficult to understand why the facts should be resisted. Donne's metaphysical style, with its bare scientific allusions and its insistently dialectical manner, seems almost completely at odds with the richly evocative language and the delight in natural creation that we find in Spenser, Marlowe and Shakespeare. Where their poetry expands imaginatively to take in great tracts of experience, Donne works tortuously towards a single, barely accessible point: his solution of a baffling intellectual problem.

If we associate the term 'Elizabethan' with discovery and colourful adventure, with richly textured speech and a sense of man's magnificence, it may be easy to feel that Donne falls short of the aureate quality that characterizes the literature of his age. His restless intellectual probing and questioning, we may feel, belong rather to the seventeenth century: not Shakespeare but Bacon is his contemporary in spirit. It is a commonplace of literary appreciation—not necessarily one to be approved—that the scientific interests revealed in Donne's poetry show him to be a forerunner of the new age of enquiry to which Bacon was herald. But it may be too readily assumed that references to spheres, maps and compasses demonstrate Donne's concern with the new science whose outlines Bacon seems to have perceived, or indeed that they indicate a scientific interest of any kind. The poets of the 1930s who mentioned gasworks and pylons were drawing attention to objects with a certain symbolic potency, not commenting on the progress of modern technology.

Shakespeare probably represents his age more completely than any other Elizabethan, but no one man can reflect every aspect of his times. Another writer may be strikingly unlike Shakespeare in style and outlook without ceasing to be typically Elizabethan. Such is Donne's case. The respects in which his thought and expression characterize the age will be discussed in later chapters of this book. For the moment, where we are concerned mainly with the biographical facts of his life, we shall find Donne typically Elizabethan in the uncertainty which dogged him throughout his career, in private belief as in material circumstances. He was born a Catholic at a time when increasing pressures were being applied to those of his faith, whose resistance endangered the newly established Anglican Church and its head, the Queen. No professing Catholic was allowed to take a degree at the two universities, nor could he hope for the kind of diplomatic or professional career to which an intelligent young man of good family was naturally inclined.

Donne's private difficulties as a Catholic epitomize the state of turbulence which England was going through during his early years. Since the reformation carried out by Henry VIII, the English Church had been twice set on contradictory courses, first under Mary who annulled all the religious changes introduced by the two previous monarchs, and then by Elizabeth who swept away Marian catholicism. When Donne was a young man there was no assurance that the Anglican Church would prove strong enough to withstand the attacks of its two enemies, Catholic and Puritan. Not only was the Anglican future in doubt: for many devout subjects of Elizabeth there were serious issues of conscience and political loyalty, and an anxious perplexity over the conflicting claims of several churches, all claiming sole authority:

> But unmoved thou
> Of force must one, and forc'd but one allow;
> And the right: ask thy father which is she,
> Let him ask his: though truth and falsehood be
> Near twins, yet truth a little elder is.

Donne's *Satire III*, in which these lines occur, proves the concern which he shared with the great body of Elizabethans who could not easily assure themselves that the form of religion authorized by the Queen was spiritually superior to the others, or that catholicism and true allegiance were incompatible. We see no evidence of this struggle in Shakespeare, even though his father may have been a recusant; and in this important respect Shakespeare proves a misleading guide to the human outlook of his times. The golden atmosphere of his early comedies may truly represent the optimism and self-confidence which the nation felt in its growing commercial strength and maritime daring, but Shakespeare gives no hint of the troubled spirit of the English Catholics, vainly trying to reconcile religious faith with their duty as loyal subjects of the Queen. For this aspect of Elizabethan life Donne acts as spokesman.

Donne's private career falls into two parts, separated by his decision at the age of forty-one to accept holy orders within the Anglican Church. The contrast between secular and religious in Donne is startling, as we might imagine by comparing one of the more scandalous of his love poems with one of the *Holy Sonnets*, or one of the many sermons which he preached as dean of St Paul's. As a student of Lincoln's Inn during the 1590s Donne was described as 'a great visitor of ladies, a great frequenter of plays', and although the writer conceded that he was 'not dissolute', the impudent and rebellious spirit of the poetry he wrote at this time suggests that this glimpse of his character as a young man does not misrepresent him. His first biographer, Isaak Walton, preferred to skirt this doubtful area of his subject and to concentrate attention upon the eagerness for study which Donne was later to attribute to himself in these early years: 'an hydroptic immoderate desire of human learning and languages'; but Walton admits that after studying from four in the morning until ten, Donne then 'took great liberty'.

There is no need to censure Donne for taking the kind of wild pleasures that often form a complement to intense intellectual activity. In his case there might have been special reasons for seeking an outlet for the impetuous energies which his poetry reveals; for according to Walton, at this period Donne had not decided whether to continue a Catholic or not. The frustration and uncertainty of his position, which beside its effects on his future had the power to disturb his emotional being whichever decision he took, was a direct encouragement to Donne to lose himself temporarily in amusement and distraction. He seems not to have done things by halves. As the student was urged by an 'immoderate desire' for learning, so the playgoer was a 'great frequenter' of theatres and a great visitor of ladies.

The charged emotional nature was to remain when Donne became a churchman, but its energies were now turned upon a very different purpose. The element of rebellious protest conspicuous in his secular poetry, which overturns conventional attitudes and modes of expression and asserts a defiant individualism, is replaced by a conservative and authoritarian outlook as Donne upholds the rights of the established Church and its head, James I. If there are reasons for associating the Donne of the *Songs and Sonets* with the intellectual movements of a new age, there are equally strong arguments for seeing the dean of St Paul's as a figure of an age about to be eclipsed: a man whose anguished awareness of mortality and corruption seems to belong less to the period of Bacon than to the medieval past. In this paradoxical mixture Donne again characterizes his times.

Early career

If the second of these two figures dominates our impression of Donne, that is because we know so much less of the younger man. His family background at least is clear. He was born in 1572, the first son of a well-to-do London ironmonger who two years later was made head of his company. His father did not enjoy his prosperity very long, for he died soon after making his will in January 1576. Donne's mother, Elizabeth Heywood, was the daughter of a minor Elizabethan writer; and both parents were Catholics. Donne was to remark in

Pseudo-Martyr, which argues against the readiness of English recusants to suffer for their faith, that no family had 'endured and suffered more in their persons and fortunes for obeying the teachers of Roman doctrine' than his own.

The Heywoods were particularly unfortunate. Donne's grandfather was obliged to flee the country, followed by Donne's uncle Elizaeus Heywood, who after being mobbed at Antwerp died at Louvain in 1578. Another uncle, Jasper Heywood, who has some literary importance as a translator of Seneca, narrowly escaped being executed with five other Jesuit priests in 1584. He remained in prison until the summer of the year following, and was allowed to be visited by his sister, Donne's mother. Subsequently he was banished on pain of death if he returned to England, and died abroad before the end of the century. Before his uncle's death Donne had lost his younger brother Henry, who died of gaol fever in August 1593 after being imprisoned for harbouring a Catholic priest, William Harrington. Such family associations cannot have made it easy for Donne to abjure the faith for which his brother had died; though the fate of these relations showed the futility of his entertaining hopes of a distinguished career while he remained a Catholic.

Of Donne's early schooling nothing is known besides Walton's statement that 'a private tutor had the care of him' until he was ten. His widowed mother had been left rich enough to educate her son privately, and probably wished him to receive his first tuition from a teacher of her own faith. In the autumn of 1584, when Donne was about twelve, he and his brother Henry matriculated from Hart Hall, a university hostel at Oxford. Even by the standards of the time, this was making an early start with a university education, but there was good reason for haste. At the age of sixteen university students were required to take the Oath of Supremacy, which affirmed Elizabeth to be head of the Church in England. This conflicted directly with the Catholic position by repudiating the Pope's claim to the same authority, which no devout Catholic could do. To avoid exposing their sons to this public test of allegiance, many Catholic parents started them at university early enough for their education to be completed before the oath could be applied. This must have been the case with Donne and his brother, who were barred from taking a university degree by the same statutory declaration. Consequently Donne left Oxford, probably in 1588, without a degree, and remained without academic title until 1610, when the honorary degree of M.A. was conferred on him by his old university.

The next certain fact about Donne's career is his admission as a law student at Thavies Inn, London, in 1591, when he was nearly twenty. A period of three or four years between these two stages of education has not been accounted for. It has been suggested, by Grierson and Leishman among others, that Donne's residence of 'some years' in Spain and Italy, to which Walton refers imprecisely, occupied the period between Donne's studies at Oxford and London. Such an experience would have been valuable for any young man, and especially stimulating for a young poet; though we should not assume that Donne needed the stimulus of foreign travel and an exciting new literature to produce the poetry which he was almost certainly writing during the years 1591–96, as a student first at Thavies Inn and then at Lincoln's Inn.

If external stimulus was needed, Donne could have found enough excitement in the London of the 1590s, where an astonishing flowering of literary genius was taking place, and where every year Shakespeare gave more abundant proof of his greatness. The 'great visitor of plays' is unlikely to have missed any of those productions, first at the Theatre and later at the Globe, which made Shakespeare's name familiar to his first audiences. Some evident borrowings from Shakespeare's narrative poems, mentioned in another chapter of this book, suggest Donne's interest in the work of his great contemporary. London was a rapidly growing city, but a small one by our standards, and we can suppose that Donne soon made contact with the body of poets and dramatists whose creative vitality he shared. Jonson's opinion, already quoted, that Donne wrote all his best pieces before he was twenty-five, may imply that the men were acquainted before the end of this productive period, which coincides roughly with the date of Donne's materially disastrous marriage.

Like other readers of Donne's early poems, Jonson could only have read them in manuscript; for Donne did not publish his work. Perhaps he could not find a publisher for the *Songs and Sonets*, whose style and manner were so strikingly at odds with the late Petrarchan fashion of the time; or he may have wished to restrict their circulation as Shakespeare had done with his sonnets, by passing them round among his friends. The sonnets were eventually published, probably without Shakespeare's consent; but either Donne's name had not the public appeal which would induce a stationer to offer a pirated edition of Donne's love poems for sale, or his private circle of readers was completely trustworthy. When Francis Davidson compiled a list of 'Manuscripts to gett' in 1606 or thereabouts, he mentioned the 'Satyres, Elegies, Epigrams &c. by John Don', but seemed not to have heard of the love-poems.*

Walton's account of how Donne divided his time between study and relaxation is to be taken seriously. The intellectual interests to which Donne himself refers in the phrase 'immoderate desire of human learning' remained a vital part of his nature throughout his life, and directly influenced his poetic style. In the first of his *Satires*, probably written before 1594, Donne gives a wry picture of himself

---

*He might, of course, have regarded them as satires, which some of them are.

This was for youth, Strength, Mirth, and wit that Time
Moʃt count their golden Age; but t'was not thine.
Thine was thy later yeares, so much refind
From youths Droʃʃe, Mirth, & wit; as thy pure mind
Thought (like the Angels) nothing but the Praiʃe
Of thy Creator, in thoʃe laʃt, beʃt Dayes.
   Witnes this Booke, (thy Embleme) which begins
   With Love; but endes, with Sighes, & Teares for ʃins.

Will: Marshall ʃculpʃit.   IZ: WA:

Engraving of Donne as a young man.

> in this standing wooden chest,
>> Consorted with these few books,

and runs through the categories which his library brings together:

> Here are God's conduits, grave divines; and here
> Nature's secretary, the philosopher;
> And jolly statesmen, which teach how to tie
> The sinews of a city's mystic body;
> Here gathering chroniclers, and by them stand
> Giddy fantastic poets of each land.

The list comprises divinity, natural philosophy or science, politics, history and finally poetry, whose authors Donne affects to slight while admitting the quality which makes them congenial to him. It is a surprising revelation from the man whom we might know simply as the unreservedly passionate speaker of *The Sun Rising* or the outrageously designing lover of *The Flea*; and in our surprise at the range of Donne's academic interests we might think that his poetry was little more than a form of recreation directed by his studies. In fact the reverse is probably true. Donne's poetry compresses and epitomizes his whole experience as a man whose intellectual curiosity is as great as his susceptibility to passionate feeling. We should not therefore regard these poems as the fruits of a busy student's moments of leisure, which reflect his absorbed reading in divinity, law, natural history and other subjects. Donne's passion for learning seems to have been as intense as we might suppose his pursuit of woman to have been, if we took the love poems at their face value. His allusions to bookish ideas are no more academic, in the pejorative sense of the term, than his straightforward references to sex: the same passionateness impels both. Seen in this way, the *Songs and Sonets* provide a reliable picture of their author during a feverishly active and strikingly creative period from the age of twenty until his marriage in 1601.

This is not to say that the love poems are true in a literal or biographical sense. They may be, but it is unwise to assume it: the poetic 'I' is often an invention. In the appeal *To Christ* which can plausibly be taken as Donne's last poem, he might be speaking of youthful indiscretions which still weigh on his conscience:

> Wilt thou forgive that sin by which I've won
>> Others to sin, and made my sin their door?
> Wilt thou forgive that sin which I did shun
>> A year or two, but wallowed in a score?

On the other hand we have Baker's specific assurance that Donne 'lived at the Inns of Court, not dissolute but very neat', and evidence within the poems themselves of Donne's wish to shock his readers by standing current literary convention on its head rather than by disclosing his adventures as a great visitor of women. Clearly it suited Donne's temperament to assault and ridicule attitudes which most Elizabethan poets respected: to scoff where they venerated, to reject the habitual idealizing of woman and to present a creature of flesh and blood, as inconstant and dishonest as the lover who speaks his poem. There is no reason to suppose that this satirical attitude was the result of any actual disillusionment which Donne may have suffered. The reader senses that poetic convention, not woman, is the real target of Donne's iconoclasm, and he is left facing the more difficult problem of what should have aroused Donne's feelings against the literary fashion generally accepted by Elizabethan poets.

We have Walton's word that at this time Donne was 'unresolved what religion to adhere to'. The death of his brother in 1593 may have brought Donne to a spiritual crisis. If he remained loyal to the faith which had already denied him a university degree, it was not unlikely that his life would be wasted as fruitlessly as his brother's had been, whether as a victim of Catholic persecution in England or as a fugitive living to no purpose in a Catholic country abroad. A young man of intelligence and promise does not easily forgo the hopes of distinction and fortune which his natural talents could win; but nor does the son of a family which had stood firm under prolonged persecution easily abandon the faith which others had upheld with their lives. The argument in *Pseudo-Martyr*, that recusants who persist in their defiance are in effect committing suicide, seems an insult to the memory of Henry Donne. It also enables us to judge how much determination Donne had to bring to the task of justifying the course he eventually decided to take. Here too there could be no half-measures.

During the years at Lincoln's Inn the torturing dilemma was still unresolved. When we see the young poet doing his best to smash one of the accepted canons of Elizabethan writing—awed respect for the mistress— we are watching an arrogantly assured innovator compel the love lyric to accept a totally new idiom, and listening while Donne gives expression to the sense of angry frustration and protest by savaging an established convention of poetry. In this sense the *Songs and Sonets* may be considered autobiographical. They do not tell us how Donne spent his nights. They suggest how he felt as he struggled with the most testing problem which he would ever meet, and which could only be solved by clamping off a vital part of himself.

This satirical impulse in Donne was encouraged by a growing movement of complaint and protest among writers of the decade. Disillusion was in the air, and by 1599 the volume of satirical writing became so great that the Privy Council, alarmed by the spread of libellous and defamatory pamphlets, forbade the publication of any further satires. Like most works of this kind, the five satires written by Donne before the end of the century are blunt and vigorously abusive; and most of their energy is directed against a society grown corrupt and vicious. So, after a visit to the court in *Satire IV*, Donne ruminates over the suitors whom he has seen there,

> and a trance
> Like his who dreamt he saw hell did advance
> Itself on me: such men as he saw there
> I saw at court, and worse, and more. Low fear
> Becomes the guilty, not the accuser: then
> Shall I, none's slave, of high-born or raised men
> Fear frowns? and, my mistress Truth, betray thee
> To the huffing braggart, puffed nobility?
> No, no: thou, which since yesterday hast been
> Almost about the whole world, hast thou seen,
> O sun, in all thy journey, vanity
> Such as swells the bladder of our court?

A settled rhythm is never allowed to establish itself in these lines, whose jerky movement strengthens the impression of the speaker's impatience and disgust. It is not only in his formal satires that Donne adopts this disturbed manner. Some of the most effective of the *Songs and Sonets* are maliciously satirical in purpose and expression, demonstrating at once Donne's personal power and the destructiveness which, as in *The Apparition*, springs from the frustration of his urge towards fulfilment. Even when, as in *The Sun Rising*, he has found complete sexual satisfaction, the satirical impulse cannot be silenced and must express itself in violent abuse of the sun, whom the lover derides as 'busy old fool' and 'saucy pedantic wretch'. In this way the language of satire runs through Donne's writing of this period, as though the angry perplexity of his private dilemma was continually demanding and finding a voice.

If we accept Jonson's judgment of this early work, we may think that the strain of this spiritual crisis contributed to the success of Donne's poetry during this tortured and decisive period of his life. Exasperation seems to have been converted into poetic energy, giving Donne's writing its thrusting impetus: a wilful force which the discipline of metre barely controls. His poems often reveal an explosive power of feeling held under pressure and determined to find an outlet, twisting and wrenching itself to reach the solution of a self-imposed problem. It may not be fanciful to suppose that the discordance of Donne's verse, and the tortuousness of his arguments, reflect his state of mind as a Catholic torn between desperate alternatives, either of which would permanently maim him.

As an Anglican apologist, Walton makes light of Donne's spiritual trouble and implies that Donne had only to apply himself to a comparison of the two faiths to recognize which was authentic: 'Indeed, truth had too much light about her to be hid from so sharp an enquirer, and he had too much ingenuity not to acknowledge he had found her.' Donne's own account of his struggle in *Pseudo-Martyr* conflicts with this suggestion of an easy victory for truth. Those who know him, he asserts, are aware 'that I used no inordinate haste nor precipitation in binding my conscience to any local religion'; and he goes on:

> I had a longer work to do than many other men, for I was first to blot out certain impressions of the Roman religion, and to wrestle both against the examples and against the reasons by which some hold was taken, and some anticipations early laid, upon my conscience; both by persons who by nature had a power and superiority over my will, and others who by their learning and good life seemed to me justly to claim an interest for the guiding and rectifying of mine understanding in these matters.

Donne is writing diplomatically, but his allusions allow us to read a little between the lines. The persons 'who by nature had a power and superiority' over him can only be members of his family, notably his mother who outlived him by dying in 1632, still a staunch Catholic. The 'examples' given by his close relations need not be enumerated. The 'reasons' seem to have come partly from his parents and partly from teachers, perhaps those responsible for his early education. When Donne speaks of the 'learning and good life' which influenced him, he may be covertly admitting that Catholic priests played some part in this schooling. With all these forces working against the urge to break with his Catholic upbringing, Donne might well confess how difficult it was for him to 'blot out' the persuasions which had formed his outlook since childhood, and what anguished wrestling led to his eventual decision to leave the Catholic Church. When the break occurred we do not know. Donne's third satire, which deals with the problem of finding the true religion, is generally ascribed to the period 1593–4. It offers no ready answer. 'Seek true religion: O where?' the poet asks; and the best solution he can offer himself is to persist in serious enquiry:

> Be busy to seek her: believe me this,
> He's not of none, nor worst, that seeks the best.
> To adore or scorn an image, or protest,
> May all be bad: doubt wisely: in a strange way
> To stand enquiring right is not to stray;
> To sleep or run wrong is.

The answer is unlikely to have come suddenly, or to have left Donne spiritually at peace with himself. Towards the end of this poem he asks himself abruptly whether he is content to let his soul be tied

> To man's laws, by which she shall not be tried
> At the last day? O will it then boot thee

To say a Philip or a Gregory,
A Harry or a Martin* taught thee this?
Is not this excuse for mere contraries
Equally strong? cannot both sides say so?

The final uncertainty of any solution could be countered only by a readiness to believe without question, and *Satire III* makes it clear that Donne was unable to give this kind of total assent. To the end of his life he continued to search for the assurance that only faith can give; seeking proof of divine mercy and trying to argue himself into a conviction that his soul might be saved. After more than fifteen years' priestly service within the Anglican Church, Donne's uncertainty had not been silenced. His ambitions had found some belated satisfaction, though not in a form which the young man could have foreseen, but he had exchanged catholicism for a faith to whose truth only his intellect seems to have responded.

In 1596, perhaps no longer a practising Catholic, Donne left Lincoln's Inn and the London playhouses to take part in an expedition against Cadiz, commanded by Essex. The fleet, comprising over eighty ships and at least six thousand trained men, reached Cadiz on 20 June and took the city completely by surprise. The attacking forces overran the Spanish defences, and to prevent a treasure-fleet in the harbour from falling into English hands, the Spaniards were obliged to sink their ships and a cargo valued at twelve million ducats. Essex withdrew his forces two weeks later, having sacked and fired the city; and before leaving Spanish waters sacked two more enemy towns. After this resounding success, a second expedition was organized in July of the following year, under Essex. His orders were to attack and destroy the ships being assembled at Ferrol in northern Spain as a second armada against England, and then to intercept the Spanish treasure-fleet at the Azores. But Essex and his fellow-commanders Howard, Vere and Ralegh were not to repeat their success of the previous year. Their expedition encountered a great gale which drove them back to port, and when they were again able to put to sea the projected attack on Ferrol had been put off. The fleet sailed directly for the Azores, where in September it failed to make its planned interception of the Spanish treasure-ships, which made safe harbour in the islands. Essex returned to England with nothing accomplished.

Donne sailed with both expeditions, in what capacity is not known. A taste of military service formed part of the liberal education of a sixteenth-century gentleman, who was expected to have some proficiency in all the main fields of human endeavour. Ophelia, we remember, sees Hamlet as a combination of courtier, soldier, and scholar: a diversity of accomplishment which after his experiences in

*Meaning the king of Spain, the Pope, Henry VIII and Luther.

18

Map showing England, Cadiz, Ferrol and the Azores.

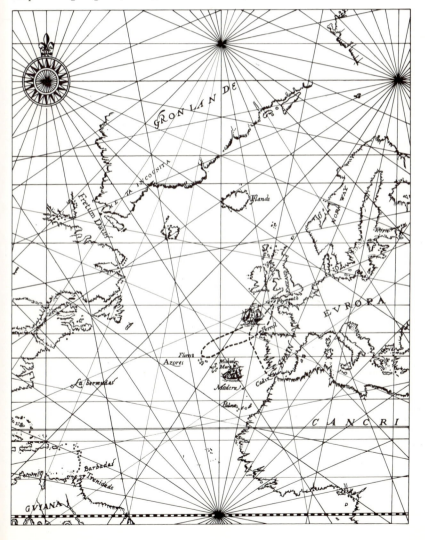

1596 and 1597 Donne could have claimed too. But Donne is not likely to have sailed with Essex for the sake of military glory, or to widen his experience as a poet; though the great storm which dispersed the Islands expedition provided the matter of a poem mocking the plight of ships and men:

> Some coffined in their cabins lie, equally
> Grieved that they are not dead, and yet must die;
> And as sin-burdened souls from graves will creep
> At the last day, some forth their cabins peep,
> And tremblingly ask what news, and do hear so—
> Like jealous husbands—what they would not know.

A companion poem, *The Calm*, won praise from Jonson, who was generally unsympathetic towards Donne's work. A well-educated Elizabethan gentleman of twenty-five, as Donne now was, must have hoped to attract favourable attention from one of the many noble and influential men of affairs which the expeditions brought together, and to be entered upon the career in public life which, with his abandoning of the Catholic faith, was now open to him. Walton tells us that Donne waited upon Essex, which may mean that he sought his patronage; but any hopes of preferment which Essex may have encouraged came to an end in 1601, when Essex paid the penalty for his abortive uprising against the Queen.

By this date Donne had in fact established himself in a position of considerable promise. One of his companions on both the voyages was Thomas Egerton, whose father was Keeper of the Great Seal and Lord High Chancellor. From a letter written by Donne four years later it appears that his friend brought Donne to his father's notice, with the result that he was appointed secretary to Sir Thomas Egerton. 'Taking notice of his learning, languages and other abilities, and much affecting his person and behaviour', as Walton tells us, Sir Thomas 'took him to be his chief secretary, supposing and intending it to be an introduction to some weighty employment in the state, for which his lordship* did often protest he thought him very fit.'

Donne's star had now risen, and with this auspicious beginning to a secular career there seemed no reason why his abilities should not have carried him to the kind of position in state affairs which Egerton had in mind. An important further step was taken in October 1601 when Brackley, a constituency controlled by Egerton, returned Donne as one of its members of Parliament; but before the end of the same year Donne saw his hopes suddenly and irretrievably ruined by a single impulsive action of his own. Since 1596 Egerton had been acting as guardian to Ann More, whose father Sir George More was Lieutenant of the Tower of London. Ann, it appears, entered the Egerton house-

---

*Walton anticipates: Egerton was subsequently created Lord Ellesmere.

hold when her aunt married Donne's employer, and continued to live there after her aunt's death in 1600. In this changed state of affairs Ann probably found rather more personal liberty than hitherto, and was now of an age to attract male interest. She and Donne fell in love, and Ann accepted his proposal of marriage. As Donne was later to acknowledge in a letter to her outraged father, he knew that he could not expect Sir George to accept him as prospective son-in-law. He was not yet able to support a wife in the circumstances which Sir George would require for his daughter; and in addition it seems that Sir George had taken an instinctive dislike to him. Knowing that to reveal their plans would have been, in Donne's phrase, 'to impossibilitate the whole matter', the lovers were married secretly in December 1601; Ann being then seventeen and her husband twenty-nine.

Marriage

This romantic but reckless step could not be immediately admitted. By marrying Ann without her father's consent Donne had committed offences against both common law and canon law, and he was naturally anxious not to disclose his secret until Sir George had been carefully prepared to learn of his daughter's marriage. The truth was eventually revealed to him by his friend the Earl of Northumberland, who had agreed to act as Donne's emissary, and who carried a letter from Donne begging his father-in-law to deal with the situation 'as the persuasions of nature, reason, wisdom and Christianity' should direct him. The plea was disregarded. The news, Walton relates, was so 'immeasurably unwelcome' to Sir George that he was transported with rage; and with complete inconsideration both for Donne and for his daughter he set about revenging himself by ruining his son-in-law's hopeful prospects. His first step was to persuade Sir Thomas Egerton, by means which Walton does not properly explain, to dismiss Donne from his service. He lost such a secretary, Egerton is reported to have said, 'as was fitter to serve a king than a subject': a compliment which if sincere suggests what pressure Donne's enraged father-in-law was able to bring to bear upon his employer. Donne seems to have realized that his dismissal meant the collapse of his fortunes, for the letter which he wrote to his wife telling her this bad news concluded with an epigram which summed up their wretched position: 'John Donne, Ann Donne, undone.'

But worse was to come. Still smarting with anger, Sir George continued his persecution by having Donne committed to prison, together with the two friends who had taken part in the marriage ceremony. Donne at once wrote to his father-in-law expressing his penitence and submission, and remarking that although Sir George might not intend 'utter destruction, yet the way through which I fall towards it is so headlong that, being thus pushed, I shall soon be at the bottom'. This appeal had no effect, but after Donne had begged for help from Sir Thomas Egerton he was allowed to leave prison, though not to enjoy complete liberty. As his spirits revived, he began to hope that he might be reconciled with his father-in-law and re-admitted to Egerton's service. The first of these hopes was answered, for Sir George was slowly induced to take a more favourable view of the man who had captured his daughter. One of Donne's spokesmen was his friend Christopher Brooke, a young lawyer who after giving away the bride at Donne's wedding had been imprisoned in the Marshalsea at her father's suit. After two weeks' imprisonment he wrote to Sir George asking to be released on the security of £1100, and including a plea for Donne: 'Were it not now best that everyone whom he anyway concerns should become his favourer or his friend who wants, my good lord, but fortune's hands and tongue to rear him up and set him out?' The commendations of Donne by men whose judgment Sir George could not ignore, and the personal attraction which Walton describes as 'a strange kind of elegant irresistible art', eventually broke down his father-in-law's resistance, and Sir George then tried to mend the harm he had done by persuading Sir Thomas Egerton to reinstate his former secretary.

In this more vital matter Donne's hopes were to be disappointed. Possibly because he had been roughly treated by More in his deter-mination to secure Donne's dismissal, Egerton was not disposed to do his bidding a second time; especially when this involved reversing his original decision. At all events, More was told that although Sir Thomas was 'unfeignedly sorry for what he had done, yet it was incon-sistent with his place and credit to discharge and readmit servants at the request of passionate petitioners'. The explanation does not ring completely true, for such yielding to pressure does not become un-dignified only when it is repeated; but there was no consolation for Donne in that. After a long and costly law-suit he had managed to obtain possession of his wife, who had been held by her father while a special commission was considering whether her marriage was legally binding. The court gave its verdict, favourable to Donne, in April 1602, some four months after their clandestine marriage; but though the couple had the happiness of reunion and life together, their future held no certainty besides their love for one another. Donne had good reason to adopt the attitude of the speaker in many of his love poems, who insists that he and his mistress constitute in themselves the whole world.

It would be pleasant to believe that after this period of shared adversity Donne and his young wife enjoyed the kind of mutual depen-dence and understanding which he describes in the tenderest and most convincing of his love poems. Walton's story of Donne's vision of his wife 'with her hair hanging about her shoulders, and a dead child in her arms', when she gave birth to a stillborn child during his absence

The front of Losely House, Surrey.

abroad, suggests a remarkable closeness of relationship. But the anecdote has another significance. Children came in rapid succession to the Donnes as to most Elizabethan families. 'I stand like a tree,' he wrote to a prospective godfather in 1615, 'which once a year bears though no fruit, yet this mast* of children.' The tone of his remark seems not entirely playful. The straitness of Donne's circumstances during much of his married life meant that every fresh increase in his family strained his resources a little further. Parents and children were repeatedly troubled by illness, and Ann Donne's strength was progressively worn down by childbearing and its attendant troubles. A letter written by Donne in 1614 gives a sombre picture of a household crushed by accumulated cares.

> There is not one person besides myself in my house well. I have already lost half a child, and with that mischance of hers [a miscarriage] my wife fallen into an indisposition which would afflict her much, but that the sickness of her children stupefies her; of one of which, in good faith, I have not much hope. This meets a fortune so ill-provided for physic and such relief, that if God should ease us with burials I know not well how to perform even that. I flatter myself in this, that I am dying too; nor can I truly die faster by any waste than by loss of children.

Protracted misfortune and worry test and sometimes break what was previously the strongest love. In the explanatory letter sent through his go-between to Sir George More, Donne had remarked and he and his wife 'both knew the obligations that lay upon us, and we adventured equally': though not, we may feel, with the expectation of such lasting distress as their adventure brought them. If Donne's secular ambitions had been a decisive factor in his rejection of the catholic faith, they are unlikely to have allowed him to marry Ann More in the knowledge that he was risking all that he had gained by this renunciation. He must have reckoned that Ann's father would reluctantly accept his *fait accompli*; and he could not have foreseen that Egerton would be coerced into dismissing him. It is not entirely cynical of J. B. Leishman to suggest that although Donne loved his wife, he could not conceal from himself that she had brought misfortune upon him, as he upon her. Donne certainly admitted his responsibility for Ann's depressed state of life. Writing to a friend in 1608, he explains that the letter has not been composed in 'my poor library' nor on the highway 'where I am contracted and inverted into myself'—his two usual places of contemplation—but from the fireside in his parlour,

> in the noise of three gamesome children, and by the side of her whom, because I have transplanted her into a wretched fortune, I

*Acorns, beechnuts etc.

must labour to disguise that from her by all such honest devices as giving her my company and discourse; therefore I steal from her all the time which I give to this letter.

This glimpse of Donne's domestic life after seven years of marriage hardly corresponds with the conception of lovers completely unified and 'interassured of the mind' which he gives in one of the most touching of his poems. With the evidence of Donne's concern to comfort his wife by distracting her attention from the realities of their situation, we may wonder whether his 'honest devices' did not include some of the poems apparently addressed to her: sincere rather in their wish to alleviate a distress of spirit than in their assertion of a relationship which adversity could not injure.

Burdened with more immediate cares, Ann Donne may not have recognized her husband's still greater need of the help which he tried to give her. The ruin of his ambitious hopes left a permanent mark upon him, and Donne seems to have convinced himself that his life had effectively come to an end in 1601. 'I have been no coward, nor unindustrious,' he wrote to Sir Henry Wotton in 1612, 'nor will I give it over yet'; but after this show of determination the letter continues: 'If at last I must confess that I died ten years ago . . . at a blow, then when my courses were diverted, yet it will please me a little to have had a long funeral, and to have kept myself so long above ground without putrefaction.' This grim quip might be taken as a flash of witty self-mockery, no more essentially serious than the lover's remark in *The Legacy*, who dies 'as often as from thee I go'; but the contradictory impulses of Donne's nature habitually lead him to present serious beliefs in a wrily comic form. He had made use of the conceit of being already dead in writing to Sir Henry Goodyer in 1608, again after referring to the ruin of his career:

> And there I stumbled too, yet I would try again; for to this hour I am nothing, or so little that I am scarce subject and argument good enough for one of mine own letters. Yet I fear that doth not ever proceed from a good root, that I am so well content to be less—that is, dead.

'I would fain do something,' he admits in the same letter, 'but that I cannot tell what is no wonder. For to choose is to do; but to be no part of anybody is to be nothing.' Again it is hard not to reflect that the love-poems tell a different story: there Donne is part of a composite being which encloses a totality of existence, and becomes 'the grave of all that's nothing' only when, in *A Nocturnal upon St Lucy's Day*, death, puts an end to this vital relationship of selves.* If he was consistent in

*It is not at all certain that this poem relates to the death of Ann Donne. Lucy was the name of Donne's patroness the Countess of Bedford.

trying to reassure his wife, Donne may not have disclosed to her the morbid depression which found some outlet in his correspondence. His melancholy sense of being nothing, or a man already dead and enduring an extended funeral, helps to explain what moved him to write his *Biathanatos*, an elaborate treatise in defence of suicide, during these difficult years. So far as his letters allow us to look into his domestic life at this time, they do not show that love brought him any real consolation for the collapse of his hopes, or that Ann Donne was able to secure him against the blackness of spirit which settled upon him as the emptiness of his existence deepened.

The first two years of the Donnes' life together were spent at Purford, a few miles from Guildford in Surrey. Two children, Constance and John, had been born to them when in 1605 they settled at Mitcham, a small town 'noted for good air and choice company' some eight miles south of London Bridge, now swallowed up in Greater London. Donne appears to have divided his time between his home and growing family—'mine hospital at Mitcham', as he was to describe it when sickness struck them—and a lodging in the Strand which afforded him some contact with men whose influence and position might benefit him. Walton asserts that 'his acquaintance and friendship were sought for by most ambassadors of foreign nations', but the only employment which Donne is known to have obtained was that of assisting one of the King's chaplains, Thomas Morton, in the task of persuading the English recusants to give up their faith. Donne must have felt the irony of his position. While at Lincoln's Inn he had undertaken a searching enquiry into the controversy between Anglican and Catholic over points of doctrine; primarily, we may suppose, in order to convince himself intellectually that it would be right to free himself of the disability which catholicism placed upon him. The special knowledge which he had acquired by this study was now useful to the established Church, and instead of regaining a position leading to employment by the state, Donne found himself drawn back into the religious conflict from which he had emerged a decade earlier. There was more than irony in the fact that Donne was now engaged as an agent of Catholic apostasy. Whether good or bad, his own decision to leave the Catholic community had come from within himself, as a choice dictated by his own reason. Those recusants whom Morton's tracts persuaded were acted upon by others; and if they sinned their guilt was shared by the assistant who helped Morton to compile his scholarly arguments. This is the more likely context of Donne's plea in his poem *To Christ*;

> Wilt thou forgive that sin by which I've won
> Others to sin, and made my sin their door?

The sin which became 'their door' was Donne's own renunciation of Catholic faith: an example which could be used to induce other

Part of Speed's map of Surrey, showing London, Losely, Mitcham, Purford and Twickenham.

recusants to give way. This reading of *To Christ* would imply that, despite his priesthood within the Anglican Church, Donne remained a Catholic at heart to the end of his life. This is not inconceivable; for while he seems to have convinced himself intellectually of the truth of Anglican doctrine, his intuitive acceptance of catholicism could not be altered. The anguish of Donne's religious verse, of which the present instance is typical, seems attributable to this conflict of faith within himself.

Donne may have disliked his work as Morton's assistant for a number of reasons, not least because it led in a direction opposite to his ambitions; and certainly because what it showed of his learning and abilities convinced Morton that Donne was needed within the church, where his talents would find full employment. When Morton was appointed dean of Gloucester in 1607 he suggested to Donne that he should take orders, offering as inducement to resign a profitable benefice in Donne's favour if he would agree. After three days' meditation, Walton relates, Donne declined; partly through fear that 'some irregularities' of his past life might be notorious enough to bring disgrace upon the Church if he were made priest, and partly because if he accepted, it might be from his eagerness to escape poverty rather than from a wish to serve God.

Donne may not have declared himself with complete frankness. According to Walton, Morton had opened his proposal by referring to Donne's expectation of state employment, and by admitting his fitness for such a post. It might seem strange that Donne did not himself allude to this long-sustained hope in his reply; for if it were still alive he cannot have wished to compromise this ambition by accepting an appointment in the Church. He may have concealed another motive for declining Morton's offer, hinted at in the comment which Walton attributes to him: 'Happy is that man whose conscience does not accuse him for that thing which he does.' Donne's resistance to the growing pressure put upon him to enter the Church, up to his capitulation in 1615, suggests that besides his unwillingness to forgo his major ambition he felt some serious moral aversion to taking orders. We are brought back again to the crucial decision which he made as a young man. If the issue had been between religious faith and secular ambition, he had made a choice which probably never ceased to trouble him, whether consciously or not. His anglicanism was not insincere, but it did not reach down to the deeper levels of his emotional being from which his catholicism had never been properly evicted. The sense of strain and unrest so habitual in his writing probably derives from this deep-seated conflict within himself. Evidently he could accommodate himself to the spiritual tension which the half-acknowledged sin of renouncing his early faith incurred; but his resistance to the step proposed by Morton in 1607, and by the King himself after the publication of *Pseudo-Martyr* in

1610, suggests that Donne could not contemplate any further and much graver compromise.

A year after his refusal of Morton's offer, Donne was relieved of his most pressing material anxiety. Sir George More was at last prevailed upon to make provision for his daughter, whose dowry he had hitherto refused to pay. He now bound himself to pay Donne eight hundred pounds at some future date as Ann's wedding-portion, and meanwhile to pay interest on this sum at the rate of twenty pounds a quarter. By Jacobean standards, eighty pounds a year was a very fair income; equivalent to nearly four thousand pounds of modern money. Not only was the family now secure against the poverty which had dogged Donne since marriage, but Donne was able to resume a modest place in society. His friendship with the Countess of Bedford, who acted as godmother to Donne's second daughter in 1608, seems to date from this time. Donne's letters show him frequently visiting Twickenham Park, where 'the good Countess' lived, and several of his poems are addressed to her. They are not the most compelling of Donne's works for a modern reader, out of sympathy with the elaborately complimentary manner of Donne's age; but they contain some gracefully turned conceits whose delicacy may surprise us after the aggressive style of the *Songs and Sonets*. So, in one of these verse letters, he tells her:

> You, for whose body God made better clay,
> Or took soul's stuff such as shall late decay,
> Or such as needs small change at the last day:
> This, as an amber drop enwraps a bee,
> Covering discovers your quick soul, that we
> May in your through-shine front your heart's thoughts see.

Walton does not admit that London and courtly society held any attraction for Donne at this time, and asserts that Donne would gladly have immersed himself in his theological studies at Mitcham. This opinion is not supported by a letter written to Sir Henry Goodyer in 1609. 'You, living at court without ambition,' Donne tells his friend, 'live in the sun, not in the fire; and I, which live in the country without stupefying, am not in darkness but in shadow; which is not no light, but a pallid, waterish and diluted one.' By speaking in the same letter of 'the barbarousness and insipid dullness' of the country, Donne shows how unwillingly he had suffered his enforced exile from the city and the society in which he had moved as a young man. Friendship with the Countess of Bedford offered Donne the *entrée* to a circle of noble and distinguished families through whom his ambitions might still be fulfilled, and with whom he might enjoy the cultured pleasures which Mitcham did not afford. His refusal of Morton's proposal might now have seemed fortunate, but Donne was not yet to realize that Morton's high opinion of his abilities had been passed on to the

King, and that James was determined to secure his services for the Church.

Among the many new acquaintances which Donne formed as his social horizon widened was Sir Robert Drury, a man of great wealth and ambition who had hopes of marrying his daughter Elizabeth to Prince Henry, the King's eldest son. In 1610 Elizabeth Drury died aged fifteen, leaving her father overwhelmed with grief. Donne had never met the daughter, and at the time of her death he may not have been acquainted with Sir Robert; but lack or slightness of familiarity with the family did not prevent him from composing an elegy of several hundred lines eulogizing the dead girl in the most strained and hyperbolic terms. In Jonson's opinion this poem was 'profane and full of blasphemies'. He told Donne that 'if it had been written of the Virgin Mary it had been something'; to which Donne answered that he had 'described the idea of a woman, and not as she was'. It might have been more honest if Donne had admitted that the poem had been designed to make one of the richest men in England his patron, for it is difficult to see any other motive in his noisy, repeated insistence that all the world's ills and disorders spring from Elizabeth Drury's death:

> She to whom this world must itself refer
> As suburbs, or the microcosm of her,
> She, she is dead, she's dead: when thou know'st this,
> Thou know'st how lame a cripple this world is;
> And learn'st thus much by our anatomy,
> That this world's general sickness doth not lie
> In any humour, or one certain part;
> But as thou saw'st it rotten at the heart . . .
> For the world's subtlest immaterial parts
> Feel this consuming wound, and age's darts;
> For the world's beauty is decayed or gone.

The pessimism which Donne proclaims so tirelessly in *The First Anniversary* was probably not assumed. His letters over the preceding years admit a growing melancholy; a weariness of life which he claimed to have felt when he 'went with the tide and enjoyed fairer hopes than now'. Although he can have felt nothing for Elizabeth Drury, her death gave him an occasion for expressing the deep misgivings which he shared with many Jacobean writers who saw the old order of life being steadily undermined by new habits of thought and belief. The best-known passage of *The First Anniversary*, in which Donne touches on the disturbing activities of the new astronomers, reveals a force of personal anxiety which

Above: *Lucy Harrington, Countess of Bedford.*
Below: *Tomb of Elizabeth Drury at Hawstead Church, near Bury.*

almost carries his hyperbolic elegy on the dead girl:

> And freely men confess that this world's spent,
> When in the planets and the firmament
> They seek so many new: they see that this
> Is crumbled out again to his atomies.
> 'Tis all in pieces, all coherence gone,
> All just supply, and all relation:
> Prince, subject, father, son, are things forgot;
> For every man alone thinks he hath got
> To be a phoenix, and that then can be
> None of that kind of which he is, but he.

The First Anniversary was published, with Donne's authority though apparently against his better judgment, in 1611: the first of his poems to be printed. By then its open appeal for Sir Robert's patronage had been successful, and Donne and his family were living rent-free in his new patron's house in Drury Lane, midway between the cities of Westminster and London proper. The 'elegant, irresistible art' exercised by Donne in his youth seems still to have been effective; for in 1611 Sir Robert proposed that Donne should accompany himself and his wife on a visit to France and the Low Countries which would take them away for several months. Ann Donne was expecting a child and was unwilling to be left, but Walton makes it appear that Sir Robert would not take no for an answer, and that eventually Donne's wife reluctantly gave her consent. Donne may have felt that Sir Robert's patronage was too valuable to be jeopardized by resisting his wishes, or his eagerness to travel may have overcome his husbandly feelings.

He was out of England from the end of 1611 until at least August of the following year, residing with the Drurys at Amiens, Paris and Brussels. It was during his absence, in January 1612, that Ann Donne gave birth to a stillborn child and Donne saw the vision recorded by Walton, in which she twice passed through the room carrying her dead baby. According to his biographer, Donne immediately sent to England for news of his wife, and learnt twelve days later that she had been delivered on the same day as her visionary self had appeared to him. But Walton is mistaken, for a letter written by Donne early in April remarks that he had received 'no syllable, neither from herself nor by any other, how my wife hath passed her danger'. It seems that the story of Donne's vision must be apocryphal; and this lack of correspondence again leaves us wondering whether his relations with Ann were as close as some of his poems imply.*

---

*To be fair to Donne, we should take account of his comment in a letter of 1614, referring to himself and his wife: 'We had not one another at so cheap a rate as that we should ever be weary of one another.' But the remark is not entirely compatible with this long absence from her.

Portrait of Donne in a ruff, by Isaak Oliver, 1617.

By September 1612 Donne was back in London, still without the position which had tantalized his hopes for so long, and apparently ready to abandon the ambition on which he had wasted himself. Now aged forty, Donne addressed an appeal to Robert Carr, a royal favourite whom James had recently created Viscount Rochester; telling him that he had resolved to make his profession divinity, and asking for his assistance. Presumably this was Donne's indirect way of bringing himself to the notice of James, who after reading *Pseudo-Martyr* had tried like Morton to persuade Donne to enter the Church. If so, he was disappointed, for nothing came of Donne's appeal besides Rochester's general patronage, admitted in a later letter when Donne speaks of having 'lived upon your bread' since their first meeting, a year before. Donne was now writing to ask the favourite to use his influence to have him appointed to the vacant post of ambassador at Venice, but this too fell through. In 1614 he was elected a Member of Parliament for Taunton, and sat during the nine weeks of its assembly in early summer. He seems to have had some other business afoot at this time, for writing to his brother-in-law at the end of July Donne complains that the arrival of a Danish embassy at court has interrupted his plans: 'Their coming have put my little court business out of the way, and dispossessed me of so near hopes as lacked little of possession. . . . I must confess my weakness in this behalf,' he adds; 'no man attends court fortunes with more impatience than I do.'

His waiting was nearly over. Later that year, probably as the result of renewed appeals to Rochester, now the Earl of Somerset, he was invited to Theobalds in Essex, where the King was residing, and promised the post of clerk to the Council which had just fallen vacant. Somerset spoke as though James could not deny his request, but he had not reckoned with the King's private purposes. 'I know Mr Donne is a learned man, has the abilities of a learned divine, and will prove a successful preacher,' he told Somerset, 'and my desire is to prefer him that way; and in that way I will deny you nothing for him.'

Ordination

Knowing that the road to secular preferment was barred by the King, Donne could only capitulate. Some lingering scruples remained, which he discussed with the King a few days later, when he agreed to accept ordination; and there were debts to be paid and other affairs to be put in order before he entered the church. But these last difficulties fell behind, and within two months of the meeting at Theobalds Donne was ordained deacon in the Anglican Church.

From this date until the end of his life in 1631 Donne enjoyed the growing distinction and material security which had eluded him throughout the frustrating years which followed his dismissal by Egerton. In 1616 he obtained two livings, in Huntingdonshire and

Kent, whose combined endowments gave him a comfortable income; and he was appointed to a well-paid post as preacher to the benchers of Lincoln's Inn. Five years later, in 1621, his fortunes were finally secured by his preferment as dean of St Paul's, which position he held until his death. But material success and the growing respect which came to Donne did not make this closing phase of his life entirely happy. In August 1617 his wife died, aged only thirty-three, a week after giving birth to another stillborn child. During their fifteen years of married life Ann had borne him twelve children, of whom seven had survived the considerable hazards of childhood. Walton, who generally seems concerned to make Donne's behaviour exemplary, tells how Donne promised his now motherless children that he would not marry again, and 'betook himself to most retired and solitary life'. A second wife might have eased his domestic problems and brought him some personal comfort, but Donne seems henceforward to have resigned himself to the bleakness of a life troubled and perhaps haunted by spiritual misgivings. The man who had regarded himself as enduring a long funeral during the empty years at Mitcham was not revived by the preferments which now came to him. So far as his poetry allows us to look into his personal feelings, it shows him threatened by increasing darkness of spirit.

Not all Donne's religious poetry was written after his ordination. One of the most striking of these poems is dated by its title, *Good Friday 1613, Riding Westward*. It is an interesting disclosure that at this time, when Donne was first expressing a wish to enter the Church and then trying to obtain the post of ambassador at Venice, he could write so heartfelt and contrite an appeal to God. His hankering after worldly distinction seems repeatedly to have collided with an equally powerful impulse towards self-abnegation and an austere religious discipline; rather as the opening lines of *Riding Westward* suggest, when Donne confesses that

> Pleasure or business so our souls admit
> For their First Mover, and are whirled by it:
> Hence is't that I am carried towards the west
> This day, when my soul's form bends toward the east.

The power of this wayward material interest makes it too strong to be mastered, and in several poems Donne appeals to God himself to discipline him by crushing the sinful impulse which alienates him from God's presence:

> O think me worth thine anger; punish me,
> Burn off my rusts and my deformity,
> Restore thine image so much, by thy grace,
> That thou mayst know me, and I'll turn my face.

Donne repeats this plea in a different form in *Holy Sonnet XIV*, where he calls upon God to break the knot that binds him to sin:

> Take me to you, imprison me; for I,
> Except you enthral me, never shall be free,
> Nor ever chaste except you ravish me.

These two passages typify the pressure of Donne's need for an assurance which only divine intervention can bring him, taking possession of him with a violence matched by his own headlong energy of language. The intemperateness of his writing as a young man persists, though his object is no longer to overwhelm his mistress's objections but to compel God to acknowledge him. 'Swear by thyself', he insists in the closing stanza of his final poem, where the urgency of his fear nerves him to demand salvation,

> that at my death thy sun
> Shall shine as it shines now and heretofore.

The thought of the last day and its awesome judgment, which earlier had figured incongruously in several of the love poems, now becomes a haunting preoccupation which rises up to strike at Donne without warning. 'I dare not move my dim eyes any way,' he admits in *Holy Sonnet I*, which ends with another moving appeal to God;

> Despair behind, and death before, doth cast
> Such terror, and my feeble flesh doth waste
> By sin in it, which it towards hell doth weigh.

Holy Sonnet XIII begins with a sudden burst of alarm as Donne recognizes that he may be called to his account before another sunrise: 'What if this present were the world's last night?' The self-assured lover of the *Songs and Sonets*, who basks in the certainty of achievement, has vanished completely, and has been replaced by a figure haggard with anxiety, whose yearning to be united with God is continually frustrated by the sins which he cannot expiate or forget.

What sin Donne had committed to be so oppressed he never reveals. His sense of indelible guilt was perhaps a product of the neurotic depression which troubled him throughout his life and which after the death of Ann Donne became increasingly severe. If he had indeed committed some moral crime, it is unlikely that the love poems give any reliable clue to its nature; and much more probable that Donne found it impossible to shake off the Catholic indoctrination that told him he was in a state of mortal sin. It seems to follow from this explanation that Donne's ministry as an Anglican priest was fundamentally insincere; but we should not assume that the issue was as simple for Donne as a plain choice between right and wrong. However strongly the buried impulse of his catholicism might protest against his decision, intellectually Donne must have argued himself into approval of the Anglican position. If he recognized any possibility that by taking orders under James he was sinning against the true Church, he might have felt that the sincerity of his dedication to God would weigh against this unwilling error. 'There are some things in which all religions agree,' he told his congregation a year before his death,

> the worship of God, the holiness of life. And therefore, if when I study this holiness of life, and fast and pray, and submit myself to discreet and medicinal mortifications for the subduing of my body, any man may say, 'This is papistical, papists do it', it is a blessed protestation; and no man is the less a protestant, nor the worse a protestant, for making it.

The quietly affirmative tone of this passage as well as its argument suggest that Donne had found the resolution of his private conflict in the belief that salvation could be reached through a direct relationship with God, not only through adherence to a single religion. Taken generally Donne's religious poems do not share this more assured mood. Rather, they reveal a degree of spiritual disturbance which only an upheaval as great as a renunciation of implanted faith might have caused.

Spiritual anxieties were not the only trouble which Donne had to contend with during this last phase of his life. His health had broken down several times during the years of privation at Mitcham, and was still precarious. In March 1619 he was appointed a member of an embassy sent to Germany in connection with the Bohemian succession, which threatened to bring Catholic rule into a hitherto protestant kingdom. Donne had no diplomatic training, and may have been sent out of England to find relief from overwork and persistent ill-health. 'I leave a scattered flock of wretched children,' he wrote to a friend before leaving for Germany, 'and I carry an infirm and valetudinary body.' To another friend he sent a copy of his poems and the manuscript of his unpublished treatise on suicide, *Biathanatos*, with the curious request that it should be neither printed nor burnt; asking that any other reader should be told when it had been composed, and that it was 'a book written by Jack Donne, and not by Dr Donne'.* Clearly he wished to be publicly dissociated from his younger self, though not to the extent that would involve destroying his earlier work. If he could not openly acknowledge Jack Donne, nor could he repudiate him entirely. Another backward glance to his youth is recorded in *A Hymn to Christ, at the Author's last going into Germany*, written before Donne embarked at Dover at the beginning of this journey. The tone of the poem suggests that Donne did not expect to return, and that he is concerned to set his house spiritually in order by renouncing all the remaining ties between himself and worldly affairs.

*Donne was made an honorary D.D. of Cambridge in 1615, at the King's insistence.

'Seal then this bill of my divorce', he tells God in conclusion,

>   to all
>   On whom those fainter beams of love did fall;
>   Marry those loves which in youth scattered be
>   On fame, wit, hopes—false mistresses—to thee.

These preparations were not yet needed. After being absent from the end of April 1619 until early January of the year following, Donne returned to London 'with his sorrows moderated and his health improved': an improvement which seems to have encouraged a revival of his worldly ambitions. In 1621, learning that the deanery of Salisbury was to fall vacant, he interested himself in securing the post. From a letter written to the Duke of Buckingham in August that year, it appears that Donne had the promise of his support. 'Ever since I had your lordship's letter,' he remarks, 'I have esteemed myself in possession of Salisbury'; but the projected vacancy had not occurred, and Donne was left still wrestling with what he calls 'a narrow and penurious fortune'. The letter concludes with an abject appeal for Buckingham's favour which contrasts oddly, and perhaps disagreeably, with Donne's passionate longing to be seized by God. 'All that I mean in using this boldness,' he writes,

> of putting myself into your lordship's presence by this rag of paper, is to tell your lordship that I lie in a corner, as a clod of clay, attending what kind of vessel it shall please you to make of your lordship's humblest and thankfullest and devotedest servant.

His letter shows that Donne could prostrate himself in the cause of private ambition with much the same eagerness and self-abnegation as he expresses in his devotional writing, where he is prepared to regard himself as clay—'wet mud walls, that waste away faster than God meant at first they should'—without the hope of ingratiating himself with a great patron. This contradiction of purposes was too deeply embedded in Donne's nature to be simply explained. He seems to be two persons, worldly courtier and ascetic; on one hand compelling himself to adopt an unremitting spiritual discipline, and on the other still actively seeking material advancement as though the service of God were not enough. Later in the same year another opportunity of preferment occurred, when the dean of St Paul's was appointed bishop of Exeter; and again Donne's ambitions prompted him to approach Buckingham, whose closeness to the King made him a powerfully influential friend in the disposing of royal gifts. According to Walton's picturesque story, Donne was commanded to attend the King at dinner; and when James was at table he told him, before beginning to eat, that

> though you sit not down with me, yet I will carve to you of a dish

S. PAULES CHURCH

Water house

Quene hythe

Three Cranes

The Eell Schies

The Gally fuste

THAMESIS

Old St Paul's, taken from Visscher's View of London, 1616.

which I know you love well; for knowing you love London, I do therefore make you dean of St Paul's; and when I have dined, then do you take your beloved dish home to your study, say grace there to yourself, and much good may it do you.

Donne was elected into his new office in November 1621. Three months later he found it necessary to resign his appointment as preacher to the benchers at Lincoln's Inn, but in his new circumstances this loss of income cannot have troubled him. Ill-health rather than financial worries was the hazard which confronted him as he accepted the physical and nervous strains which fell upon him as dean of a great cathedral. In the autumn of 1623 he suffered a serious breakdown of health, and became so dangerously ill that he was not expected to survive. This illness, which lasted just over three weeks, allowed Donne's markedly introspective mind to pore over its most fascinating subject, studying and ruminating upon the changes of bodily and mental condition which succeeded one another as the sickness ran its course. The results of this unusual self-analysis were published early the following year as *Devotions upon Emergent Occasions*, a prose work whose popularity led to three further editions within the next four years. Probably no other work of Donne's reveals him so clearly, or shows how strongly his outlook was coloured at this time by the idea of death. As a sick and possibly dying man he becomes, in his own macabre judgment, a symbolic figure, repesenting both the morally diseased state of man and the steadily worsening condition of the natural world. In the *First Anniversary* Donne had taken the death of Elizabeth Drury as an emblem by which 'the frailty and the decay of this whole world is represented'. Twelve years later he has himself become this ghastly emblematic figure; and he returns to his theme with the feverish interest of a man absorbed in the spectacle of his own approach to physical dissolution. 'Man, who is the noblest part of the earth,' he writes in Meditation II,

> melts so away as if he were a statue not of earth but of snow. We see his own envy melts him, he grows lean with that; he will say another's beauty melts him. But he feels that a fever doth not melt him like snow but pour him out like lead, like iron, like brass melted in a furnace: it doth not only melt him but calcine him, reduce him to atoms and to ashes; not to water but to lime. And how quickly? Sooner than thou canst receive an answer, sooner than thou canst conceive the question.

In Meditation IV, repeating the familiar argument that man is a microcosm of the greater world he inhabits, he shows how both contain and breed evils which seek to destroy them.

> As the other world produces serpents and vipers, malignant and venomous creatures, and worms and caterpillars, that endeavour

to devour that world which produces them ... so this world, our-selves, produces all these in us, in producing diseases and sicknesses of all those sorts: venomous and infectious diseases, feeding and consuming diseases, and manifold and entangled diseases made up of many several ones. And can the other world name so many veno-mous, so many consuming, so many monstrous creatures, as we can diseases of all these kinds?

The tolling of a bell for another man, less fortunate than himself, brings Donne to recognize in Meditation XVIII that he too must be considered dead. In the prayer which follows he revives the paradox of himself as a living corpse, an idea found in Donne's writing before he had considered entering the Church. 'That voice, that I must die now,' he recognizes as the bell tolls, 'is not the voice of a judge that speaks by way of condemnation, but of a physician that presents health in that. . . . I am dead, I was born dead; and from the first laying of these mud walls in my conception they have mouldered away, and the whole course of life is but an active death.'

In his morbid preoccupation with death and disease Donne takes on a symbolic character which he himself could not have perceived. An age was dying with him, and many of the most gifted writers of his time shared his neurotically depressed outlook. The elation and con-fidence of late sixteenth-century poetry—a spirit which Donne had caught in the masterful boldness of his early writing—waned and collapsed as the new century advanced, giving way to the melancholy foreboding which the tragedies of Webster express through their picture of a terrified and helpless humanity waiting to be struck down. For Donne, the macabre imaginings displayed in his *Devotions* were no new development. Several of the love poems startle the reader by in-troducing incongruous allusions to the lover's grave or his skeleton, to shrouds and corpses, and to the practice of disinterring bodies to make way for new burials. We may suppose that Donne used such images partly for their bizarre effect; but incongruity of this kind is native to him, and the interest in mortality which he wittily exploits in his early writing points ahead to the obsessive concern with death which dominates so many of his sermons. What seems an odd fancy in the love-poems has grown to envelop his mind, forcing him into a mesmerized contemplation of what both appals and fascinates him. 'Thou pursuest the works of the flesh, and hast none,' he argued in a sermon preached at Lincoln's Inn, 'for thy flesh is but dust held to-gether by plasters. Dissolution and putrefaction is gone over thee alive: thou hast overlived thine own death, and art become thine own ghost and thine own hell.'

Argued and illustrated again and again, this obsession with physical decay and the dissolution of the body pursued Donne to the end of his final sermon, delivered shortly before his death in 1631 and

A Rod *for* Run-awayes.

In which flight of theirs, if they looke backe, they may

behold many fearefull Iudgements of God, sundry wayes pro-
nounced vpon this City, and on seuerall persons, both
flying from it, and staying in it.

Expressed in many dreadfull Examples of sudden Death, falne vpon both young and
old, within this City, and the Suburbes, in the Fields, and open Streets, to the
terrour of all those who liue, and to the warning of those who are to
dye, to be ready when God Almighty shall bee pleased
to call them.

With additions of some new Accidents.

Written by T H o. D.

Lord, haue mercy on London.

I follow. We fly

Wee dye.

Keepe out.

Printed at London for *Iohn Trundle*, and are to be sold at his Shop in Smithfield. 1625.

published as *Death's Duel* shortly afterwards. 'For us that die now, and sleep in the state of the dead,' he told his congregation,

> we must all pass this posthume death, this death after death, nay, this death after burial, this dissolution after dissolution; this death of corruption and putrefaction, of vermiculation and incineration, of dissolution and dispersion in and from the grave. . . This is the most inglorious and contemptible vilification, the most deadly and peremptory nullification of man, that we can consider.

The shadow of the shroud

During the closing years of Donne's life his health deteriorated steadily. Repeated attacks of fever left him emaciated and wasted, as though to illustrate the paradoxical view which Donne had taken of himself as a man long dead who had become his own ghost. He survived the major epidemic of plague which swept London in 1625 and almost halted the life of the city, by taking refuge in Chelsea with Sir John and Lady Danvers. There, in the household of the old friend whom he had previously known as Magdalen Herbert, he spent the summer revising and preparing many of his sermons—a letter mentions eighty of them—for publication; and he may have written *The Autumnal* as an unconventional poetic tribute to his hostess. The plague followed Donne to Chelsea, but he was not to join the thousands of Londoners buried every week as the disease ravaged a terrified city. Donne's end was to take a form poetically appropriate to the prolonged conflict of mind and spirit which had exhausted his once vigorous energy and self-confidence: that of a man reduced to the shell of himself, whose life had been a long funeral preparation for the final act of dying. Two further serious breakdowns of health, in 1628 and 1629, left him unable to carry out his duties for several months. He was unable to preach in St Paul's on Christmas Day 1629, and during the winter following illness again prevented him from preaching before the King at Christmas. In December 1630, recognizing that he might not have much longer to live, he made his will; a document which throws some interesting light on Donne's personal tastes and acquisitions.

Its unexpected disclosure is that Donne had been something of a collector of paintings, four of which he left to his executor Henry King. A picture of Adam and Eve, another of the Virgin Mary, and a Deposition of Christ form three more bequests. Another close acquaintance was to receive his painting of Mary Magdalen; and to the dean of Gloucester Donne bequeathed 'the picture called the Skeleton which hangs in the hall', presumably a *memento mori*. The

Title-page of Dekker's A Rod For Runaways, *1625.*

Corporis hæc Animæ sit Syndon, Syndon Jesu
Amen.

Martin ℞ scup. And are to be sould by RR and Ben: ffisher

old friend who had put himself in jeopardy nearly thirty years earlier by marrying Donne to Ann More was remembered by the gift of 'the picture of the Blessed Virgin and Joseph which hangs in my study', while four large pictures 'of the four great prophets' were to remain in the deanery. Several other paintings to be chosen by Donne's beneficiaries are not identified by subject, but the last to be mentioned is described in terms which must arouse interest. To Robert Ker, his friend and correspondent for many years, Donne bequeathed 'that picture of mine which is taken in shadows and was made very many years before I was of this profession'. This must be a portrait of Donne, unusual in showing the sitter 'in shadows' instead of evenly lit, as was the Elizabethan custom. The remark about its being painted 'very many years' previously seems to imply that Donne wished to disclaim his connection with this younger self. The portrait may have depicted him as an arrogant man of fashion, extravagantly dressed; or it may have hinted too clearly for Donne's later comfort at the wildness which he had outgrown. By the end of his life all physical traces of the fiery young man whom he had been were obliterated, and Donne had purposefully shaped himself into the grim and self-mocking image which he intended to bequeath to St Paul's: an effigy of his own corpse, made ready for the burial which he felt had been so long delayed.

Walton relates how Donne's final portrait was painted, in the costume and posture appropriate to the identity which Donne was about to take over in earnest. He obtained a wooden urn, large enough for him to stand on, and then dressed himself in his winding-sheet,

> so tied with knots at his head and feet, and his hands so placed, as dead bodies are usually fitted to be shrouded and put into their coffin or grave. Upon this urn he stood with his eyes shut, and with so much of the sheet turned aside as might show his lean, pale and deathlike face, which was purposely turned toward the east, from whence he expected the second coming of our Saviour.

The full-length portrait was then placed at Donne's bedside, 'where it continued and became his hourly object till his death'. It is not mentioned in Donne's will, but Walton records that it passed into the hands of Henry King, who commissioned the effigy in white marble which was executed from the portrait by Nicholas Stone, the most eminent sculptor of the time. The effigy was then set up in St Paul's, where it still stands, virtually undamaged by the Great Fire which destroyed almost every other trace of the medieval cathedral known

Engraving of Donne in a shroud, prefaced to Death's Duel, *1632*

to Donne. The lucky chance which spared this monument enables us to bring a study of Donne's personal life to an end on perhaps the most revealing indication of his inner self which he left to the world. When Walton mentions that he has seen 'many pictures of him, in several habits, and at several ages and in several postures' we are not surprised. Donne never escaped from himself, or broke loose from the introspective habit which made him probe and question the workings of his own mind and spirit. His evident fondness for having his portrait painted at every stage of life is not an admission of vanity, but another mark of the tireless curiosity about himself which is most openly declared in his *Devotions*. So persistent a desire to see himself objectively represented and shown to exist might have been impelled by a private fear in Donne that he had no real existence: that he had already been annihilated, and was nothing. Such a suggestion is in fact made in some of the love poems, where Donne argues that absence 'withdrew our souls, and made us carcasses', and that he and his mistress 'are nothing then, when on a divers shore'. It would be wrong to regard such remarks as merely playful. Suitably amended, they reappear in his devotional writing when Donne expresses an agonized fear that God may reject him, 'let my soul fall out of his hand into a bottomless pit, and roll an unremovable stone upon it, and leave it to that which it finds there . . . and never think more of that soul, never have more to do with it.'

The fear of desertion which preyed upon Donne's mind could never be completely silenced; yet for the man who had encouraged himself to think of himself as a corpse awaiting burial the prospect of physical annihilation, that 'most deadly and peremptory nullification of man', cannot have been entirely unattractive. As a dead man, perhaps, he would possess the positive reality which had eluded him in his search for the substantial identity of John Donne. He was so far from fearing death in his last illness, Donne told his physician, 'which to others is the king of terrors, that he longed for the day of his dissolution'. Death had been the king of terrors for Donne too; but the dead were beyond reach of such fears. 'We die every day, and we die all the day long,' he had told his congregation ten years previously, 'and because we are not absolutely dead we call that an eternity, an eternity of dying: and is there comfort in that state? Why, it is the state of hell itself; eternal dying, and not dead.'

The portraits 'in several habits and in several postures' known to Walton represented Donne's lifelong attempt to externalize himself as a living reality, and to break away from the conviction that he was at best a creature 'not absolutely dead'. But the conviction proved irresistible. By the end of his life it so far dominated his mind that the only image which he could willingly leave to posterity was the corpse-like figure within the knotted shroud which still perpetuates him, in Donne's last and most paradoxical attempt to portray himself.

Critical reputation

Donne's reputation as a poet, and his influence on other writers, were chiefly posthumous. His sermons made him famous and respected throughout the city, while his poetry was a private occupation, little known outside the circle of friends and fellow-writers who saw his work in manuscript. If we can believe Jonson, these copies of Donne's poems may have been harder to come by after his ordination, for 'now since he was made doctor [he] repenteth highly and seeketh to destroy all his poems'. Donne's divided feelings towards *Biathanatos*, which was neither to be published nor burnt, make it seem unlikely that he wished to destroy any of his writing; though as priest he might well have felt anxious that his love poems should not come into the wrong hands. He was spared any such scandal. The poems were first published in 1633, two years after his death. Two further editions appeared in 1635 and 1639, in which the poems were divided into the groups familiar to modern readers—*Songs and Sonets*, Elegies, Satires, Letters, Divine Poems* and some lesser categories. Evidently Donne's family was not consulted by his anonymous editor, and it is clear that no permission to publish the poems had been given. In 1637 the younger John Donne petitioned the Archbishop of Canterbury to forbid the printing and publishing of the 'many scandalous pamphlets' issued under his father's name since Donne's death, speaking as though these works were entirely spurious. The list includes the poems, published 'very much to the grief of your petitioner, and the discredit of the memory of his father': a comment which does not specifically deny that the poems were Donne's, but which shows how unwelcome the disclosure of his youthful character had been to his family.

The reputation which Donne's son thought in danger was solidly upheld in 1640, when the great folio collection of eighty sermons was published. The son could not have known that the most authoritative critic of the age had acknowledged Donne 'the first poet in the world in some things'; and presumably he was unimpressed by the tributes from Donne's fellow-poets printed as a preface to the collected poems. The best known of these was contributed by Carew, who generously admits Donne's originality and inventiveness:

> The Muses' garden, with pedantic weeds
> O'erspread, was purged by thee: the lazy seeds
> Of servile imitation thrown away,
> And fresh invention planted. Thou didst pay
> The debts of our penurious bankrupt age.

---

*Sonets, as distinct from sonnets, are described as short poems or pieces of verse. The title misrepresents the character of Donne's love-poems by suggesting a predominantly lyrical tone.

His praise of Donne is more than uncritical eulogy. Carew recognizes that his style is generally rough and unmusical, and argues that Donne deserves credit for turning the stiffness and inflexibility of English to his advantage:

> Thou mayst claim
> From so great disadvantage greater fame,
> Since to the awe of thy imperious wit
> Our stubborn language bends, made only fit
> With her tough thick-ribbed hoops to gird about
> Thy giant fancy, which had proved too stout
> For their soft melting phrases.

But although Donne's inventive wit appealed strongly to the gentleman poets of this time, Jonson's insistence upon clarity and natural expression stood against any inclination they may have felt to imitate the sometimes brutal forcing of language to which Carew refers. The damning remark that Donne, 'for not keeping of accent, deserved hanging', implies that Jonson misunderstood one of the most important characteristics of Donne's poetry: its substitution of colloquial speech rhythms for the regular metrical patterns which most Elizabethan poets had adopted. Seen from the viewpoint of conventional writing, Donne's poetry often contained more syllables, stressed words, caesuras and other metrical irregularities than the lines seemed able to contain without losing rhythmical pattern altogether. But Donne had not tried to write regular verse. His rhythms are continually shifting and varying as he follows the accents of the speaking voice, now rapid with impatience, now dragging with resignation; twisting and misshaping language structure as he compels words to accept his argument, as though against their will. The result is one of the most strikingly individual forms of expression contrived by a poet: a style which justifies itself by representing the poet's struggle to realize curiously involved ideas within the framework of a literary form, and one which could not be imitated.

During the second quarter of the seventeenth century there were few English poets who resisted Donne's influence as the master of witty contrast and analogy. As he had represented the relationship of parted lovers by an image of compasses, so Lovelace could describe a lady's glove as a farm with five tenements, and Marvell a glow-worm as a country comet. But their quaint and consciously mannered images were set in poems that were rhythmically smooth and regular; and the roughness that came from Donne's wrestling with words was imitated only by a few later satirists, who believed that abusive writing should be metrically discordant. The important difference between Donne and the most prominent of these imitators was neatly defined by Dryden. 'We cannot read a verse of Cleveland's without making a face at it,' he wrote in 1668, 'as if every work were a pill to swallow: he gives us many times a hard nut to break our teeth, without a kernel for our pains. So that there is this difference betwixt his satires and Dr Donne's; that the one gives us deep thoughts in common language, though rough cadence; the other gives us common thoughts in abstruse words.'

But although at this date Dryden could give his approval to the roughness of Donne's style, twenty-five years later the change in literary taste towards urbanity and correctness led him to take a different attitude towards the same subject. 'Would not Donne's Satires,' he asked, 'which abound with so much wit, appear more charming if he had taken care of his words and of his numbers?' He seems to have adopted Jonson's unsympathetic view of Donne's unevenly stressed lines, and to have lost his respect for what he had previously called 'deep thoughts'. Dryden now complains that Donne 'affects the metaphysics, not only in his satires but in his amorous verses, where nature only should reign; and perplexes the minds of the fair sex with nice speculations of philosophy, when he should engage their hearts and entertain them with the softnesses of love'.

This passage is remembered chiefly for its association of Donne's poetry with metaphysical ideas, which Dryden was first to make;* but we should also notice its rejection of speculative argument as a fitting subject of poetry. New literary standards were beginning to crystallize, and wit was soon to be defined as the expressing of familiar ideas in new and elegant form: a criterion which Donne's startling originality of thought and uncouth energy could not satisfy. One eminent eighteenth-century critic dismissed Donne's poetry as 'nothing but a continued heap of riddles', and Pope complained that his style was 'rugged and most unmusical'; though he recognized that Donne's language had not become out of date. The objections which eighteenth-century readers felt towards metaphysical poetry were summed up when Dr Johnson wrote a critical essay on Cowley in his *Lives of the Poets*, published in 1778. Cowley, who flourished a generation after the death of Donne, is not much regarded by modern critics, and it says a good deal for the general lack of appreciation which Donne's poetry suffered that Cowley's timid manipulation of metaphysical stock-in-trade should have been preferred to the inventive vigour of Donne.

Johnson's critical strictures are directed at metaphysical poetry in general, and he does not often refer to Donne in particular but assumes that the same complaints can be made of him as of Cleveland

---

*Metaphysics is defined as a branch of speculative enquiry dealing with such concepts as being, substance, time, identity and so on. More commonly, it is taken to be the study of abstract and immaterial things, like the angels whose nature Donne discusses in *Air and Angels*. Not many of his poems justify Dryden's use of the term 'metaphysics' in this way.

and Cowley. Few modern readers would agree; but it is interesting to see how Donne appeared to this great eighteenth-century conservative. 'The metaphysical poets were men of learning,' Johnson remarks, 'and to show their learning was their whole endeavour.' This may be true of Donne's imitators, who delighted to find bizarre analogies between common experience and bookish ideas—Marvell sees the mowers as Israelites passing through the green sea of the meadow— but Donne does not simply put his learning on show. His allusions to science and Scholastic philosophy are brought in not to decorate his poems, but as part of the argument which is their *raison d'être*. When Johnson asserted that the metaphysical poets 'neither copied nature nor life, neither painted the forms of matter, nor represented the operations of intellect', he was only partly right; for although Donne never describes his mistress and ignores the natural world almost completely, his poems represent the process of thought by which Donne moves towards an intellectual goal. But Johnson evidently found it difficult to distinguish between the genuine oddity of Donne's thinking and the consciously fantastic style which later poets developed from his example. 'Their thoughts are often new, but seldom natural', Johnson complained, including Donne with his imitators,

> they are not obvious, but neither are they just; and the reader, far from wondering that he missed them, wonders more frequently by what perverseness of industry they were ever found . . . The most heterogeneous ideas are yoked by violence together; nature and art are ransacked for illustrations, comparisons and allusions.

The main task of poetry, Johnson believed, was to renew the appeal and interest of ideas which every generation rediscovered; and he criticized the metaphysical poets for searching so much after intellectual novelty and surprise that they lost touch with common truth. 'Great thoughts are always general,' he insisted, certain that fondness for the unusual could only produce trivial ideas. Those writers who lay in watch for novelty, he argued, 'could have little hope of greatness, for great things cannot have escaped former observation'. This disposed of Donne's originality, but Johnson's prejudices did not prevent him from appreciating that despite their mistaken respect for the odd and the fanciful, the metaphysical poets sometimes produced arresting ideas. If they frequently threw away their wit upon false conceits, he conceded, 'they likewise sometimes struck out unexpected truth. If their conceits were far-fetched, they were often worth the carriage. To write on their plan, it was at least necessary to read and think.' This just comment will seem more generous in a critic of Johnson's time when we remember that he is speaking more particularly of Cowley than of Donne; but although we must respect the critical honesty of this admission, we should probably not wish to praise metaphysical poetry for its 'unexpected truth'. Unlike Johnson, a modern reader does not look for instruction from poetry: he expects to share an experience which the poet causes to happen by releasing the energies of language. But this was not an aspect of Donne's poetry which an eighteenth-century critic was likely to praise, had he recognized it.

Johnson's essay helped to fasten the description 'metaphysical' more firmly to this group of poets, despite its inappropriateness. When De Quincey protested against the title in 1828 it was too late to resist what had become settled practice. 'Metaphysical they were not', De Quincey wrote; 'Rhetorical would have been a more accurate designation.' He went on to explain that he was using the term in its original sense, 'as laying the principal stress upon the management of the thoughts, and only a secondary one upon the ornaments of style'. This hints at a clearer understanding of Donne's purpose than any previous critic had shown; and the comment which followed shows still more critical perception: 'Few writers have shown a more extraordinary compass of powers than Donne; for he combined—what no other man has done—the last sublimation of dialectical subtlety and address with the most impassioned majesty.' But for De Quincey as for earlier commentators, the colloquial rhythms of Donne's verse were still so far from being heard that he could complain of the 'intolerable defect of ear' that marred Donne's poetry. His misunderstanding was widely shared by other nineteenth-century writers, who must either have missed or disregarded a remark made by Coleridge and published in the *Lectures* of 1818. To read Dryden or Pope, Coleridge pointed out, 'you need only count syllables; but to read Donne you must measure *time*, and discover the time of each word by the sense of passion. . . . Not one in a thousand of his readers has any notion how his lines are to be read—to the many, five out of six appear anti-metrical.' Wordsworth confirms the impression that Donne was generally undervalued or ignored at this time, when after praising *Holy Sonnet X* he admits that 'to modern taste it may be repulsive, quaint and laboured'. A little later, in 1839, Tennyson's friend Hallam went much further in a sweeping condemnation of Donne's poetry, which he found uncouth and unintelligible; and allowed himself a disapproving sniff directed towards the love poems:

Donne is the most inharmonious of our versifiers, if he can be said to have deserved such a name by lines too rugged to seem metre. Of his earlier poems many are very licentious; the latter are chiefly devout. Few are good for much; the conceits have not even the merit of being intelligible; it would perhaps be difficult to select three passages that we should care to read again.

But not all Victorian poets were ready to dismiss Donne as abruptly as this. Browning and Swinburne both admired him, and towards the end of the nineteenth century the critic Edward Dowden suggested that some of the difficulties confronting the reader of Donne could be removed by appreciating the literary traditions of his age. Dowden was not prepared to recognize Donne as the founder of a school of English poetry. 'I do not believe in the existence of this so-called "metaphysical school"', he wrote; and he pointed out that a delight in subtleties of thought, ingenuity and fantastic ideas is character- istic of Elizabethan writing. This was a timely observation, for hitherto Donne had been regarded as a poet who broke away from the central tradition represented by Shakespeare to develop a new literary interest. Donne was coming to be recognized both as a typical Elizabethan in the extravagance of his wit, and as a poet whose work was to be judged not by the irrelevant criterion of metrical form but by its passionate feeling.

Writing in 1896, George Saintsbury felt obliged to admit that 'no one with the finest sense of poetry as an art could have left things so formless' as some of Donne's poems; but he asserted that for the reader who knew something of human passion 'there is no poet and hardly any writer like Donne'. This great change in critical attitude made it possible for Saintsbury to see what earlier commentators had hidden from themselves by supposing that the irregularity of Donne's verse was inadvertent: that his style might be 'an index and reflection of the variety and rapid changes of his thought and feeling'. What had been mistaken for clumsiness and insensitivity was Donne's means of indicating the growth of excited feeling, by varying stress and movement to match the fluctuating emotions behind the argu- ment. Unlike Dryden, who had rebuked Donne for perplexing his mis- tress with philosophical talk, Saintsbury perceived that these seeming- ly detached arguments were driven by a passionate energy which Donne never describes, but represents through the irregular move- ment of his verse. In a picturesque analogy, Saintsbury admitted that this passionate energy was not always able to master the intellec- tual concepts which Donne heaped upon it. 'But the fire is always there,' he went on, 'overtasked, overmastered for a time, but never choked or extinguished; and ever and anon from gaps in the smoul- ering mass there breaks forth such a sudden flow of pure molten metal, such a flower of incandescence, as not even in the very greatest poets of all can be ever surpassed.' Admiration of Donne was now moving his critics to rapture. Four years later Sir Walter Raleigh defended the poet against another familiar charge by asserting that there was little extravagance in Donne's conceits: 'The vast over- shadowing canopy of his imagination seems to bring the most wildly dissimilar things together with ease.'

In 1899 Edmund Gosse produced a biography of Donne in two volumes which included many long extracts from the poet's letters.

Although Gosse assumed without right that the poems could be used as biographical material, his picture of Donne's life was a helpful adjunct to the literary work, and a means of widening the common appreciation of Donne. Then in 1912, when Herbert Grierson's edition of the poems was published with a full critical apparatus, Donne at last received the accolade of scholarly recognition. After this milestone, the last important contribution to the understanding of Donne that need be mentioned here was made in 1921, in the now famous essay by T. S. Eliot which appeared under the title, 'The Metaphysical Poets'. Like some of his predecessors, Eliot was disposed to question the appropriateness of this term, though for reasons very much his own. He recognized no intellectual bias in Donne's poetry, and insisted that, to the contrary, Donne and some of his contemporaries were men who 'incorporated their erudition into their sensibility: their mode of feeling was directly and freshly altered by their reading and thought'. Where other critics had found bare dialectical argument, Eliot saw a fusion of thought and feeling: in his own words, 'a direct sensuous apprehension of thought, or a re-creation of thought into feeling'. In a passage of his essay now perhaps better known than any other critical comment on metaphysical poetry he explained:

> When a poet's mind is perfectly equipped for its work, it is constantly amalgamating disparate experience; the ordinary man's experience is chaotic, irregular, fragmentary. The latter falls in love, or reads Spinoza, and these two experiences have nothing to do with each other, or with the noise of the typewriter or the smell of cooking; in the mind of the poet these experiences are always forming new wholes.

This ability to combine disparate kinds of experience, Eliot believed, was especially marked in poets of the early seventeenth century, who possessed 'a mechanism of sensibility which could devour any kind of experience'. Their importance for Eliot was increased by what he called a 'dissociation of sensibility' as the combined influence of Milton and Dryden came to bear upon English poetry. Language became more refined, while feeling became cruder; and later poets had been unable to recover the power of fusing the two elements of experience in what Eliot called a direct sensuous apprehension of thought. His theory of the dissociation of sensibility, at first widely accepted, had lost most of its appeal by the middle of this century, but it had served a valuable purpose by stimulating a fresh appraisal of Donne's achievement and a new approach to the poetry of his age. It was largely in consequence of his own critical reassessment of Donne that Eliot could affirm in 1931 that Donne's literary standing had been permanently improved. His merit, Eliot observed in his summing-up, was to have substituted a natural conversational idiom for a conventional one, carrying out a revolution of the kind 'which has to occur from time to time . . . if the English language is to retain its vigour'.

The Elizabethan settlement

In respect of religious affairs, the reign of Elizabeth was an unquiet age. For this the Queen was hardly to blame. She inherited a kingdom whose religious traditions had already been seriously disturbed, and constitutional wisdom required her to steer a course between extremes of faith, in an attempt to bring as many of her subjects as possible within a new communion—that of the Anglican Church. The disturbance of established religion had its beginnings twenty-five years before her accession, when her father Henry VIII set himself against the authority of the Pope and declared himself head of an independent Church of England. There was no sudden disappearance of Roman Catholic ritual and practice, for the king had no sympathy with the Protestant movement initiated by Luther in Germany; but there was some modification of Catholic doctrine, the clergy was enjoined to preach sermons, and an authorized translation of the Bible was published in 1535. Such changes, with the destruction or removal of images, the dissolution of the monastic houses and the desecration of religious shrines, transformed the appearance of English Catholic life; and by making the scriptures accessible to the unlearned, and cutting away much that was inessential to faith, these changes tended towards the simplicity and self-reliance of Protestantism. On the other hand, when an order was issued for the celebration of communion, as distinct from mass, the statute disclaimed any intention of condemning other forms of the same rite; and mass was not immediately rejected. The new Prayer Book published in 1548 was a compromise between the traditional and the reformed, though entirely in English. Under the guidance of Cranmer, the new Church was steadily feeling its way towards a version of modified catholicism, tempered to the outlook of a people who had grown resentful of alien authority and inclined towards a simple form of religious expression.

The wish for change was not universal, but the power of the crown working through the archbishops who were no longer appointed by the Pope would probably have assured the eventual establishment of Anglo-catholicism without any great protest. The hope of peaceful transformation was lost in 1553, when the shortlived Edward VI was succeeded by his half-sister Mary I, an ardent Catholic. Acknowledging the authority of the Pope, Mary reunited her kingdom with the Catholic world from which her father had separated it, annulled all the changes and reformations brought about in the previous twenty years, and began a persecution of her Protestant subjects which did more to injure her cause than had their heresies. Before her death in 1558 some three hundred English men and women were burnt at the stake as martyrs to their faith, as Mary attempted vainly to stamp out the religion which had been taking shape since the Reformation. The memory of this savage persecution was to remain in the popular mind throughout the reign of Elizabeth, causing catholicism to be feared and hated by the great body of her subjects who regarded themselves as members of the English Church. Any hope of reconciling the conflicting outlooks of Catholic and Protestant within a single communion was now lost, as each side adopted a fiercely dogmatic position which could only be satisfied by complete victory over the other.

Unlike her half-sister Mary, Elizabeth* had no strong religious persuasion; and did not act as though she felt obliged to impose religious belief upon her subjects. Throughout her reign, she and her ministers showed more concern for the political unity and stability of the realm than for religious dogma, of whatever form; and at different times the religious extremists among her people, whether Protestant or Catholic, were treated with the same severity. Evidently she was prepared to be tolerant and to allow differences of private faith, so long as there was outward conformity with the established religion and no attempt to challenge her authority as head of the English Church. But many of her subjects could not accept such a compromise. Those who were Catholics were bound by their faith to recognize the supreme authority of the Pope, and could not subscribe to the principles of another faith without committing heinous sin. On the other side the Protestant extremists, many of whom had gone into exile during the Marian persecution, were noisily discontented with the moderateness of the ecclesiastical reforms carried out under the Queen. Exile had brought them into contact with Calvinism, a doctrine which appealed strongly to the general disposition of Protestants to reduce the outward forms of religion to a bare minimum, and to regard the Bible rather than the priest as the mouthpiece of God's purposes.

In their clamour for still greater reforms within the English Church, and in their disrespect for Elizabeth's bishops and clergy, these Puritans—to give them their distinguishing title—were as great a cause of unrest and anxiety to the Elizabethan establishment as the Catholics, whose loyalty to the crown could never be wholehearted. Thus although Elizabeth might have preferred to allow her subjects a measure of religious freedom, as political ruler she could not afford to be tolerant. However dissimilar in other respects, Catholic and Puritan were alike in believing it their mission to overthrow the established faith, and to replace it by a form of religious

*Mary was the daughter of Henry VIII's first Queen, Catherine of Aragon; Elizabeth the daughter of her successor, Anne Boleyn.

extremism such as England had suffered under Mary. Simple political expediency, to say nothing of self-preservation, made it inevitable that Elizabeth should herself accept some degree of religious persecution and repression for the sake of stable government.

She began her reign by returning to the position taken up by Henry VIII. By the Act of Supremacy, which became law in 1559, the Queen was declared supreme head of the Church as her father had been; his anti-papal statutes were revived, and the reactionary laws passed under Mary were annulled. The Anglican prayer book was restored to use in churches throughout the country, and clergy who refused to comply with the order were made liable to fines and imprisonment. More stringent forms of punishment were reserved for those who refused to take the oath of supremacy, or who declared that any foreign prince, prelate or potentate had authority within the Queen's realm. This clause was directed principally against the Catholic contention that the Pope remained head of the English Church; and the oath had the effect of barring professional life to all sincere Catholics. It was to be sworn by all clergy, judges, mayors, and royal officials; and also by those receiving university degrees and religious orders. Since it involved denying the authority of the Pope, the educated Catholics in Elizabethan England were forced to decide between abjuring their faith or forgoing qualifications or preferment within their chosen calling.

The Act of Supremacy began to bite as soon as it was put into force. All the bishops but one refused to take the oath, and were deprived of office; but the parish priests installed under Mary ignored this example, and with only few exceptions they adapted themselves to the new regime. Their compliance with the Act was an encouragement to their congregations to follow this lead. We should remember that however different the form of divine service under Elizabeth, it was celebrated in the same parish churches as the Catholic worshipper had attended under Mary; and that to continue an old habit was easier than to turn aside to a service held in secret by a Catholic priest. Those who refused to attend Anglican services for reasons of conscience were fined as recusants, and later were likely to be questioned about their loyalty. It seems probable that most Catholics neither embraced the new faith nor abandoned the old, but contrived an uneasy compromise between their duty as loyal subjects of the Queen and their spiritual obligations; joining both in the communion and in the mass. The state encouraged such equivocal behaviour by not enquiring into the private belief of the individual, and by being satisfied if there was outward conformity.

Catholic recusants

The new Church was given a settled body of doctrine in 1571, when parliament sanctioned the Thirty-nine Articles which had been drawn up eight years earlier. The delay was due to the Queen's refusal to allow parliament to introduce a bill affecting religion, which she held to be a matter for her own prerogative as head of the established Church. The same objection was to frustrate attempts by Puritans to introduce further religious reforms later in the reign, where again the Queen held up changes that many of her subjects would have resented. However, in 1570 an event occurred which made it impossible for Elizabeth to continue the policy of giving a broad measure of religious tolerance to the Catholic recusants. In February 1570 the Pope passed a sentence of excommunication upon the Queen, declaring her a pretended ruler and deposing her forthwith. The intention of this papal bull, which was surreptitiously published in London three months later, was to make it impossible for English Catholics—who were believed in Rome to be ready to rise against her—to continue to behave as loyal subjects of the crown. After 1570, those who obeyed the Queen's laws and respected her authority put themselves in hazard of the same sentence of excommunication. The compromise adopted by most Catholics, which admitted loyalty both to the Queen as political head and to the Pope as religious authority, was now ruled out; and it became the duty of the English recusants to seek the downfall of Elizabeth and her ministers. In fact the Queen was in no great danger. Only shortly before the Pope's sentence she had put down a rising in the north of England, where recusancy was strongest; and by suppressing this rebellion she had disabled those who were most likely to have rebelled against their excommunicated ruler. The common people seem to have been unimpressed by the Pope's action, and an outburst of scurrilous pamphlets ridiculed his presumption, 'as if no prince in the world might rule without his sufferance'. None the less his bull had brought the Queen and her government into a hazard which could not be ignored, especially when it was seen that recusancy increased and hardened in consequence of the papal decree. Further measures against the Catholics followed inevitably.

If the Pope's sentence against Elizabeth was to be made effective, the Queen would have to be deposed by force; either by armed rebellion or by foreign invasion. When the threat of invasion came to a head in 1588, it was met by a nation united behind their Queen; and the destruction of the Spanish armada was received as proof of God's support of the Protestant cause. After this decisive repulse of a would-be invader the danger of foreign intervention could be discounted, but Elizabeth continued to be troubled by the activities of Catholic seminarists, or trained missionaries, who risked death by defying her edicts. Shortly before the papal pronouncement against Elizabeth, a college had been set up at Douai in northern France to provide education for the families of English Catholics who had gone into exile for conscience' sake. This scheme proved so successful that its purposes were soon extended to the training of young men for the fight against Protestantism and the re-establishment of the old faith in England. Despite Elizabeth's attempts to prevent young Catholics from going abroad to join this seminary, they left England in such numbers that similar colleges were instituted at Rome, Valladolid and Seville to accommodate them.*

These seminarists submitted themselves to seven years' rigorous training of mind and body, pledging themselves to receive holy orders and to return to England 'for the salvation of souls' whenever the superior of the college directed. The fact that their activities were treasonable cannot blind us to their courage and religious devotion, for Elizabeth's secret service was constantly on the watch for seminary priests, who could expect the most horrible of deaths if they were captured. But we have also to recognize that their undoubted concern with the salvation of souls necessarily involved them in political subversion. By strengthening the Catholic cause in England, they were siding with the authority which had excommunicated and deposed the Queen; and even had these missionaries wished to confine them-selves to pastoral duties, they were nourishing a force which would, if it became strong enough, overthrow not merely the English Church but the political establishment. Their presence in the country—at least a hundred of them had returned to England by 1580—con-stituted a more dangerous threat to the safety of Elizabeth's realm than the prospect of military invasion, and she took up the challenge savagely.

Elizabeth's persecution of the Catholics in the years following 1580 may seem better justified when we learn that by this date the new Pope had gone well beyond his predecessor's measures against Elizabeth. Not only had he encouraged plans of invading England through Ireland or the Low Countries, but he had discreetly published his opinion that the assassination of Elizabeth in the cause of religion could not be held a sin. By advocating regicide to the English Catholics he gave the Queen the best of reasons for sharpening the penalties which she had already imposed for recusancy. The fine for non-attendance at Sunday service, hitherto fixed at a shilling, was increased to the huge sum of £20 per month; and the offender was obliged to find a further £200 as security for his future compliance with the act.†
If a recusant was unable to pay the fine, the crown was entitled to

*We cannot suppose that all English Catholics approved and supported the activities of the seminarists. Many of the gentry hoped to find a compromise between their religious obligations to Rome and their patriotic feelings as subjects of the English queen.

†To appreciate the value of Elizabethan money, we might remember that Shakespeare paid £60 for his house at Stratford-on-Avon.

seize all his goods and two-thirds of his land and other property. For saying or singing mass a fine of two hundred marks—about £125—was now to be levied, and the offender to be imprisoned for a year; and each member of such a congregation was to pay a hundred marks' fine and suffer the same term of imprisonment. Any Catholic priest who attempted to make converts from those of the established faith made himself guilty of treason, a capital offence. All seminary priests and Jesuits were ordered to leave the country on pain of death, and those of the Queen's subjects studying in foreign seminaries were ordered to return to England and to prove their loyalty by taking the oath of supremacy; in default of which they would be declared traitors. Suspected priests who refused to answer a judge's interrogation might be held in prison indefinitely; and to check the movement of recusants about the realm such persons were ordered not to travel more than five miles from their homes, on pain of forfeiting all their property. Those who uttered slanderous or seditious rumours about the Queen were to be set in the pillory, to lose both ears and to be fined £200; and the publishing of seditious books was made a felony punishable by death.

The severity of these anti-Catholic laws, and the ghastly apparatus of torture and lingering death which awaited many of their victims, suggests that the persecution of the Catholics under Elizabeth grew to be as brutal and inhumane as Mary's attempts to stamp out protestantism thirty years earlier. In defence of Elizabeth it can be argued that where some two hundred and fifty Catholics were martyred for their faith during twenty years of her reign, Mary had sent three hundred protestants to the stake in five years; but the greater horror of the Marian persecution should not encourage us to see Elizabeth's behaviour as humane and enlightened. By accepting the rack, the pillory and the disembowelling-knife as instruments of policy she called the moral right of her government into question, and gave her enemies some apparent justification for seeking her overthrow. But a Catholic successor would have been obliged to use the same instruments of persecution and terror to break the will of Protestant England, and to bring its Church again under the rule of the Pope. At a time when Spain was known to be preparing an armada against England, and when every English Catholic was obliged by his faith to regard the Queen as a desposed heretic, it is hard to see that Elizabeth could have acted otherwise. Her mildness towards the old religion at the beginning of her reign, and her obvious hope that Catholics would adopt a compromise of conscience as loyal subjects, shows that unlike Mary she had no wish to make private faith a matter for persecution; but as a ruler with the material interests of her subjects at heart she could only resist the determined attempts of a Catholic minority to dethrone her, with the probable consequence of a religious war in England.

The Puritan experiments

It is certain that a no less dedicated body of Puritans and Protestant extremists would have risen against any Catholic seizure of power. From the early years of Elizabeth's reign this Puritan element, strongest in London and the south-eastern counties, had made itself heard in complaints against the lingering traces of catholicism in ecclesiastical ritual and outlook; and although Elizabeth could not afford to take measures against protestant extremism in the early years of her reign, the efforts of Puritans in parliament, within the established Church and in the country at large to bring about radical reforms were to cause almost as much trouble as the Catholic recusants. In Puritan eyes, the reformation of the English church had stopped well short of its proper objective. By denying the authority of the Pope, substituting communion or 'the Lord's supper' for the mass, introducing an English liturgy and casting out what were considered superstitious and idolatrous images from the churches, a welcome start had been made; but the Puritans were impatient to obliterate all traces of Catholic ritual from the new religion. The reason for their impatience lay in their refusal to admit that the Church of Rome was a Christian institution. The Anglican reformers had no such quarrel with catholicism. They granted that it was substantially the true faith, but corrupted and overlaid by false practices which had accumulated during the Middle Ages; and their stated purpose was to recover the genuine form of Christian worship as it had existed in the fourth and fifth centuries. To the Puritan this was not enough. In his belief, the only true and pure form of Christianity lay still further off, in an epoch before the early Fathers of the Church had produced the commentaries on holy writ which constituted the basis of Christian learning. The Puritans wanted no commentaries, and no scholarly interpretations of scripture. Assured of their ability to grasp God's purposes without any such learned exposition, they asked for nothing more than the English Bible which Coverdale had given them, and such elders as they would themselves freely elect. To persuade them that matters of religious doctrine and practice should be determined by the secular authority of the Queen would be as difficult as to make the Catholics accept the same point.

The first dispute between the Puritans and the establishment arose over the question of the vestments to be worn by the new clergy. To many parish priests the decision to retain a form of dress associated with Catholicism seemed a betrayal of Protestant principle, and the injunction which prescribed the wearing of vestments was angrily resisted. It was argued that the priest should be at liberty to choose how he dressed, that the clergy should be distinguished by their behaviour and not by special clothing, and that congregations would be confused by seeing these marks of the old religion in a church which purported to have rejected Catholic doctrine and ritual. Their protests were ignored, for the Queen could not allow her prerogative of determining the order of religious services to be successfully challenged. Frustrated on this point, the Puritans brought their indignation to bear upon other relics of catholicism which had been allowed to remain—kneeling during the Lord's supper, making the sign of the cross at baptism, using a ring in the marriage ceremony, and supplementing the services with organ music.

To us such protests seem merely quaint and absurd; partly because the Elizabethan dramatists—whose theatres became the target of puritan indignation and abuse—succeeded in making such scruples of conscience seem ridiculous. The ludicrous remark given to Ananias in Ben Jonson's play, *The Alchemist*, 'Bells are profane: a tune may be religious', suggests how easily the oddities of Puritan outlook could be exploited by the comic satirist. But Jonson is being less than fair to his victims when he presents them as monsters of hypocrisy and greed, who use religion as a mask for self-aggrandisement and fraud; and by making it seem that the Puritans constituted a race apart, an outlandish and eccentric enclave on the fringe of Elizabethan society. Like the Catholic recusants, by the end of the century the Puritans had proved the sincerity of their faith by their readiness to endure persecution and death for their beliefs. When in 1566 Matthew Parker, Elizabeth's first primate, published his *Book of Advertisements* or notices directing how church services were to be conducted, over a third of the clergy in the diocese of London refused to comply with his directions. Hitherto it had been possible for the extreme Protestants among them to avoid such elements of ritual as they found incompatible with a reformed Church, but this had led to such diversity of practice that the Queen had felt obliged to require 'an exact order and uniformity' in all religious ceremonies. Parker's directions could only offend the extremists who saw antichrist in every survival from the past, many of whom preferred to give up their livings rather than put his orders into practice. Others persisted in their puritanism despite the archbishop's decree, and Parker was forced to make a further show of authority; but not all the bishops whom he required to discipline their clergy were ready to support his measures, for several of them shared the puritan dislike of vestments and ritual.

Here again popular Elizabethan literature is likely to mislead us by suggesting that the Puritans were a lower middle-class sect, without learning or social distinction. In fact, the movement found adherents not only among Elizabeth's bishops and clergy, but among nobles, courtiers and members of parliament; nor were the universities untouched by it. The man who emerged as the leader of puritan thought in this early phase, Thomas Cartwright, was professor of divinity at Cambridge and a scholar of great talent. From this eminent position within the Anglican establishment, Cartwright threw his weight against the new order by declaring his belief that Elizabeth's moderate protestantism was in total conflict with the principles of the primitive Christian Church. He found no authority in the New Testament for a hierarchy of bishops and archbishops, and contended that it should be swept away, to be replaced by elected ministers and elders who would be responsible for ecclesiastical discipline. His arguments were too formidable to be ignored, for they were firmly based on the scriptures, and too dangerous to be allowed free expression. After being deprived first of his professorial chair and then of his fellowship at Trinity College, in 1574 Cartwright was forced to leave the country to avoid arrest. But although he ceased to trouble the ecclesiastical authority with his presence, the ideas which he had planted would continue to impel puritan attacks upon the bishops, upon Anglican ritual, and upon the control of the Church by a secular power.

The Puritans in parliament made a number of attempts to bring about reforms in the Church by constitutional means. Parliamentary assent had been a necessary part of the religious settlement at the beginning of Elizabeth's reign; and as the puritan sympathies of parliament increased it seemed possible that the terms of the settlement might be emended. But this was to reckon without the Queen, who stood rigidly upon her prerogative and refused to allow religious matters to be discussed without her assent. When Walter Strickland introduced a bill for the reform of the prayer book in 1571, he was summoned before the privy council and forbidden to appear in parliament. A year later two bills 'touching rites and ceremonies' were impounded by the Queen before they could be discussed. In the decade following parliament showed much greater temerity by agreeing to consider the radical proposal that all existing legislation concerning the Church should be repealed, and a system of calvinist discipline put in its place. Again the Queen refused to permit any discussion of the bill, and when Peter Wentworth tried to open the subject of parliamentary privilege he was committed to the Tower. We should resist the temptation to see Wentworth and others as martyrs in the cause of free speech; for although they were prepared to risk their lives in challenging the prerogative which stifled them, a puritan state would no more have permitted free speech or religious dissent among those of other beliefs than had Mary. It was not puritan faith itself which Elizabeth was acting against, but the refusal of the Puritans to acknowledge the secular authority which she expressed through the Church. She might allow them to dissent, as she was willing that Catholics should subscribe to their private faith so long as they paid outward respect to her religious establishment; but she would not permit either Catholic or Puritan to bring her authority into question. Nor would she allow the Puritans in parliament to introduce measures designed to harass their particular enemies, the English Catholics. When in 1571 parliament passed a bill which would have compelled the recusants not merely to attend Anglican services but to take communion, Elizabeth vetoed it.

By the middle of Elizabeth's reign it had become clear that the Puritans could not be persuaded to accept either episcopal authority or crown control of religious affairs, and that they would continue to resist the royal prerogative. After Edmund Grindal, who succeeded Parker as archbishop in 1575, had himself challenged the Queen over the matter of puritan 'prophesyings', Elizabeth found herself obliged to move against this rebellious element within the church. These 'prophesyings' had been organized by the clergy, who met weekly or fortnightly in several south-eastern dioceses to study and discuss the scriptures. They also set up courts of discipline to improve public morals, a practice which respected the puritan ideal of bringing the life of the community under the rule of its elected presbyters or elders. Not without reason, Elizabeth suspected that these meetings might encourage the growth of Puritanism among the laity who were allowed to attend the 'prophesyings' as audience; and she ordered Grindal to suppress them forthwith. But her archbishop stood firm, refusing to carry out her command and remonstrating that the Queen's peremptory demand was no better than the 'antichristian voice of the Pope'. The tone of the phrase is revealing; and after the abrupt departure of Grindal from Canterbury Elizabeth seems to have taken care that no puritan sympathizer took his place. The man she appointed, John Whitgift, had already proved his loyalty to her Church by resisting the growth of puritanism at Cambridge, where he had been Cartwright's main adversary. In his arguments with Cartwright, Whitgift did not choose to meet his opponent on the thorny ground of how the early Christian church had been organized: the point at issue was not whether their assumptions were correct, but whether the present time and circumstances were right for such a sweeping reformation of the Church as the Puritans proposed; 'whether . . . it may stand with godly and Christian wisdom to attempt so great an alteration as this platform must needs bring in, with disobedience to the Queen and law and injunctions of the church, and offence to many consciences'.

Elizabeth was not disappointed in her new archbishop. In 1583 he acted decisively against the Puritans among his clergy, by framing six articles which all priests were to accept without qualification; requiring them to recognize the Queen's supremacy over the Church, the book of common prayer and the Thirty-Nine Articles. He appointed an ecclesiastical commission to ensure that his test was rigorously applied, with the consequence that over two hundred members of the clergy in East Anglia and Kent were suspended. Those whom the commissioners summoned to their court were asked to take an oath binding them to return true answers to a searching interrogation of their religious belief and allegiance: if they incriminated themselves by their answers they were fined or imprisoned without right of appeal, and if they refused to take the oath they were sent as suspects to the Court of Star Chamber to be punished. This practice aroused strong puritan protests, for it introduced a form of legal procedure contrary to principles of English law. The suspects were not examined in public, they were condemned by evidence they themselves were compelled to give, and they were declared guilty by their examiners, without reference to a jury. Such extreme measures could only be justified by Whitgift's determination to remove the puritan clergy from the church, for in many parishes the minister was so popular that his congregation would have refused to give evidence against him. In consequence of Whitgift's measures, and of the deaths of several puritan leaders in the early 'nineties, by the closing decade of her reign Elizabeth seemed to have mastered this second threat to the authority of her Church.

The Stuart Church

Thus when James came to the throne in 1603 he found the established Church in no immediate danger. Persecution of the Catholics had seriously reduced their numbers; for many—like Donne himself—had yielded either to practical expediency or loss of faith in the old religion, whose traditions were now part of an age outside the experience of most Englishmen. The Puritan movement was temporarily without any strong leader, and the new king was sufficiently confident of his royal authority to suppress any stirrings of dissent. This he showed very early in his reign, when a body of Puritan ministers presented their Millenary Petition, for which they claimed the support of a thousand of the clergy. Their petition amounted to a deferential request that certain ritual practices which the Puritans had always resisted—the use of a ring in the marriage ceremony, and the sign of the cross in baptism—should be dropped, and that other established customs should be left optional, such as the wearing of cap and surplice by the clergy. James went so far as to allow a conference to be called at Hampton Court in 1604, where he himself presided over a debate between the heads of the established Church and four Puritans; but the Puritans obtained no other satisfaction from this conference than the airing of their views. Their arguments left James completely unconvinced, and at the end of the conference he told the Puritan speakers that he would either force them to conform to established practice or drive them out of his kingdom. His own speech left no doubt that he intended to see that his subjects respected 'one doctrine and one discipline', and that he would resist any attempt to weaken the authority of established religion as an attack upon his own prerogatives as king. His frequently repeated phrase, 'No bishop, no king', summarized his belief that those who wished to bring about new reformations in the Church were also likely to undermine his position as divinely appointed sovereign.

As king of Scotland before his accession to the English throne, James had enjoyed a much less eminent and powerful position. During the reign of Elizabeth the Scots had given themselves the kind of presbyterian church that the English Puritans hoped for, which did not allow the king to impose his own policy upon ecclesiastical matters. James was naturally gratified by the supremacy in Church affairs which he acquired as king of England, and just as naturally disposed to react strongly against Puritan attempts to weaken the power of his bishops, who did most to uphold the doctrine of divine right which James adopted. For this reason he gave his full support to the bishops against their Puritan opponents in parliament, and they in return encouraged their flocks to offer no resistance to the king's decrees. Thus a situation was brought about in which neither Church nor State could be criticized; for criticism of the king was regarded as blasphemous, and opposition to the established religion treated as seditious. To impose such checks upon free discussion at a time when traditional assumptions about political and relirious authority were being actively questioned could only increase resistance to the king and his bishops, though for the moment the opposition was not strong enough to challenge their reactionary power. When it came, the popular rebellion was more determined because its grievances had been suppressed for so long.

Woodcut from The Bishop's Last Goodnight, *1642.*

More than this, the combined authority of Church and Crown had deliberately outraged Puritan feeling by a number of ill-advised acts, some of which attracted popular sympathy to the Puritan cause. In 1624 it became illegal to print or to publish any book dealing with religion or church government without official approval—a form of censorship designed to protect the establishment against its Puritan opponents, who by this date were incensed by the king's assumption of divine right. The Arminians, the supporters of a high Anglican movement within the Church, were free to argue in favour of this divine prerogative as noisily as they wished, while all Puritan objections were to be silenced. When this edict against unlicensed printing was strengthened in 1637, a number of Puritan writers including William Prynne and John Lilburne suffered punishment by mutilation, whipping or the pillory for their pamphlets against the king's religious policy; but the great crowds who watched these scenes of cruelty, and who heard their victims' appeals for individual liberty, saw their savage treatment as evidence of tyranny. More popular indignation was aroused by attempts in 1618 and 1633 to crush the Puritan opposition to Sunday games and sports after church service, which were a traditional feature of English country life. With the growth of Puritan feeling, such recreations were coming to be regarded as ungodly, and in some parts of England Sunday games were actually suppressed by local authorities. The king replied to this move by ordering a declaration permitting lawful sports to be read from the pulpit throughout the kingdom. This edict was probably designed to discourage discussion of state affairs, to which men might turn if Sunday games were banned, rather than to preserve a venerable custom; but in the changing temper of the times this attempt to legitimize behaviour which a great number of the king's subjects considered sinful could only bring his divine right more deeply into question. He aroused further popular feeling by an order of 1622 which severely limited the range and subject matter of sermons to be preached by the clergy. Commentary upon texts taken from the creed or the Lord's prayer did not allow the preacher to pursue the line of argument which congregations had come to expect, and which for the Puritan was the most vital part of the service: the direct application of texts from Holy Writ to the political and ecclesiastical issues of the times. By this move the establishment silenced another source of criticism, and sharpened the desire for reform which it feared.

Such measures had the effect of widening the differences between Anglican conformity and puritanism. Under Elizabeth the Puritan objections to the established form and ritual of the English church were not severe enough to prevent his joining in its services. Many of the clergy were in general sympathy with Puritan aims and outlook, not disposed to challenge the crown's prerogative in ecclesiastical matters but sharing the Puritan dislike of customs and of ritual that they felt to be unreformed elements of catholicism. Such members of the clergy and their congregations would not have regarded themselves as Puritans, partly because the state still allowed a degree of latitude in religion which gave them a place within the established Church. Under James and Charles this degree of latitude was reduced to the point where those with Puritan inclinations and sympathies were forced outside the Anglican community. Typical of the measures which completely alienated an important part of the Anglican congregation was the directive of 1640 that the altar should be set at the east of the church and railed off, and that worshippers should bow towards the altar when they entered the church, and again when they left. To many this seemed a revival of popery, and an outraging of the Protestant ideal behind the Reformation; and by this date the king had identified himself so closely with the Arminianism of his bishops that those who wished for a radical reform of the Church knew themselves committed to a struggle against the sovereign. In this way the controversy over matters of religious outlook and practice merged with political issues which eventually could only be settled through civil war and the execution of Charles.

In its simplest terms, the war between king and parliament was the manifestation of a struggle between traditional loyalties and the demands of individual conscience, which gave men the will and determination to oppose the established power of sovereign and bishop. There was much blindness and bigotry on both sides. It is too great a simplification to suggest that where the royalists were the defenders of prerogative, their opponents were the guardians of liberty and justice. But it seems true to say that where the royalists were interested in preserving a traditional system of authority under the king, which did not allow the subject to criticize or obstruct his decisions, the parliamentarians were impelled by a genuine concern with the rights of the individual to challenge law and custom where they caused injustice or strained private conscience. In this respect they were breaking away from a constitutional system essentially unchanged since the late Middle Ages, and reshaping traditional ideas about the relationship between king and subject. In consequence, the authoritarian basis of English society was being weakened, and the individual was gaining a greater measure of personal freedom and protection under the law.

This did not come about at once. During the Commonwealth, Puritan control of English life piled so many restrictions and moral prohibitions upon the common man that, two years after Cromwell's death, the nation rose against this restrictive regime and welcomed

Portrait of James I by Simon de Passe, 1616.

Crounes haue their compaſſe, length of dayes their date,
Triumphes their tombes, felicitie ßee fate :
Of more then earth, can earth make none partaker,
But knowledge makes the KING moſt like his maker.

Simon Paſſeus ſculp: Lond.   Ioh: Bill excudit.

back Charles II as king. The restoration of monarchy was a second manifestation of the people's new-found power. They would now be governed by their consent, and not by virtue of any unalienable right in the ruler himself. The break with the constitutional past was complete, and with its passing many ideas and attitudes which had maintained a tenuous link with the previous age disappeared for good. When Dryden, referring in 1670 to the work of Shakespeare and Jonson, calls it the poetry 'of the last age', he seems to be looking back over a vast expanse of time. In fact barely fifty years had passed; but in those years literature, like society itself, had undergone profound changes. Dryden was right to suggest the extent of the transformation. An exhausted tradition had succumbed to pressures aroused by its own inflexibility and resistance to change, and had been replaced by the vigorous and confident outlook of a new society, eager to demonstrate its independence of the past.

3 The intellectual background

Any discussion of Donne's intellectual background can be expected to begin by remarking that during his lifetime the frontiers of knowledge were being vigorously pressed back, and that the excitement of discovery was gradually qualified by the doubts which new facts and theories brought to bear upon the traditional structure of belief. The discussion may go further than this, and assert that by undermining the authority of the old science this influx of new ideas had a deeply disturbing effect upon religious and intellectual outlook; and that much of the evident pessimism and anxiety of Jacobean literature can be attributed to the crumbling of faith in an established order of things. Donne himself, in his *First Anniversary*, is often brought in as witness to the truth of this assumption. Whether we accept this view or not, it is clear that new ideas about universal order, the nature of man and the aims of scientific study which were produced in Donne's lifetime helped to form the body of new science which, by the end of the seventeenth century, had replaced traditional habits of thought and belief over a great range of subjects. We have some encouragement, therefore, to regard the age of Donne as a bridge joining an old and a new philosophy, or as a sometimes confused interval between waning of one intellectual authority and the enthronement of its successor; and to expect of Donne some direct commentary upon the struggle of ideas, or evidence in his poetry of the uncertainty which it caused. We shall be in a position to judge how far Donne was affected by the intellectual upheaval of his times, and to what extent his work reflects new philosophical interests, when we have some acquaintance with both traditions of thought.

Ancient opinion

The old philosophy, which retained its authority until the end of the sixteenth century at least, was a medieval compilation of ideas drawn from much earlier sources. The philosophers of the Middle Ages had no talent for original work in the various fields of scientific enquiry, and too much respect for the great speculative thinkers of the ancient world to question their teaching. Medieval learning in the fields of astronomy, physics, medicine, cosmography and biology, as in such less important subjects as dream lore and physiognomy, was firmly based on the received opinions of Aristotle, Pliny, Ptolemy, Galen and other ancient scientists whose works made up a comprehensive body of knowledge. The fact that these writers were pagans whose pre-Christian era denied them the full illumination of truth did not prevent the medieval Church—the immediate source of contemporary learning—from recognizing the importance of their work, or from accepting it as the embodiment of scientific truth about the nature of man and his universe. Some modifications had to be made where the ancient philosophers' opinions were at variance with Christian doctrine, but these were not great enough to change the essential form and character of the ideas which the Church absorbed. The main contribution of the medieval Schoolmen to this body of knowledge was to collate and arrange its beliefs into an organized scheme, relating its parts together and educing the patterns and correspondences which were to appeal so strongly to the Elizabethan mind. The writer John Maplet in 1581 adopts a familiar demonstration when he observes:

> Amongst all kinds of birds the eagle is president; among beasts the lion. In fresh and salt waters the mightiest fishes rule, as the whale in the sea and the pike in pools. Man ruleth over all living creatures; and in man, compounded of body, soul and understanding, the soul commandeth over the body, and the understanding over the desire.

He sees the correspondence extending to the family, whose head rules over its various members, and then to the state, where a sovereign or governor is set over the people as political ruler. The habit of thinking in such parallel terms, which Scholastic outlook directly encouraged, must be reckoned as an influence upon Elizabethan poetry when Shakespeare, 'heaping examples', builds up a list of like actions or qualities to reinforce an argument:

> As many arrows, loosed several ways,
> Come to one mark; as many ways meet in one town;
> As many fresh streams meet in one salt sea;
> As many lines close in the dial's centre;
> So may a thousand actions, once afoot,
> End in one purpose.
>
> *Henry V*, I. ii. 106–10.

Belief in the correspondences which related events throughout the hierarchies of created life was more than a picturesque fancy. By defining the sympathetic links between beings and substances of like nature, and showing the ordered design to which the myriad forms of universal life had been shaped, the old philosophy gave a close-knit unity to the whole of creation. Every being, however, trivial, had its appointed function in the cosmic scheme: every phenomenon and feature of the material world had its useful purpose; for the earth and the system of heavenly bodies surrounding it were the handiwork of the divine architect who made nothing at random or without its place in the great moving fabric of the universe. To discover the purpose which individual objects and creatures served within this unified design, and not to study their actual behaviour, was the aim of medieval science. It was not until the rise of experimental science in the seventeenth century that the erroneous beliefs of the old philosophy were brought to light. Assumptions which had gone unchecked for nearly two millenia were put to the test, and found to be mistaken. The new science could justifiably claim to be substituting exact knowledge for venerable hearsay; but the price of this more reliable information was the loss of the comforting assurance that the universe was centred on man, and that all its creatures—trees, minerals, birds, planets, insects, four-footed beasts—had specific places and functions in the minutely organized design which God had set upon his work.

The frame of order

The general form of this universal design will be familiar to readers of Elizabethan literature. It may be helpful to begin not by describing the Ptolemaic system of planets, moving about the fixed point of the earth, but with the simple proposition that, by God's special appointment, 'all things in the world serve to the community and use of mankind, whom God had made lord and master of all'. The opening chapter of Genesis left no doubt about the sovereignty imparted to man over all other forms of life. Man was not merely invited but bidden to regard the world as his own, created for his use and benefit; and to see all other creatures as existing to serve his purposes. The beasts produced flesh and skins so that he might be fed and clothed; trees had been created to supply him with timber for houses and boats; the earth contained metal so that he might possess tools and arms; the sun existed to give him warmth and light, and the stars to guide him through the darkness. The creation of man could be explained by seeing a need for God to be praised by a being capable of appreciating his goodness: the rest of creation then fell into God's design by ministering to man's needs.

Modern man has outgrown the habit of supposing that universal life revolves about him and exists for his exclusive benefit: we know ourselves to be the inhabitants of an unremarkable planet, held by the influence of a sun itself dwarfed by the magnitude and brilliance of distant stars, in a universe whose full extent we have no means of computing. What we know of the sheer immensity of cosmos, and of the insignificance of our own tiny planet, makes it impossible to believe that man is the centre of universal attention, and the being whom all other creatures exist to serve. But before Copernicus suggested that the earth did not stand at the centre of an easily imaginable universe, it was difficult to reach any other conclusion. The Hebraic view of man's dominating rôle was confirmed by Ptolemaic astronomy, which saw the sun and the other planets acting as satellites to the earth. Thus together Holy Writ and ancient science encouraged man to consider every other part of creation as determined by his needs and directly related to himself.

With this encouragement it is not surprising that the old philosophy should have taken man as its central principle, seeking to explain natural phenomena by showing their beneficial effects upon man's life, and the wisdom of the order which had disposed them to man's advantage. The sun, according to Ptolemy, was placed midway between the earth and the sphere of the fixed stars which limited the heavens; having the moon, Mercury and Venus on one side, and Mars, Jupiter and Saturn on the other. The arrangement was fitting; for the size and brilliance of the sun made it like a king among the planets, and his station gave him three attendants on either side. But there was a more practical reason why the sun should have been set midway between earth and the fixed stars: that in any other position the sun would have given either too much or too little heat to sustain life on earth. 'For if the sun were placed next to the earth,' John Maplet explains in another passage of his *Dial of Destiny*,

> the earth by his excessive heat must needs be brent up and consumed, and all things and creatures also upon the earth must needs die and perish; and contrariwise, if the sun had the highest place and were in that room where Saturn continueth, the earth here below should be void and destitute of sufficient heat, and all things living should periclitate and be in danger of decay.

It was proof of God's forethought and kindly concern for man that he had avoided these extremes, and given the sun a position that would most benefit life on earth. The placing of Saturn furthest from the earth was a similar mark of benevolence and wisdom; for this malignant planet, 'cold and dry, malicious and hurtful', had an entirely baleful influence upon living things; and it was as well for man that Saturn, 'of all other planets the cruellest, should be most remote and furthest off'. So long as medieval science concerned itself with explanations of this kind, taking the facts for granted and attempting to account for natural phenomena in terms of divine providence, it could learn nothing about the laws which govern the behaviour of material objects. On the other hand, it gave man the assurance of knowing that cosmos had been planned and fashioned according to his needs, and that every facet of its structure provided evidence of God's interest in the wellbeing of mankind.

Since the whole universe was God's personal handiwork, its beauty and symmetry were no more in question than the usefulness of its creatures. Seeing day matched by night, summer by winter and youth by age, the old philosophers supposed that such opposition was a fundamental principle of created life, and that every being and object had its antithesis, towards which it felt a natural antipathy. This sense of a symmetrical weighing of type against antitype throughout creation prompted a further belief that the sea contained marine versions of all the plants and animals found on land, and that the same kind of symmetry extended to geographical features of the southern hemisphere. Thus when Magellan discovered a south-west passage into the Pacific—mistaking Tierra del Fuego for the tip of an antarctic continent—the cosmographers supposed that a corresponding passage would be found in the north-west; for God's disposition of the four known land masses was as carefully contrived as the rest of his work.

Belief in the symmetry of creation found weighty support in the Aristotelian principle that all material objects were constituted of one or more of four elemental substances—earth, water, air and fire; and that in these elements the opposite qualities of hot and cold, wet and dry, were held in balance. The natural antipathy between fire and water—one hot and dry, the other cold and wet—gave each of these two elements a restraining influence over the other; and in the same way the heavy element of earth was offset by the lightness of air. The medieval mind saw each of the elements struggling to assert itself over the other three, with consequences that would be disastrous for life on earth. The form of such a universal cataclysm is suggested by Lear, when he calls upon the elements of air, water and fire to destroy all living creatures:

> Blow, winds, and crack your cheeks: rage, blow!
> You cataracts and hurricanoes, spout
> Till you have drenched our steeples, drowned the cocks!
> You sulphurous and thought-executing fires,
> Vaunt-couriers of oak-cleaving thunderbolts,
> Singe my white head!
>
> *King Lear* III. ii. 1–6.

But again the providence of God had placed safeguards upon the destructive potential of the elements, so that no such disaster could occur. The antipathy of water to fire, and of earth to air, assured that each element was kept in check by the contrary nature of its counterpart, and that no single element could gain ascendency over the others. From time to time—during great floods and tempests, or a summer of great heat—it might appear that the elemental balance had been disturbed; but always order reimposed itself through the resistance of a second element, and the disposition of the whole system towards stability.

Elements and humours

Since all things were compounded of the elements, man himself was framed of these four substances: he breathed air, was kept warm by the elemental fire in his bodily constitution, and took the liquid element of blood from water; and at death the heavier parts of his body reverted to earth, from which they were made. The element of fire was, in addition, responsible for the indispensable condition of man's bodily existence—the spirit of life itself; which as the Elizabethan psychologist Timothy Bright explained, had its origins in very thin blood, 'which being purified and as it were distilled with the hotness of the heart, engendereth a most subtle breath, much like a flame of fire; which passeth from the heart, and walking throughout the whole body, doth minister and yield unto every member a lively heat, which is called vital spirit'.

There was the same need to preserve an elemental balance within man's body as in the macrocosm, and for similar reasons. Undue preponderance of one element threw his constitution out of gear, and produced illness whose nature reflected this imbalance. To give a more accurate explanation of disease, and a clearer basis for medical treatment, the old philosophy held that the body contained four fluids called 'humours', each corresponding to one of the elements; and that good health depended upon their harmonious relationship. The element of fire gave its hot, dry quality to choler; a humour which in excess produced burning fevers. When Donne suggests, in *A Fever*, that his wife's illness might be the fire which 'shall burne this world', he is not being as fanciful as a modern reader might suppose. The watery element had a corresponding element in phlegm, whose preponderance could be recognized in dropsy and running colds; and the earthy humour of black bile was the cause of melancholy and depression. The remaining element, air, shared its warm moist quality with the humour of blood; and by imparting its characteristic lightness to the constitution, encouraged liveliness and gaiety to offset the depression arising from black bile. Excess of blood led to illnesses such as apoplexy, which might be relieved by bleeding the patient, to reduce the preponderance of this humour.

Ideally, the four humours should be so equally balanced that body and mind should remain in perfect health; but as from time to time the elements became unstabilized and produced floods and tempest, so the human constitution tended to favour one or other of the humours; and the temperament developed with a particular bias for some characteristically 'humorous' form of behaviour and outlook. In the sixteenth century as during the Middle Ages, individual temperament was referred to as 'complexion'; a term which now means only the facial colouring by which temperament could be recognized. Of the four complexions—sanguine, phlegmatic, choleric and melancholic—each had its characteristic marks in bodily appearance and manner. According to Galen, the sanguine man would be found to be 'of a purple and ruddy colour; soft, warm, and smooth-skinned;

comely of stature and of reasonable feature; fleshly bodied and a little rough; auburn haired, red or yellow bearded, and comely bushed'—that is, with a great spreading head of hair.

Galen, and the generations of medical practitioners who followed his beliefs, saw blood as the best of the humours—'this lovely and amiable juice', as one Elizabethan writer described it—and supposed that the sanguine man would be distinguished by his good temper, robust physique, personal charm and liveliness. A preponderance of any of the other three humours was much less of an advantage. In the choleric man, natural moisture was severely reduced by the undue heat of 'the great store of choler which is in him'; and the resulting dryness impeded healthy growth and quickly exhausted the vitality of the body. Such men were found to be 'naturally fierce, arrogant, imperious, stately, untractable and unruly'; and could be recognized by their mean stature, leanness, rough skin and frizzled hair, as well as by their quickness of movement and rapid speech. Very different was the temperament of the phlegmatic man, whose cold, moist complexion made him naturally sluggish and drowsy; whose body was fat and pallid, and whose wits were feeble, being 'drowned in moist quality and cold humour' which left him stupefied and incapable. But least fortunate was the melancholic man; for where healthy life and growth required warmth and moisture, the mixture of dry and cold in his complexion threatened him with decay, and deprived him of all lively energy and good spirits. This disordered state of health might be brought about by prolonged grief or suffering; and could also be produced by exhausting the mind by studying too hard, 'by leading a peakish and solitary life, by hunger, penury, and strict fare; or else by using some kinds of nourishments whereby such men brought themselves into a cold and dry distemperature'. A man suffering from such a disorder would be ill-advised to eat root vegetables taken from the earth, for they would increase his imbalance towards melancholy; in the same way as eating fish from the cold, moist element would increase phlegm, and highly spiced food would increase choler.

Where modern medicine determines diet by calculating the amount of protein or vitamin which a given food contains, the old philosophy made its recommendations in the belief that every kind of meat and drink took on the properties of its natural evironment or source: that because birds lived in the air their flesh would contribute to the associated humour of blood, and that wine gave merriment and liveliness by adding to the vital spirits which animated the whole body. We may find such beliefs as absurd as the many scientific assumptions which the old philosophy promoted without ever examining the facts; but there is something humanly attractive in the notion that living creatures share the qualities and character of their environment, and are related by natural ties which the layman easily understands. Here again we see the strong basic tendency of the old philosophy to bring things into relationship and association: refusing to regard the universe as a random collection of objects and creatures—stones, planets, flowers, carnivores—dissociated by species, and existing in separate compartments. The whole universe was one entity, and through its network of sympathy and correspondence every single part was in communication with the rest.

Alchemy

The belief that all created objects were organized into systems and relationships supported one of the most persistent hopes of the old science—that of discovering the so-called philosophers' stone, by which base metals could be transmuted into gold. Like algebra, alchemy was one of the sciences brought to Europe during the Middle Ages by the Moorish invasion of Spain; but it proved to be a less useful form of knowledge. What persuaded generations of alchemists to waste time, money and ingenuity in a fruitless search for the philosophers' stone was a characteristic assumption that the metals, like all other created things, formed a hierarchy in which each kind had its appointed place. It followed from this that each metal was distinguished from the others not merely by its physical qualities but by its place in the natural order; so that to the medieval mind the sovereignty of gold or the baseness of lead were attributes as real as their weight and colour. The kingly quality of gold, the alchemists seem to have supposed, came in part from its inclusiveness: it summed up the qualities of metal as comprehensively as a king did those of his subjects, and in this way represented an epitome of their individual natures. If this were so, they evidently argued, it must be possible to make gold by combining elements of all the basic metals and related substances, like clay and ashes. This belief stands behind the numberless attempts of medieval alchemists to combine what they hoped were the right ingredients in the true proportions, so that when their mixture melted the result would be pure gold. The Canon's Yeoman asks his fellow-pilgrims in Chaucer's tale (lines 758–63):

> What sholde I tellen ech proporcion.
> And bisye me to telle you the names
> Of orpyment, brent bones, iren squames,   [scales.]
> That into poudre grounden been full smal;
> And in an erthen pot how put is al,
> And salt yput in, and also papeer,
> Biforn thise poudres that I speke of heer?

'Thise poudres' suggest the special ingredient which every alchemist trusted to bring the final transformation about; though for this much more was required than a simple melting of elements. Chaucer's Yeoman, who has been assistant to an alchemist, speaks of the work of 'sublymyng, amalgamyng and calcenyng,' and of the apparatus needed for this long process; the 'sondry vessels maad of erthe and glas,' urinals, descensories.

> Violes, crosletz, and sublymatories,
> Cucurbites and alambikes eek,
> And othere swiche, deere ynough a leek.

The lists of ingredients and apparatus are still longer in Jonson's play, *The Alchemist*, which was first performed in 1610. By this date alchemy had fallen into general disrepute by its long-standing association with such cheating and trickery as both Chaucer and Jonson describe; but so far as the scientific theory could be held apart from the frauds which it encouraged, there was still no reason to doubt its central assumption. Jonson's villains offer a different explanation of the scientific principle involved in the transmutation of metals. It would be absurd, Subtle argues, to suppose that gold suddenly came into existence in its perfect state: nature first creates a rough and imperfect substance, and then gradually refines it. The task of the alchemist is to accelerate this process by giving base metal the qualities which gold acquires through its long natural maturing, so that the change can occur overnight. To us, this idea must appear even more absurd than the other, but it conformed with the Elizabethan belief that gold was the final expression of qualities which the other metals shared to a smaller extent. Here again, the old philosophy insisted upon likeness and relationship within its hierarchies, and assumed that the character which philosophers attributed to an object were indeed part of its nature.

Maps of wit

The sense of correspondence and relationship between objects entirely different in form and species directly encouraged the natural impulse of the poet to discover likenesses in things apparently dissimilar and unconnected. When Donne came of age, a vogue for witty writing gave further encouragement to the poet to seek out relationships that were sometimes absurdly improbable or fanciful; but such strained comparisons as Donne himself contrives may contain an element of seriousness. The old philosophy itself proposed connections between planets, animals and stones hardly less bizarre to modern judgment than the old associations which metaphysical poetry came to offer. The link between Scholastic beliefs and poetic practice was strengthened by the taste for intellectual attitudes and allusions in later Elizabethan writing, which developed with the widespread interest in formal rhetoric, described in a later chapter of this book. Wit, in its broad Elizabethan sense, could be displayed by references to ideas and beliefs of the old philosophy, which represented the only body of organized scientific opinion available to writers of the age.

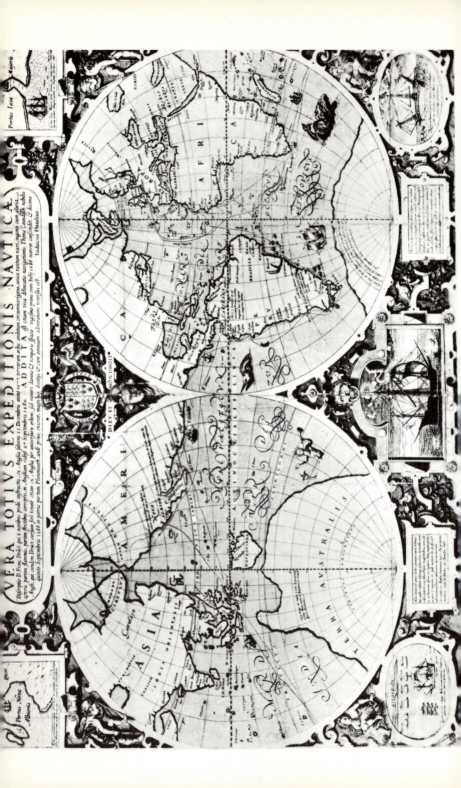

It is in this spirit that Shakespeare makes Maria compare Malvolio's face to 'the new map with the augmentation of the Indies'; an image both fantastic and learned, though referring to one of the discoveries which were proving the limitations of the old science.

The ancient geographers had assumed, reasonably enough, that the earth was divided into three continents meeting about the Mediterranean, which formed the physical centre of the known world. Their mistake was brought to light by the voyage of Columbus in 1492; and in the century following numerous expeditions and navigations to both the Americas revealed the magnitude of the error. In this major respect at least the old science had been proved fallible, and we might expect to find a marked decline in the authority of its cosmographers in consequence, and a rejection of the intellectual habits which they had encouraged their readers to adopt. In fact neither happened. Instead, while sixteenth-century navigators, merchants and poets agreed in placing America firmly on the map, they continued to respect established authority by speaking as though the world had only three parts. This ambivalence of outlook is well illustrated by Donne himself, who in one poem can address his mistress as 'my America! my new-found-land', yet in another adopt the assumption of the old cosmography that three continents make up the world:

> On a round ball
> A workman that hath copies by, can lay
> An Europe, Afrique, and an Asia,
> And quickly make that which was nothing, all.
> *A Valediction: of Weeping*

Frobisher's attempts to find the North-West passage, the efforts to colonize Virginia, and Ralegh's expedition up the Orinoco were all too well publicized for the reality of this new continent to be doubted; yet Donne's conceit shows that even an unusually intelligent Elizabethan could continue to write as though the old cosmography had not been disproved. Although he knew that there were not three continents but four, the habit of thought implanted by traditional beliefs was evidently too deep-rooted to be checked, even when it was so obviously erroneous. Whatever the facts of the situation, which were fully acknowledged where practical considerations of trade and navigation were involved, in other respects Donne and his contemporaries seem to have found it more convenient to ignore the new map of the world, and to return to the appealing conception of a world divided into three neighbouring land-masses. This impulse to leave America out of account is not likely to have been motivated by respect for the old cosmography alone. It seems more probable that the habit of expecting all creation to be laid out according to a logical design made it difficult to accept the existence of America imaginatively. However vast, it stood entirely outside the ordered scheme of the

Map of the world showing Drake's circumnavigation of 1586–8,

old world, refusing to combine with the other three continents in the intelligible order which must inform all the work of God. America might be accepted as a geographical fact, but its existence seems to have posed theological questions which Donne's age was not ready to examine.

Before the bases of empiricism had been established, there was no immediate case for discarding a scientific theory when it had been shown to conflict with observable fact. Such evidence did not form the basis of Scholastic science, which had been laid down dogmatically or by arguing the likely behaviour of objects from their supposed natures. Thus it was believed that, because it was heavier, a large stone fell more rapidly than a small one; where a practical test would have shown that they fell at the same rate. But where intellectual outlook was dominated by the authority of Scholastic dogma, there could be no inclination to submit beliefs to any form of practical test; for this was not the means by which the philospher arrived at the truth. The opinions held by Aristotle or Ptolemy were not to be regarded as hypotheses which later scientists might challenge and modify, but as statements of absolute fact to be pondered and repeated. Bacon was to complain justly that 'knowledge derived from Aristotle and exempted from liberty of examination, will not rise again higher than the knowledge of Aristotle,'* but the habit of testing theories experimentally, and of searching for truth in the actual behaviour of natural objects, rather than in received opinions, had still to establish itself. During Donne's lifetime, intellectual curiosity reached a point where a few outstanding scientists began to make such observations, and to question some of the fundamental assumptions of the old philosophy; but as yet there was no general movement towards the rejection of its authority. Some of the new ideas aroused hostility and contempt, but for the most part they seem to have been met with indifference and incomprehension. It is not difficult to understand why. The old philosophy was a closely integrated system of belief, which could not be dismembered piecemeal. Once fallibility was admitted, the whole system was in danger of falling apart; for such a concession would involve admitting not only that it was mistaken on some particular point, but that its characteristic method of arriving at the truth by what Bacon called 'tumbling up and down in their own reason and conceits' was completely unreliable. To recognize that scientific truth must come through painstaking observation of nature, as Bacon insisted, required a major readjustment of intellectual outlook, which could not be accomplished overnight. Further, before the old philosophy could be abandoned, an alternative system of belief had to stand ready to take its place. In Donne's lifetime, only a few tentative steps had been

* *Advancement of Learning* I. iv.

taken towards the position which was securely established with the publication of Newton's *Principia Mathematica* in 1687. Even when faults in the old system were admitted, there could be no will to exchange the current conception of universal law for a still unformulated body of new ideas. Over a long transitional period, new scientific discoveries had to be accommodated, with varying degrees of discomfort, within the system of belief which they contradicted.

One of the earliest and most persistent of them was the argument that the earth did not, after all, stand at the centre of cosmos, but was a satellite of the sun. This argument had been advanced by Pythagoras six centuries before Christ, but to have regarded the earth as a moving observatory would have greatly complicated primitive astronomy, and—no less serious—the theory did not conform with the religious doctrine of the medieval world. Pythagorean astronomy was therefore forgotten, and when Copernicus revived its argument in 1543 he appeared to be making a new and startling suggestion. The Church of Rome moved to defend orthodox faith by placing *De revolutionibus orbium coelestium* on its index of proscribed books, but although—as this action admitted—Copernicus was threatening to unsettle the basis of established belief, his theory seems to have made little impression upon the general outlook of the age. Some modern commentators have too readily assumed that an assault upon so central a tenet of scientific thought could only have produced disorder and uncertainty. If it did, the disturbance was either very localized or well concealed. More probably, Copernicus simply failed to shake popular faith in a Ptolemic axiom whose truth was self-evident to the humblest observer: that the earth stood still in the heavens, while the sun revolved about it. Even in this more enlightened age we speak of sunrise, not of earthdip; for intellectual judgment has little force against man's instinctive sense of standing on a motionless earth. The threat posed by Copernicus was largely academic: an affront to theological opinion but not an idea that could distress the common man, whose observation told him how foolish it was. Those English writers of the early seventeenth century who resist the Copernican theory refer to him in amusement and contempt, not with anger or with the sense of resisting a dangerous heresy. Donne, we shall see later, was among those who disbelieved Copernicus but treated his ideas indulgently.

Most English readers must have become acquainted with Copernicus through Thomas Digges, whose *Perfit Description of the Coelestiall Orbes* was published in 1576. His simple presentation of the argument makes it easier to understand why this challenge to the old philosophy was so quietly assimilated. If the authority of Ptolemy is brought into question, there is no hint of disrespect for the power which ordains universal order, and no suggestion that God's wisdom is less admirable in this new cosmic design than in the old. To the contrary, Digges calls attention to the majesty and wondrousness of the great system by which the earth is contained:

> Herein can we never sufficiently admire this wonderful and incomprehensible huge frame of God's work proponed [set forth] to our senses; seeing first this ball of the Earth wherein we move to the common sort seemeth great, and that in respect of the Moon's orb is very small; but compared with *orbis magnus* wherein it is carried, it scarcely retaineth any sensible proportion, so marvellously is that orb of annual motion greater than this little dark star wherein we live. But that *orbis magnus* being—as is before declared—but as a point in respect of the immensity of the immoveable heaven, we may easily consider what little portion of God's frame our elementary corruptible world is; but never sufficiently be able to admire the immensity of the rest: especially of that fixed orb garnished with lights innumerable, and reaching up in spherical altitude without end.

This passage serves as a helpful corrective to the assumption that the Copernican theory could only have aroused alarm and deep misgivings among Elizabethan readers. Copernicus continued to regard the sphere of the fixed stars as the motionless abode of angelic spirits, and its height above the earth as the measure of its spiritual purity; and his theory confirmed anew the inherent orderliness and beauty of the whole cosmic design. His argument introduced a new concept which disputed Aristotle's authority in one area of science, but except in the field of theology presented no radical challenge to the old tradition of thought. The notion that man did not, after all, stand at the centre of God's creation could be accepted without abandoning the Scholastic position to which it belonged. Alternatively the issue might be set aside with the kind of mild rebuke which Milton was to express through Raphael:

> Whether heaven move or earth
> Imports not, if thou reckon right; the rest
> From man and angel the great Architect
> Did wisely to conceal, and not divulge
> His secrets to be scanned by them who ought
> Rather admire.
>
> *Paradise Lost* viii. 70–5

The disturbing effect of the Copernican theory has been exaggerated by commentators of our own times who recognize its deeper implications. If Copernicus was right, then the whole system of Ptolemaic astronomy was based upon an error great enough to invalidate its picture of universal order, and it would be necessary to reject this traditional belief altogether. But to Donne and his contemporaries such a total rejection of Ptolemy would have been impossible. We do not discard one form of belief until an alternative offers itself, and until Newton published his *Principia Mathematica* much later in the seventeenth century no such alternative existed. A modern reader looking back over the centuries of new science sees Copernicus in a context which Elizabethans could not dream of. To us he is a bold fore-runner of the scientific thought which was to develop a century later: to them he was hardly more than an amusing crank.

The impact of Galileo's discoveries upon the popular mind has probably been overstressed in much the same way. By observing the planets through the newly invented telescope, Galileo found that Jupiter had a number of attendant moons which moved about the greater body of the planet. This observation was in conflict with an important point of Scholastic doctrine, which asserted that the forces of change and decay did not extend beyond the sphere of the terrestrial moon. Above that—higher, to the Scholastic way of thinking, and thus

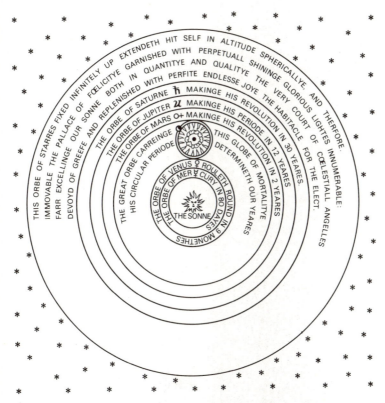

Diagram of the Copernican system, redrawn from Thomas Digges's Perfect Description of the Celestial Orbs, *1576*

in a purer form of existence—the planets were fixed in an unchanging, incorruptible order, wheeling about the earth with a regularity unmatched by any sublunary body. This sense of faultless perfection was seriously compromised by Galileo's discovery. Evidently the heavens contained satellites which recognized not the earth but Jupiter as their centre, and which did not conform to the great general principle which made all the planets turn about the same fixed point. Furthermore, above the sublunary sphere which was accepted as the boundary of change and decay were other moons, if Galileo's testimony could be believed; and a moon could only be associated with the forces of growth and decay which were held to extend no further than the sphere of mutability which enclosed the earth.

This was not the only blow which Galileo struck at the old philosophy, for from other observations he learned of the existence of sunspots. Such blemishes might be accepted in the moon, which lay within the sphere of change and decay; but physical blots could only be seen as evidence of imperfection which no philosopher of the old school could admit in the planetary system. When the professor of astronomy at Padua refused to look through Galileo's telescope to confirm his discoveries, he was not trying to obstruct the course of science. A scientist had not established the truth when he had proved a fact experimentally: he was not expected to establish truth at all, for that had been done centuries earlier by the Schoolmen. If facts and appearances sometimes conflicted with Scholastic doctrine, there could be no possibility of preferring a chance event to a settled opinion confirmed by ages of agreement. It is difficult for us to project ourselves intellectually into the Scholastic habit of working from written authority and of ignoring the actual behaviour of the natural world; but medieval science was firmly based upon such received opinion. There was no need to look through Galileo's telescope: the nature of the heavens had been defined by the greatest of philosophers, and a child's toy was not to disprove the teaching which had gone unchallenged for so many centuries. None the less, it was with the telescope that Galileo found the Galaxy or Milky Way to be composed of myriads of stars: a discovery to which Donne probably makes one of the earliest allusions in the first stanza of his poem *The Primrose*.

Profit, observation and experiment

This uncritical veneration for the voice of the long past was a feature of the old science which came under attack in Bacon's *Advancement of Learning*, published in 1605. As a long reasoned evaluation of the intellectual outlook of his times, the first book of the *Advancement* is probably both a more significant and a more potentially influential contribution to seventeenth-century thought than any of the scientific theories or discoveries that might be mentioned. This is not to say that

Bacon's ideas had an immediate impact on seventeenth-century readers. The considerable interval of twenty-five years elapsed before the *Advancement* was published for the second time, and Bacon's importance as the forerunner of a new attitude to scientific learning was not fully appreciated until still later in the century. Few of his first readers can have been much affected by his arguments; but as his ideas lay germinating they helped to turn the movement of contemporary thought in a new direction, and to encourage a more radical questioning of traditional attitudes of mind. The simple, perceptive remark which he directs against the authority of the greatest of the old philosophers may have seemed merely rebellious: 'Knowledge derived from Aristotle and exempted from liberty of examination will not rise again higher than the knowledge of Aristotle'. [I. iv. 12]. But the remark forms part of an argument whose purpose is to encourage enquiry, and not simply to dethrone Aristotle. Pupils owe their teachers, Bacon declares, 'only a temporary belief and a suspension of their own judgement till they be fully instructed, and not an absolute resignation or perpetual captivity' [*ibid*.], and although it is right to give ancient authors their due, that respect must not prevent the general advance of enquiry, whose end is 'further and further to discover truth'. When he considers the defects and weaknesses of the prevailing attitudes towards knowledge, Bacon calmly challenges some of the central tenets which, in his clear-sighted view, have been responsible for stagnation and error in the field of scientific knowledge. Among the more important of them, he suggests, has been 'a kind of adoration of the mind and understanding of man', which has prompted philosophers to account for natural phenomena by working out a likely explanation in terms of divine purposes. The old scientists were confident of their ability to understand natural events by reasoning their causes, and did not trouble to make the observations which might have revealed the working of natural laws. 'Men have withdrawn themselves too much from the contemplation of nature,' Bacon complains, 'and have tumbled up and down in their own reason and conceits. . . . They disdain to spell, and so by degrees to read in the volume of God's works; and contrariwise by continual meditation and agitation of wit do urge and as it were invocate their own spirits to divine and give oracles unto them, whereby they are deservedly deluded' [I. v. 6]. This criticism is more serious than its measured tone may suggest, for it amounts to a thorough discrediting of the mode of scientific enquiry adopted by the old philosophers. Galileo's findings could be disregarded because their method was untraditional and invalid: truth lay in Holy Writ or the writings of the ancient astronomers, not at the further end of a telescope.

By joining issue with the Schoolmen on this crucial point, Bacon was shaking the fabric of their philosophy; but in discussing the greatest error of contemporary learning—'the mistaking or misplacing of the last or furthest end of knowledge'—he delivered a still greater blow against Scholastic tradition. The philosophers of the ancient world had studied their environment out of a desire for knowledge as disinterested as ever prompted scientific enquiry. The medieval Church inherited their findings without either their spirit of enquiry or their respect for scientific knowledge as an end sufficient in itself. Man was now to study the natural world in order to grasp the inexpressible wonder of divine creation, and thus to subordinate scientific enquiry to religious feeling. This attitude is expressed by Sir Thomas Browne in *Religio Medici*, published in 1642, when he remarks that 'Those highly magnify [God] whose judicious enquiry into his acts, and deliberate research of his creatures, return the duty of a devout and learned admiration'. The characteristic form of medieval enquiry which appealed so strongly to this well-trained physician is indicated in his comment:

> In the causes, nature and affections [influences] of the eclipse of the sun and moon there is a most excellent speculation; but to propound farther, and to contemplate a reason why his providence hath so disposed and ordered their motions in that vast circle as to conjoin and obscure each other, is a sweeter piece of reason and a diviner point of philosophy.

Browne's 'why' could not be answered by an account of the natural forces and movements that are involved in an eclipse: his 'most excellent speculation' would end in an explanation of God's purposes in causing an eclipse to occur. The example shows how natural philosophy had become a minor province of theology, treated as an invitation to ruminate over the finally insoluble question of divine will and not to weigh, measure and observe the behaviour of natural objects. Bacon had already condemned such speculation by remarking that if human intellect cuts itself off from 'the contemplation of the creatures of God', and works upon itself 'as the spider worketh his web, then it is endless, and brings forth indeed cobwebs of learning, admirable for the fineness of thread and work, but of no substance or profit' (I. iv. 5).

The keyword of this argument is 'profit'. Bacon wished learning to be useful, as it could never be while it remained the form of agreeable diversion which Browne found it. Learning would attain its proper end, in Bacon's view, when this merely speculative element of thought had been separated from all that was purposeful and of practical interest in natural philosophy, 'that knowledge may not be as a courtesan, for pleasure and vanity only, or as a bondwoman, to acquire and gain to her master's use, but as a spouse, for generation, fruit and comfort' (I. v. 11). Although Bacon is understandably careful not to offend religious feeling, it is clear from his argument that the idea of studying natural phenomena in order to admire the ingenuity of God's handiwork was to him an irrelevant pursuit. Knowledge was to serve an essentially practical end; not by enriching its possessor but by enabling man to achieve what the arrogant modern phrase calls the control of his environment. In his picture of an ideal state where learning has been directed to such practical ends, Bacon describes a society organized about an institution for scientific research, whose head outlines their purposes as 'the knowledge of causes and secret motions of things; and the enlarging of the bounds of human empire, to the effecting of all things possible'.

New Atlantis was written later in Bacon's life, and published in 1627 a year after his death. Its ideas, and its prophetic glimpse into a future when telephones, submarines and refrigerators would have been invented, consolidate the position which Bacon takes up in *The Advancement of Learning* and build upon its suggestions. In his wish to have knowledge of the 'causes and secret motions of things' Bacon seems to be associating himself with the impulse that led Dr Faustus to destruction; but the fear of enquiring too far, which seems to be justified in Marlowe's play, was now beginning to lose its power of daunting research. The secret motions which Bacon's scientists set themselves to discover were not to be considered as forbidden to man's knowledge. In declaring their freedom to pursue enquiry beyond the bounds of theological approval—more simply, in divorcing natural philosophy from divinity—they were reducing the authority of God as it had been accepted hitherto. Whether for good or evil, desire for scientific knowledge was becoming more powerful than such traditional respect. This change of outlook reflected a slow but comprehensive shift in man's conception of his own nature and competence which eventually led him to abandon the old tradition of thought.

The scientific discoveries of the new age deserve to be remembered as milestones in the establishing of truth based upon observation and experiment. But as poets, Donne and his contemporaries were not directly involved in these discoveries; and a literary historian must be more concerned with the intellectual outlook which prompted Bacon to write his *Advancement*, or Harvey to make the enquiries that led him to discover the circulation of the blood. Such challenges and such discoveries came about as the result of a disposition to question and re-examine which was beginning to show itself after centuries of intellectual conformity; and this intellectual stirring may not have been confined to scientists. Something new was in the air which the sensitive antennae of a poet might have picked up and incorporated into his writing, not in explicit terms but as an echo of the changed attitude underlying the shift of scientific outlook. It is generally assumed that Donne's poetry gives body to these intellectual undercurrents, and that he expresses a direct interest in the outlook of the new science which his age was bringing into being. This suggestion is immediately attractive. It seems to explain why so many of Donne's

A seventeenth century compass.

images are taken from broadly scientific subjects, and why he adopts an argumentative method in developing his theme, where other Elizabethan poets seem to be impelled only by feeling. Despite its plausibility, however, this is a suggestion to be treated with reserve.

The fact is that Donne's scientific allusions are drawn entirely from the old philosophy. No alternative was open to him, for at the period of his *Songs and Sonets* at least, if not throughout his life, there existed no coherent body of thought which might have been recognized as a new scientific outlook. This fact has been obscured by the mistaken belief that in *The First Anniversary* Donne refers explicitly to 'the new philosophy': a mistake encouraged by Grierson's oversight in the introduction to his *Metaphysical Poetry*, where the line is misquoted. What Donne wrote was 'And new philosophy calls all in doubt,' and although a modern reader may reasonably suppose the phrase to carry much the same meaning, Donne is using 'philosophy' to mean the study of nature. He seems to be referring generally to the new

ideas of his age, but in fact he intends a particular and limited refer-
ence to the Copernican theory, already half a century old. Donne uses
the phrase again in *Sermon LXXX* when, discussing the impermanence
of earthly things, he remarks: 'I need not call in new philosophy, that
denies a settledness, an acquiescence in the very body of the earth,
but makes the earth to move in that place where we thought the sun
had moved: I need not that help, that the earth itself is in motion,
to prove this.' The phrase appears again in his *Devotions*, a series of
prose pieces recording the progress of a serious illness which Donne
underwent in 1623. When the fever abates, and he is allowed to
leave his bed, he writes:

> I am up, and I seem to stand, and I go round; and I am a new
> argument of the new philosophy that the earth moves round. Why
> may I not believe that the whole earth moves in a round motion,
> though that seem to me to stand, when as I seem to stand to my
> company, and yet am carried in a giddy and circular motion as I
> stand?
>
> *(Meditation XXI)*

With these examples before us, we have to abandon any notion that
Donne's 'new philosophy' involved a prevision of Newtonian physics,
or the recognition of any other organized body of new scientific ideas.
We have also to take the no less important point that Donne is so far
from expressing anxiety over the Copernican theory that he can make
it the subject of a light-hearted conceit. The passage describing
himself as 'a new argument of the new philosophy' should send us
back to *The First Anniversary* with a more critical awareness of Donne's
tone. When he complains that, in consequence of the Copernican
argument, 'The element of fire is quite put out' (l. 206) Donne is
playing on two senses of the expression 'put out', and showing more
witty detachment than disquiet. To judge from his playful remarks
in the *Devotions*, Donne gave Copernicus very little serious consider-
ation. Harvey, who published his discovery of the circulation of the
blood well within Donne's lifetime, seems not to have persuaded
Donne to revise his traditional belief that the heart served merely to
heat the blood. In a sermon preached in 1626 Donne summed up his
intellectual allegiance by remarking, in respect of man's knowledge:
'We look upon Nature but with Aristotle's spectacles, and upon the
body of man but with Galen's, and upon the frame of the world but
with Ptolemy's spectacles.' There can have been few members of his
congregation for whom this generalization was not true, as it certainly
was for the preacher himself.

The poet's position

We do not read Donne in order to learn about the old philosophy, nor did he write in order to air his knowledge. There are in fact fewer scientific allusions in his poetry than are sometimes supposed. The popular notion that his writing abounds in references to navigation, alchemy, mathematics, the elements and human anatomy needs only to be tested against a few poems to be seen as mistaken. Here and there we find the scientific analogies and parallels which were to become characteristic of metaphysical poetry: in *The Funeral* (ll. 9–11), for instance, where Donne follows the old anatomy in regarding the sinews as though they were nerves, feeding information to the brain:

> For if the sinewy thread my brain lets fall
>> Through every part,
> Can tie those parts, and make me one of all:

or in *The Dissolution* which speaks of the lover's

>> fire of passion, sighs of air,
> Water of tears, and earthly sad despair,

and affirms conventionally that these elements 'my materials be'. Another of the *Songs and Sonets* contains a well-known reference to the belief, shared by theologians and physicians, that the vital spirits served to unite the bodily and the spiritual identities of man (*The Ecstasy*, 61–4).

> As our blood labours to beget
>> Spirits as like souls as it can,
> Because such fingers need to knit
>> That subtle knot which makes us man.

But Donne's allusions to contemporary philosophy are seldom as elaborate or as specific as these passages suggest. Moreover, by isolating such references we may overlook their function in the poem, which is to support an argument and not to display Donne's learning. *The Funeral* continues, after suggesting its physiological parallel,

> These hairs which upward grew, and strength and art
>> Have from a better brain,
> Can better do't:

maintaining that the bracelet of woman's hair which Donne wears can tie him together more effectively than the 'sinewy threads' in his own body. Similarly, in *The Ecstasy*, Donne uses the reference to the 'subtle knot' of man's mixed nature to argue that lovers' souls must not ignore their physical senses, but find expression through them. The illustration drawn from science or theology is not itself the focus of Donne's interest, but a means of bringing attention to bear upon the idea which he is working out. This is the aspect of his poetry which has probably caused most surprise, and in some ages given most offence, to Donne's readers; who suppose for the most part that poetry is concerned with passions and sensations rather than with dialectic, and that its images are drawn from the natural world rather than from the sciences. But Donne, as will be suggested in a later chapter, seems to have been imaginatively impelled to define his experience; and to serve this purpose his images had to have an exactness of meaning that sensation cannot render. His comparison of the separated lovers to 'stiff twin compasses'—or as we should say, to a pair of dividers—in *A Valediction forbidding Mourning* makes its point by excluding all terms of feeling, and by forcing us to consider the lovers' relationship in its starkly essential form. The oddity of the image, and its unlikeliness as a figure of love poetry, are incidental to Donne's purpose: what matters is the clarity and firmness of his definition, which only an intellectual parallel can provide.

Compasses, maps, globes and spheres suggest a common interest in navigation and cosmography, and encourage a modern reader to suppose that Donne took a lively interest in the geographical discoveries of his age. We should not press this point too far, but recognize that Donne also shows himself aware of the less momentous common affairs of his day. Thus he refers to the portraitist Hilliard, to the chronicler Holinshed, and to Bajazeth, a character in Marlowe's *Tamburlaine*. If at one time he speaks of America, at another he mentions Westminster, Aldgate and Charing Cross, and alludes to books which were the fashionable reading of the times. Such passages help to correct any impression that Donne's intellectual interests were limited to academic and scholarly subjects. They were far more comprehensive. It is the generality of his interests, both erudite and everyday, finding expression first through images of alembics and atomies, and then by referring to sundials and bedstaves, which should prevent us from assuming that Donne was either medieval or modern in outlook. He belonged to his time, and embraced its characteristic beliefs; more consciously than most of his contemporaries, perhaps, but not separated from them by any appreciation of how short a time the authority of the old philosophy had still to run. As a young poet, writing verse that was often challengingly bold and original, he might have been seen as the forerunner of a literary movement supported by a vigorous disposition to challenge and remould traditional ideas. As dean of St Paul's he had lost this defiant energy. The sermons reveal a sombre awareness of moral corruption, feeding itself on a pessimistic evaluation of man which lames the hope of an intellectual advance. 'We are all conceived in close prison,' he told his congregation in 1619, 'in our mothers' wombs we are close prisoners all; when we are born we are born but to the liberty of the house, prisoners still, though within larger walls; and then all our life is but a going out to the place of execution, to death.'

Donne's obsession with decay and mortality, embodied in the effigy in St Paul's Cathedral, was shared by other Jacobean writers who could not shake off the sense of moral contamination which man had inherited from the Fall. Their attitude of mind, and the defeatism it encouraged, were seen as a direct challenge to the new ideas which were slowly establishing themselves, and to the half-formed promise of progress in learning offered by Bacon. It became an urgent task of the new movement of thought to resist the pessimistic conviction of man's ignorance and helplessness which Donne's sermons admit so frequently. We should see the gloom and foreboding that darkens Jacobean outlook, perhaps, as the characteristic response of men whose familiar landmarks were crumbling, and who could not re-establish themselves in the world of mixed values and uncertain standards from which, after an interval of open confusion, the outlines of a new system would emerge. Donne was not among the handful who sensed in advance what this form was to be. Intellectually and by emotional inclination he was rooted in his epoch; coming of age during its great upsurge of optimism and self-confidence, and dying when the afterglow of Elizabethan splendour was about to be finally extinguished. His mind had been a storehouse crammed with current ideas and intellectual concepts drawn from sources which epitomized the nature and range of Elizabethan belief. It is significant that what his poetic followers borrowed from him most eagerly was the oddity or quaintness which Donne's intellectual figures had then acquired.

4   The literary background

Metaphysical style

Donne is commonly considered as the great literary innovator of his age: a poet who although much less accomplished than Shakespeare, shaped for himself a much more individual style. Shakespeare emerged from the main stream of Elizabethan poetic tradition where Donne, it might seem, forced himself into the literary limelight by the sheer energy, impudence and originality of his writing. This view of Donne is put forcefully by Carew in his elegy to the dead poet, when he comments in a famous passage (lines 25–8):

> The Muses' garden, with pedantic weeds
> O'erspread, was purged by thee; the lazy seeds
> Of servile imitation thrown away,
> And fresh invention planted.

Set beside the flamboyance and lavishness of much Elizabethan verse—qualities which obviously appealed to Spenser, Marlowe and the young Shakespeare—the bare, taut, unceremonious language of the *Songs and Sonets* can make Donne seem like the poet of a different age and a distinct tradition. It would be unjust to deny the importance of the qualities which separate Donne from other Elizabethan poets and establish his individual greatness; but it would also be mistaken to suppose that Donne's 'fresh invention' was entirely independent of current trends of Elizabethan writing. Although much that Donne wrote was surprising, it was not always new; and in one major respect at least he was continuing to develop a line of interest which several Elizabethan poets had already found absorbing.

It was as monarch of wit that Carew finally described Donne, whose style in prose and poetry is dominated by a taste for intellectual argument and demonstration, often by means of the conceit: a fanciful or ingenious notion worked into the train of thought. Donne surpassed other poets by going further, by straining comparisons and relationships of idea to the point where they seem about to crack; but this extremism does not disguise Donne's association with a literary fashion which had been growing for at least twenty years before he began to write. The line of wit has its roots in formal rhetoric, which was being rediscovered and popularized during Shakespeare's boyhood. Its practices, schematized in such handbooks as Wilson's *Art of Rhetoric*, 1553, were taken up enthusiastically by writers of fiction and raised to a point of elaborate artifice in Lyly's *Euphues*, published in 1578. The subtitle of Lyly's prose tale, 'The

Anatomy of Wit', defines his purpose. His story is a flimsy outline serving as basis for an astonishingly versatile display of rhetorical tropes and figures, arranged in counter-balancing patterns whose sense is always subordinate to Lyly's euphuistic style. The wit of his subtitle is displayed in the sheer inventiveness of his writing, which draws upon every variety of rhetorical figure to produce its fantastic embroidery of speech:

> Alas Euphues, by how much the more I love the high climbing of thy capacity, by so much the more I fear thy fall. The fine crystal is sooner crazed than the hard marble, the greenest beech burneth faster than the dryest oak, the fairest silk is soonest soiled, and the sweetest wine turneth to the sharpest vinegar; the pestilence doth most rifest infect the clearest complexion, and the caterpillar cleaveth unto the ripest fruit; the most delicate wit is allured with small enticement unto vice, and most subject to yield unto vanity. If therefore thou do but harken to the Sirens thou wilt be enamoured: if thou do haunt their places and houses thou shalt be enchanted.

The attraction of this metronomic style soon palls, and after a blaze of popularity euphuism was to fall out of fashion as suddenly as it had burst upon Elizabethan readers; but the urge to display unwearied inventiveness that is so marked in Lyly's writing did not share his eclipse. The young Shakespeare's fondness for multiplying examples—one of the figures of formal rhetoric—is clearly shown by this characteristic passage of his first published work, *Venus and Adonis* (ll. 163–8).

> Torches are made to light, jewels to wear,
> Dainties to taste, fresh beauty for the use,
> Herbs for the smell, and sappy plants to bear:
> Things growing to themselves are growth's abuse.
> > Seeds spring from seeds, and beauty breedeth beauty:
> > Thou wast begot; to get it is thy duty.

The poet displays his wit by calling up a rapid series of illustrations to support the speaker's argument; but there is wit of a tougher kind in the argument itself. Where Lyly chooses images for an effect of colour and variety without disciplining his ideas at all strictly— sweet wine does not in fact produce the tartest vinegar—Shakespeare keeps a firm grip on the point being debated, and makes the illustrations serve this purpose. In this way his variation on Lyly's style acquires a much stronger intellectual element than euphuism had included, and Shakespeare gives impulse to a more demanding form of wit which depends more upon subtle presentation of ideas than upon sheer copiousness. He sometimes pursues this intellectual element of his poetry to the verge of mere cleverness (*Venus and Adonis*, 961–6):

> O how her eyes and tears did lend and borrow;
> Her eye seen in the tears, tears in her eye;
> Both crystals where they viewed each other's sorrow:
> Sorrow that friendly sighs still sought to dry.
>   But like a stormy day, now wind, now rain,
>   Sighs dry her cheeks, tears make them wet again.

We recognize here incipient forms of the conceit which Donne was to make a conspicuous feature of his poetry. Shakespeare's play of ideas aims at a pretty, half-comic effect, and stops where Donne would begin to apply analytical pressure; but in this stanza Donne might have found the starting-point of at least two extended conceits. Such borrowing or adapting of Shakespeare's playful analogies is more clearly seen in a passage of Donne's *Elegy IX, The Autumnal*, which develops its metaphysical line of thought from Shakespeare's fanciful account of the 'pretty dimple' in Adonis's cheek (*Venus and Adonis*, 242–7):

> Love made those hollows, if himself were slain,
> He might be buried in a tomb so simple;
>   Foreknowing well if there he came to lie,
>   Why, there Love lived, and there he could not die.
> These lovely caves, these round enchanting pits,
> Opened their lovely mouths to swallow Venus' liking.

By comparing the dimple to a tomb, to caves and pits, Shakespeare prefigures the kind of strained analogy typical of Donne; but in a context of courtly feeling—'lovely', 'enchanting'—which softens and modifies the sense of striking unfamiliarity. When Donne treats the same idea in *The Autumnal* he makes the comparisons bluntly, forcing us to acknowledge their oddity and the deviousness of his wit (ll. 13–18):

> Call not these wrinkles graves: if graves they were,
>   They were Love's graves, for else he is nowhere.
> Yet lies not Love dead here, but here doth sit
>   Vowed to this trench, like an anachorit;   [anchorite]
> And here, till hers—which must be his death—come,
>   He doth not dig a grave, but build a tomb.

Like Adonis's dimple, Lady Herbert's wrinkles are seen as a tomb; but only after Donne has suggested four times that they are graves, and has transformed the figure of dead Love into a living hermit uncomfortably confined in a trench: a pointedly unromantic notion. Unlike Shakespeare, Donne makes no attempt to clothe his odd ideas in appealing terms: his language is bare and uncompromising, and in the absence of poetic decoration his argument stands out as a hard plain structure. As a result, the whole sense of the passage is dominated by Donne's wit, which does not so much play with a charming conceit, as Shakespeare does—'Love made those hollows'—as hammer out a strenuous pattern of ideas; beginning with a forthright injunction, 'Call not these wrinkles graves', and qualifying its own conclusions as the argument thrusts forward, following the twists of the poet's mind. If Lady Herbert's wrinkles were graves, they must be the graves of Love: but Love is by no means dead, he lives in her wrinkles like a hermit in a cell, and will do so until she dies and those wrinkles become his tomb. Once Donne has fastened on to the central idea of considering the wrinkles graves, he clings to it tenaciously, wringing out every bizarre consequence that the image can be made to yield. It is this intense intellectual working of a single concept which distinguishes Donne's handling of the idea first treated by Shakespeare, whose appeals to sensation—'pretty dimple' and 'opened their mouths'—find no parallel in Donne's forceful argument. The difference in feeling between the two passages is implicit in their central ideas: the bewitching and youthful dimple, and the unromantic brand of old age.

If the comparison reveals how abruptly Donne broke away from the line of richly sensational poetry followed by Shakespeare, it also suggests how far this movement of dissent was prompted by a tendency which Donne found in the main stream of Elizabethan poetry. The essential novelty of his writing lay in what it left out: in its isolating of the intellectual element which in Shakespeare was combined with what may conveniently be called poetry of feeling. Donne made this isolated element of wit the dominating force of his writing. He pared down the abundant language of Elizabethan poetry to a comparatively narrow measure, discarding terms whose imaginative overtones would blur the clear, hard statement of the ideas which he struggles to define; and he sacrificed attributes of poetry which other writers would have considered indispensable—melody, courtly grace, mythological enrichment—in order to concentrate upon the intellectual argument or demonstration which his poems habitually work out. Shakespeare too can devote himself to the kind of playful dialectic which proves the truth of paradox (*Venus and Adonis*, 1015–20):

> O love, quoth she, how much a fool was I,
> To be of such a weak and silly mind
> To wail his death who lives, and must not die
> Till mutual overthrow of mortal kind?
>> For he being dead, with him is beauty slain;
>> And beauty dead, black Chaos comes again.

But the argument is offered with too little energy to be intellectually impressive: Shakespeare knows that his paradox rests precariously on a form of words, and submits it as an amusing trifle. When Donne treats the same paradox in *A Nocturnal upon St Lucy's Day* he goes far beyond Shakespeare in hyperbole; but he develops his argument with such single-minded deliberateness that we might accept what he says as the expression of profound personal feeling (ll. 28–37):

> But I am by her death, which word wrongs her,
> Of the first nothing the elixir grown.
>> Were I a man, that I were one
>> I needs must know: I should prefer,
>>> If I were any beast,
> Some ends, some means: yea, plants, yea, stones detest
> And love: all, all some properties invest.
> If I an ordinary nothing were,
> As shadow, a light and body must be here.
> But I am none; nor will my sun renew.

Both language and structure of this passage are determined by its intellectual purpose, which is to prove—absurdly, as it might seem—that Donne has no existence. This argument is in itself a manifestation of wit far more striking than Shakespeare has attempted, and Donne's passing references to points of scientific belief—the first nothing, the elixir, the properties of plants and stones—give particular emphasis to the intellectual standpoint of his poem. Where another poet would use images to evoke feeling, Donne brings in allusions to cosmology and natural philosophy to resolve his ideas more sharply. He is not a man, nor an animal; he is not even a plant or a stone, but nothing; even less than the nothing of a shadow that is cast by a solid object. As he presses forward his fantastic thesis, these references to contemporary belief help to concentrate attention upon his ideas, where imagery drawn from the realm of feeling would diffuse it over a wider field of interest.

Colloquial energy

It is probably for this reason that Donne uses conventional images so seldom, preferring to express himself in vigorous, undecorated language whose emotional impact is brought about by its colloquial directness. The speaker seems to make no concessions to formal literary style, but to blurt out his feelings with the choking impatience or excitement of a man too deeply absorbed in his private experience to impose discipline upon what he writes. The actuality of emotional engagement is there, in the rough language and uneven phrasing of protest or passionate statement, where any considered literary effect would immediately lower the temperature of his utterance:

> 'Tis true, 'tis day: what though it be?
> O wilt thou therefore rise from me?
> Why should we rise because 'tis light?
> Did we lie down because 'twas night?

Break of Day, which opens with these lines, warns us not to assume that Donne is always writing about his actual experience, for here the speaker is a woman.

The *Songs and Sonets* are not poetry of spontaneous impulse, as the frequent elaborateness of their stanza-form makes clear; but they are poems written to create an effect of actual happening in the world of common fact. In this respect Donne dissociates himself from general Elizabethan practice very sharply. It is not his disrespectful rebuke to the sun in *The Sun Rising* that makes this poem so surprising, but Donne's emphatic rejection of the studied idiom reserved for poetry. The opening lines of Shakespeare's Sonnet 33 are typical of the formal literary manner by which the poet indicates the noble elevation of this theme. He is not attempting to describe the actual world, but to transmute a commonplace experience in the way that Sidney suggests, by turning its base metal to gold:

> Full many a glorious morning have I seen
> Flatter the mountain-tops with sovereign eye,
> Kissing with golden face the meadows green,
> Gilding pale streams with heavenly alchemy.

The creative power of the poet is made to work the same change upon its subject matter as the 'heavenly alchemy' of the sun upon the pallid landscape. It brings about this transformation by using language and forms of speech that have almost nothing in common with the spoken English of popular life. The opening phrase 'full many', used for 'several', tells us at once that the poet is adopting a manner too lofty to accept terms of popular speech. The outburst of feeling that begins *The Sun Rising* (lines 1–8) has just the opposite effect:

> Busy old fool, unruly sun,
> Why dost thou thus
> Through windows and through curtains call on us?
> Must to thy motions lovers' seasons run?
> Saucy pedantic wretch, go chide
> Late schoolboys, and sour prentices;
> Go tell court huntsmen that the king will ride;
> Call country ants to harvest offices.

In these eight lines only 'pedantic' falls outside the idiom of spoken English so convincingly represented in the phrasing of Donne's sentences. From the outset we are firmly placed in a familiar, everyday context of windows and curtains, schoolboys, apprentices and harvesters; where both language and forms of speech are irrevocably linked with common human feelings and experience. Where Shakespeare abounds in metaphor, 'flatter the mountain-tops . . . kissing the meadows', Donne speaks directly and with an entirely literal purpose: his windows and curtains are not part of a poetic analogy but objects taken from real life. The whole character of his poem is directed by a desire to represent the actuality of passionate experience. With this intention Donne refuses to employ the forms of poetic ornament which most Elizabethan writers adopted as a matter of course, limiting himself to a kind of basic English vocabulary which renders impressions in terms as stark as the grave-digger's discovery: 'a bracelet of bright hair about the bone'. This famous line from *The Relic* epitomizes Donne's power of making direct statement act upon the reader with the dramatic effect of figurative speech. Alliteration gives the phrase the emphasis of heightened feeling, but this is the only literary device which Donne uses here. He relies upon the force of plain colloquial terms to evoke an impression of sensational contact as sharp and immediate as a physical blow, which makes the discovery of the relic happen to the reader.

This may explain why, when Donne uses figurative expressions, he draws images and comparisons most readily from the field of science and allied studies. It would be mistaken to think of Donne simply as an Elizabethan highbrow or intellectual, for although his learning and intelligence are indisputable, his poetry is clearly the writing of a deeply passionate man. The so-called metaphysical images which are taken to characterize him are not designed to show his learning, and do not in fact represent any unusual degree of erudition. Any literate Elizabethan knew something about the celestial spheres, human anatomy, America and the nature of angels; though he may not have been accustomed to seeing these subjects referred to in love poetry. Donne brings in allusions to science and theology because he is trying to reach a state of finality or absoluteness through his writing, and because points of scientific belief are more helpful than natural images in such a task. This aim of reaching a condition of fixed security is most easily recognized in the closing lines of some of Donne's best known poems: *The Sun Rising*, for instance, (lines 29–30).

> Shine here to us, and thou art everywhere;
> This bed thy centre is, these walls thy sphere.

The same impression of complete resolution is evoked by the closing statement of *A Nocturnal upon St Lucy's Day*, (line 45) as the poem settles into the immobility of grief:

> This
> Both the year's, and the day's, deep midnight is.

A more familiar example occurs in the final stanza of the *Hymn to God the Father* (lines 15–18) which is generally accepted as Donne's last poem, when the poet stills his disquiet and rests in the assurance of divine grace:

> Swear by thyself that at my death thy sun
> > Shall shine as it shines now and heretofore;
> > > And having done that, thou hast done:
> > > > I have no more.

These poems end in the resolution of a spiritual or intellectual problem which Donne has announced at the outset. There is no need to remark that this process of working out some form of puzzle, or of proving a paradox, is highly characteristic of Donne; for it is the argumentative scheme of his poems which does most to justify their being called metaphysical. As exercises in logical reasoning they are usually very faulty, and the means by which Donne develops and rounds off his argument displays more wit than respect for dialectical method. 'On a round ball', he remarks in *A Valediction of Weeping*, (lines 11–16):

> A workman that hath copies by, can lay
> An Europe, Afric, and an Asia,
> And quickly make that which was nothing, all.
> > So doth each tear
> > Which thee doth wear,
> A globe, yea world, by that impression grow.

The argument only seems logically connected: an unmarked globe is not nothing, and does not become 'all' when the continents are engraved on it; nor do the lover's tears become worlds when they hold an image of his mistress. Donne knows this well enough, but his poetic impulse can only be satisfied when it has presented its ideas in the form of an argued demonstration. However far from logical truth in fact, he must seem to follow, step by step, a process of thought leading from initial thesis to final proof; and to a greater or lesser degree his poems fit themselves to this argumentative form.

We may suppose that Donne imposed this character upon his work because it suited his bent of mind, or because it gave the fullest play to his wit; but more probably the sense of proving and demonstrating which the poems communicate is a condition which Donne felt imaginatively impelled to create. As the colloquial directness of his language gives his poetry the sense of actual happening, and of an immediate contact with reality, so his dialectic seems to confirm the impression of solid truth which such familiar and spontaneous speech evokes. Donne's writing is perhaps to be understood as an attempt to make out of poetry a form of imaginative reality more positive and secure than Donne found in the world about him. His personal life was assailed by doubts and troubling uncertainties which seem only to have been temporarily stilled by marriage. His poetry is his answer to the insecurity which dogged him: an imaginative making of the dependable reality which he needed for peace of mind, and whose absence impelled him to create this synthetic equivalent.

It is important to reach some understanding of the private motives which urged Donne to write and which determined his style, for through this understanding we recognize that the curious 'metaphysical' features of his poetry are not modish decoration but an essential means of expression. The involved, sometimes almost tortured working-out of attitudes and relationships, the strained analogies and uneven rhythm which characterize his writing are an integral part of its meaning: a reflection of the mind labouring to organize the incoherent matter of private experience into systematic order, and to give the world of feeling a structure as positive and constant as a Euclidian demonstration. No poem can be represented by a paraphrase of its explicit sense, for part of its total effect on the reader is brought about by the unperceived working of rhyme and metre upon his feelings, and still more by a mysterious chemistry of words. This is especially true of Donne. His style seems at first gratuitously noisy and conspicuous, distracting attention from the substance of his poem to its mere manner of delivery or its oddities of thought. Later we come to realize how much of Donne's meaning is carried by what we had mistaken for superficial effects. The experience which he communicates to us is represented in large part by the almost physical difficulties of realizing ideas; by a laboured process of working-out and resolving which we are made to feel directly through disturbed patterns of speech and rough wordsounds. Donne's reference to climbing the Hill of Truth, a famous passage recalling the tradition illustrated in our cover picture, shows how forcefully such effects contribute to the plain sense:

> On a huge hill,
> Cragged and steep, Truth stands; and he that will
> Reach her, about must and about must go,
> And what the hill's suddenness resists, win so.
> *Satire III*, 79–82

Both metrically and in syntax the sentence is broken into disjointed phrases, which join the aspirates of 'huge hill' to represent the difficulties of approaching Truth. The word-sounds are unmusical throughout, and the irregular stressing—felt particularly in the unstressed rhyme-word 'will'—denies the passage all sense of steady movement: the commentary seems to follow the climber as he heaves and scrambles breathlessly towards his goal, which he finally reaches in the climax, 'win so'.

This characteristic passage of Donne's writing shows how integral his mode of expression is to the sense of his poetry. If his ideas were expressed in some other form—more gracefully, with a steadier rhythmical pulse—they would no longer describe the experience which Donne seeks to define. The oddities of metaphysical style do not stand on top of an otherwise plain poem, like fantastic ornament set on an inconsequential building: they are the poem, which has been compelled to assume this strangely idiosyncratic form by the pressures urging Donne to create. For him, metaphysical style was not merely a natural means of expression. It was the only mode by which he could represent the sombre intellectual searching of his religious life, and the persistent effort of the lover to prove himself and his mistress fused into a single, self-contained world of being. With his successors, who formed a 'school' only in the loosest sense of the term, this was not so. Such a strongly individual style was bound to admit imitators, who adopted what they could of Donne's manner without his justification. Donne wrote as he did because what he had to say could not be expressed otherwise: his purpose determined his means. There could be no school of Donne, for his style was a uniquely personal instrument which could not serve the need of other poets. What they took from him was at best a dilution of his racked and involved manner, and more usually a domesticated form of the conceit which missed the inner logic of Donne's bizarre parallels, and offered instead mere quaintness. Rather than being integral to the general style of their poems, these metaphysical effects stand out like plums in a cake; and their literary context derives not from Donne but from Jonson.

The significance of Ben Jonson

Though a much less talented poet, Jonson far more than Donne set English poetry on a new course, and by the end of the seventeenth century had proved himself an innovator of deep and lasting influence. Unlike Donne—or indeed, most other Elizabethan poets of moment—Jonson declared his literary standards in a small body of critical writings, and preached these ideas to the group of young poets who accepted him as master. Some of the most trenchant of his critical comments are directed against the popular drama, whose romantic excesses Jonson felt to be ludicrous and unworthy of serious art:

> To make a child, now swaddled, to proceed
> Man, and then shoot up in one beard and weed
> Past threescore years, or, with three rusty swords

And help of some few foot-and-half-foot words
Fight over York and Lancaster's long jars.

Every Man in his Humour, Prologue, 17

His own plays are usually set in the London of his own times, with characters drawn from common life; and by observing the Unities Jonson does still more to limit attention to a credible everyday world, and the 'deeds and language such as men do use'. His comments, some directed almost explicitly against Shakespeare, indicate the strong bias towards classical restraint and disciplined expression which marks Jonson's critical outlook in general. He speaks out against the literary taste of his age as bluntly as he attacks the implausible scope of the romantic drama. 'Now nothing is good that is natural', he writes in *Discoveries*; 'Right and natural language seem to have the least of wit in it; that which is writhed and tortured is counted the more exquisite . . . No beauty to be had but in wresting and writhing our own tongue. Nothing is fashionable till it be deformed; and this is to write like a gentleman'.

Many of the particular comments, and probably the critical inspiration of *Discoveries*, come from Jonson's reading of the ancient Roman authors whose work constituted the basis of classical criticism throughout the Renaissance and during the two following centuries. It was Jonson who made the first determined attempt to graft these classical principles upon the native tradition of English poetry, both by direct instruction and by the example of his own writing. He began to introduce Horatian standards and principles to English audiences at a time when native poetry was more vigorously individual and adventurous than in any previous age, and as much unlike the ideal advanced by Jonson as English writing has ever been until the present. Where it was wild and exuberant, he wished it to be restrained and urbane; where—as in Donne's poetry—it was intensely personal, Jonson argued for a measured detachment of feeling, and where Elizabethan writing at its greatest tended to be involved and dense with meaning, Jonson required it to be simple and clearly expressed. 'The chief virtue of a style is perspicuity,' he remarks in *Discoveries*, 'and nothing so vicious [defective] in it as to need an interpreter.' This axiom condemns a great deal of Shakespeare's most powerful dialogue as well as much of Donne's writing; and we shall not be surprised to hear Jonson's opinion that Shakespeare 'needed art', or that he admired Donne for two poems which are either more restrained or less agitated in metre and feeling than the others: 'His verses *The Lost Chain* he hath by heart, and that passage of *The Calm*, "That dust and feathers do not stir, all was so quiet"'. So Drummond of Hawthornden reported, after Jonson had visited him in 1619; and although we know the first poem as *Elegy XI*, and barely recognize his quotation as coming from *The Calm*, (lines 17–18):

> No use of lanterns; and in one place lay
>   Feathers and dust, today and yesterday;

there is no reason to doubt the general truth of Drummond's report. Another of his guest's remarks on the current literary scene was the apparently irritated opinion that Donne 'for not keeping of accent deserved hanging': a comment which shows that Jonson could not be won over by the emotional dynamism of Donne's poetry when so great a dislocation of rhythmical structure was involved. Evidently Jonson was not prepared to concede that strong passion should display itself in the kind of metrical upheaval so often found in Donne. The poet was not to write for the private relief of discharging profound feeling, but was to use the disciplines of his art to mould impulse into a temperate and well-balanced statement. When the poet allowed his personal involvement to wrench and distort language, forcing words to bear more meaning than they could express in clear terms, he was debasing the standards of good writing. 'Our style should be like a skein of silk', he writes; 'to be carried and found by the right thread, not ravelled and perplexed; then all is a knot, a heap.'

By introducing Horatian standards under the very shadow of Shakespeare's greatness, Jonson was breaking with all the traditions of English writing and issuing a direct challenge to the strain of emphatic individualism that seems to run through Elizabethan poetry. Singling out Lyly, Spenser, Marlowe, Nashe and Donne as five of the most strikingly talented writers of the quarter-century which brought Shakespeare into prominence, we see how each fashioned for himself a uniquely personal style by which he is instantly marked out and identified. In his great comedies Jonson himself is no less distinctive, for one of his principal satirical weapons is language as rhetorically inflated or overloaded as he attacks in his criticism: merely by speaking, his victim makes himself ridiculous. In this way Jonson may have been satisfying a deep imaginative urge to write in the exuberantly personal style which as critic he opposed, yet without exposing himself to a charge of inconsistency. But in his non-dramatic poetry he provides a copybook example of the restrained, emotionally detached and lucid manner which his criticism recommends. His translations of Horace, which render the felicities of Latin with a homely bluntness, must interest us for their attention to the points of style which Jonson felt important—clarity, conciseness, and simplicity of language:

> The poplar tall he then doth marrying twine
>   With the grown issue of the vine;
> And with his hook lops off the fruitless race,
>   And sets more happy in the place;
> Or in the bending vale beholds afar
>   The lowing herds there grazing are;

Or the pressed honey in pure pots doth keep
    Of earth, and shears the tender sheep;
Or when that autumn through the fields lifts round
    His head, with mellow apples crowned,
How—plucking pears his own hand grafted had,
    And purple-matching grapes—he's glad!

The Praises of a Country Life, 9–20

This is neither great nor memorable poetry: it lacks the energy
of committed writing, is cumbrously expressed, and in leaving
nothing to suggestion or personal feeling it fails to excite more than
passing interest. But Jonson is roughing out a new literary style
which was not to reach its completely resolved development for
another century, and in its earliest form this new tradition should
interest us by its intentions rather than by its achievement.

The controlled vigour of his style is seen to better advantage in
To Penshurst, the first of a number of seventeenth-century poems extol-
ling a country house and its family, in which Jonson presents an ideal-
ized picture of life that is industrious, pious and humane: the moral
positive which might stand behind the images of corruption and folly
dominating his satire. The country estate is the hub of an innocent and
harmless system of life, whose tenants show their master a dutiful res-
pect which recalls an earlier and more settled social order (lines
48–56):

But all come in, the farmer and the clown,
And no one empty-handed, to salute
Thy lord and lady, though they have no suit.
Some bring a capon, some a rural cake,
Some nuts, some apples; some, that think they make
The better cheeses, bring 'em; or else send
By their ripe daughters, whom they would commend
This way to husbands, and whose baskets bear
An emblem of themselves in plum or pear.

Here the clarity of Jonson's writing is enriched by its frank appeal
to sensuous feeling; and although he loses none of the perspicuity
which he values as critic, he begins to communicate with his reader
through word-sounds and imaginative suggestions as well as by
explicitly stated ideas. His comment about the 'ripe daughters'

          whose baskets bear
An emblem of themselves in plum or pear

fuses wit with a joyously realized image which sets young womanhood
in a context of warm and rounded maturity. But this sensuous expan-
sion is unobtrusively controlled, and Jonson is not diverted from his
main task of praising Penshurst through these images of natural

abundance. A balance has been established between the appeal of simple, evocative language—'the purpled pheasant with the speckled side', 'the blushing apricot and woolly peach'—and the need to give his poem the organization of a readily intelligible commentary, on which the poet's private feelings do not obtrude. The phrase describing the pheasant has a verbal richness akin to the effect of metaphor, but is in fact closer to impersonal statement. Jonson is showing the way to temper emotion to a conscious literary discipline, and to shape poetry by the standards of a polite culture hitherto alien to English writing.

Unlike Donne, whose style ceased to justify itself when it was imitated, Jonson offered his fellow-poets literary precepts and a manner of writing which he meant them to adopt. Because his style was not a reflection of individual temperament but a considered and impersonal literary form, it could serve other poets equally well; and we are not surprised to find writers of the Caroline period working within this new tradition and at no great distance from Jonson's particular example. *To Penshurst* was imitated by several poets* who either repeated or extended its idealized conception of a contented, self-sufficient community practising the civilized virtues of hospitality and moderation, and paying respect to established customs which in the world at large were being progressively eroded. Perhaps by the single example of this poem Jonson successfully implanted an idea of human culture which, although increasingly at odds with the disturbed state of English society under Charles, continued to appeal to educated taste and to encourage attempts to realize its promise of quiet and well-ordered existence.

The promise was not to be effectively fulfilled until the early eighteenth century, when English social culture reached the point of urbane development which it had willed itself to achieve; but in literature at least the main form of this achievement had been clearly foreshadowed only a few years after Jonson's death in 1637, by the courtier and poet John Denham. In *Cooper's Hill*, one of the first topographical poems, he summed up the classical ideal of poetry in two couplets addressed to the Thames:

> O could I flow like thee, and make thy stream
> My great example, as it is my theme!
> Though deep, yet clear; though gentle, yet not dull;
> Strong without rage, without o'erflowing full.

In both idea and expression these lines look forward to Pope, whose most decisive work was to be written more than seventy years later. Behind Denham stands the unmistakable influence of Jonson, whose

*Thomas Carew, *To Saxham*; Andrew Marvell, *Upon Appleton House*, John Dryden, *To my honoured kinsman John Driden of Chesterton*. The tradition extends to Pope's *Moral Essay IV*.

The frontispiece of Hatfield House, 1611.

efforts to deflect the course of English poetry towards this classical tradition of lucid, concise, forceful yet well-disciplined writing were now beginning to yield fruit.

Jonson had not been alone in wishing to curb the flamboyance and excess so characteristic of the Elizabethan spirit, and which in his eyes marred even the work of Shakespeare. At the time when Jonson was censuring popular taste, and trying to wean audiences away from their romantic diet of freaks and drolleries, a new and severe architectural style was announcing a similar break with the elaborate and overloaded tradition then current. The great houses built in the closing decades of Elizabeth's reign offer suggestive parallels in form and feeling with the prevailing literary style. They are majestically formal, enriched with architectural conceits of every kind, and dressed in a visual rhetoric so elaborate that we may wonder whether the imposing facade overlies any genuine purpose, or is itself its *raison d'être*. Inigo Jones, an architect who worked with Jonson in designing court masques, helped to introduce a completely different building style which seems even more in advance of its times than Jonson's innovations in poetry. The Queen's House at Greenwich and the Banqueting House at Whitehall, both built during the lifetime of Donne, impose the same kind of ordered restraint upon architectural form and decoration as Jonson was bringing to literary practice. Emphasis passes from ornament to structure: architectural features are relieved of the elaborations which smothered them and redefined in strong outline. Where the great Elizabethan houses might lead us to expect their inhabitants to be splendid yet curious half-mythical creatures, the new style reduces both the scale and the ostentatiousness of Elizabethan architecture to a point where simple human associations replace grandeur and display. Jonson praises Penshurst, with its medieval hall, for its lack of flamboyance; and ends his poem by suggesting that Penshurst is above all a home and not an empty showpiece (lines 99–102):

> Now, Penshurst, they that will proportion thee
> With other edifices, when they see
> Those proud ambitious heaps, and nothing else,
> Will say their lords have built, but thy lord dwells.

Marvell addresses the same compliment to Fairfax in *Upon Appleton House*, (lines 3–4) condemning the arrogance of architects who

> unto caves the quarries drew,
> And forests did to pastures hew;

and refusing to apologize for the unpretentiousness of the house which the great soldier has chosen for his retirement (lines 61–4):

> And yet what needs there here excuse,

The Caroline façade of Kirby Hall, 1640.

Where everything does answer use?
Where neatness nothing can condemn,
Nor pride invent what to contemn?

The poet judges the architect's work by standards which he observes in his writing; but even a cursory acquaintance with native building style during the reign of Charles will show how completely the characteristic opulence and lavishness of high Elizabethan architecture had fallen out of fashion. The change can be appreciated particularly well by comparing the frontispiece of Hatfield House, built in 1611, with the north range of Kirby Hall in Northamptonshire, which is dated 1640. The contrast between the self-assertive splendour of the older building and the graceful reserve of the other indicates not merely a shift of fashion but a growth of civilized awareness, which was not limited to any single field of human activity.

Jonson's literary principles, and the example of his writing, made a ready appeal to the young courtiers and intelligentsia—the 'mob of gentlemen', as Pope was to describe them—who wrote much of the minor poetry of his age. English society was becoming increasingly conscious of divisions and differences within itself, and not least in the literary tastes of the courtly and middle classes. Shakespeare, it is often observed, addressed himself to a compound audience made up of all classes and callings. This is less true of his last plays, which incline towards the tastes of a more discerning clientèle, and appeal to the gentler feelings of an audience able to pay for seats in the private theatres. Beaumont and Fletcher, his immediate successors, widened the gap between courtly and popular by writing almost exclusively for this new audience, which evidently expected its finer sensibilities to be brought into play. For his part, Jonson made the mistake of presenting to popular audiences plays both unfamiliar in genre and intellectually over their heads. The disappointment of failure prompted him to condemn popular taste outright, and to look for appreciation only from the cultured and discriminating readers who could recognize his worth. Predictably, he found his disciples among the young gentlemen who shared his educated background, and who were pleased to prove their courtly credentials by adopting a literary style so distinct from the native tradition which popular taste approved.* By embracing Jonson's Horatian manner they identified themselves with the courtly society to which they looked for employment or preferment.

But accepting Jonson did not necessarily involve rejecting Donne, even though Donne probably offended more of Jonson's critical principles than any other important writer of the age. In his impudence and wit as a love poet, Donne made a powerful appeal to the same

*The so-called 'tribe of Ben' included Suckling, Carew, Randolph and Herrick.

body of young writers. He too was a minority poet, barely known outside the circle of readers with access to manuscript copies of his work; and the markedly intellectual character of his poetry must have limited its appeal very severely outside this special audience. This could only have increased its attractiveness to its devotees. Jonson might persuade his young disciples to avoid Donne's roughness and to organize their writing on a firm and lucid structure, but not annul the fascination of his wit; in particular of the conceit. The result was a literary compromise. The poets of Jonson's 'tribe' followed his lead in the general matter of poetic style, producing well-turned verse whose easy negligence was to earn Pope's slight, and adding a courtly form of the conceit for an effect of intellectual elegance. Carew's inscription for the tomb of Lady Mary Wentworth, who died aged eighteen, includes a typical example of this blending of influences within a manner that is essentially courtly. The first stanza has the neatness of idea and expression which Jonson urged:

> And here the precious dust is laid,
> Whose purely tempered clay was made
> So fine that it the guest betrayed.

The compliment is unobtrusive and deftly managed, served by a wit which gives polish to the sentiment. The second stanza develops this idea by offering an alternative explanation of the lady's early death, and at once Carew loses his balanced manner in pursuing an intellectual conceit:

> Else the soul grew so fast within,
> It broke the outward shell of sin,
> And so was hatched a cherubin.

The image betrays Carew's readiness to re-use conceits brought about in another poet's struggle to realize his ideas. The passage of Donne's *Second Anniversary* (lines 179–184) from which Carew has borrowed his conceit allows us to watch Donne working towards the idea, which then comes about as the natural climax of a train of thought dominated by the notion of release:

> But think that Death hath now enfranchised thee;
> Thou hast thy expansion now, and liberty:
> Think that a rusty piece, discharged, is flown
> In pieces, and the bullet is his own
> And freely flies. This to thy soul allow:
> Think thy shell broke, think thy soul hatched but now.

Donne represents the process of excogitation, and his conceit of a soul hatching out forms an organic part of his argument: Carew, on the other hand, produces the idea out of nowhere, and cannot make it integral to his poem. Transplanted from its native setting in *The*

113

Second Anniversary, its function becomes mainly decorative; and thus what appears at first sight to be a metaphysical poem merely simulates the process of thinking so vital to the character of Donne's writing, offering instead an inert conceit transferred from its living context.

The school of Donne and the school of Jonson

Such borrowing and imitation of Donne's ideas continued throughout the seventeenth century, as lesser poets associated themselves with the line of wit which he had initiated. Of Donne's courtly imitators it might be said at once that the habitual clarity and ease of their writing showed how little genuine need they felt to express themselves through the involved arguments and abstruse analogies that were natural to Donne. Their aim was to produce a metaphysical effect: to amuse and perhaps to astonish by the sheer outlandishness of ideas and comparisons, but without taxing the understanding of their readers. Thus Lovelace begins a poem to his mistress's glove, 'Thou snowy farm with thy five tenements', Marvell describes the flowers at Appleton House as musketeers discharging volleys of scent, and Crashaw, writing of Mary Magdalene's tears, suggests that in heaven

> Where the milky rivers creep,
> Thine floats above, and is the cream.

Unless the poet's intention were simply to advertise his ingenuity, such imagery would be self-defeating, for it distracts attention from the subject to the sheer oddity of the comparison. Donne is perhaps hardly less bizarre when he sums up man as 'a province packed up in two yards of skin'; but his image justifies itself both by his energy of expression and by the imaginative recognition which it compels the reader to share. We have no grounds for rejecting a poet's curious account of his experience unless his writing fails to persuade us that he is representing it truly; and most of Donne's successors are clearly trying to heighten the interest of a commonplace event or perception by forcing alien associations upon it. When Donne brings heterogeneous ideas together, he shows us why or how his mind has discovered their hidden likeness. The analogies of the *Hymn to God my God* may strike us as absurdly farfetched (lines 6–9):

> Whilst my physicians by their love are grown
>   Cosmographers, and I their map, who lie
> Flat on this bed, that by them may be shown
>   That this is my South-West discovery;

but later the inner logic of Donne's argument persuades us to accept his extraordinary point of view. The attitude of his doctors, watching intently for any change in his condition, suggests the complete absorption of cosmographers bent over their maps; and after making this visual comparison Donne clinches the analogy by arguing that his death will provide the issue from 'these straits' into the Pacific Sea of everlasting life. These conceits are the basis of his poem, which could not exist without them. It is a proper question whether his imitators, whose conceits float on the surface of their poems as witty embellishment, should be described as metaphysical poets.

Some reservations have to be made in this general criticism. Some forms of human experience are in themselves bizarre and unaccountable, and during the second quarter of the seventeenth century awareness of oddity and enigma beyond the range of normal understanding seems to have quickened; as though in protest at the growth of more rational trends of thought. Browne is perhaps an example of a writer who deliberately encouraged himself to become lost in spiritual and intellectual puzzles; but some of his contemporaries may have verged upon a kind of genuinely mystic insight such as poets would not undergo again until the Romantic Revival. Marvell is one of them. A man of unusually alert intelligence, he occasionally writes as though he had been taken off his guard by a sense of an indefinable power in the natural world, which immobilized his reason. The word 'green' recurs in his poems as a term whose charged significance has an almost mesmeric effect on his mind. When he describes himself plunging through the meadows at Nun Appleton, where the summer grass is ready for mowing, he admits a sense of awed incomprehension that is only half playful. In the great gulf of greenery his rational intelligence is drowned, and looking up in his abasement he sees the giant insects crowing over him from remote spires of grass, far above his head (*Upon Appleton House*, lines 369–376):

> And now to the abyss I pass
> Of that unfathomable grass,
> Where men like grasshoppers appear;
> But grasshoppers are giants there.
> They, in their squeaking laugh, contemn
> Us as we walk more low than them;
> And, from the precipices tall
> Of the green spires, to us do call.

While Marvell's intelligence is offering a witty commentary on the quaintness of his rural experience, his deeper feelings are stirred by the huge vitality of the grass which engulfs and dwarfs him. His phrase 'that unfathomable grass' is at once bantering and serious; for although Marvell merely pretends that the grass rises high above him in 'precipices tall', its silent energy presents a puzzle which his mind cannot deal with. What he senses or half-sees in the natural world is an overwhelming and single-minded force of growth which, if not actually threatening man, challenges his domination of the earth.

The occasional hints of quasi-mystic experience in Marvell's poetry justify some of his odder conceits, which are not always prompted by the kind of fantastic wit which sees the fishers with their coracles as 'Antipodes in shoes'. An element of strangeness had shown itself in metaphysical poetry from the outset, and continued to dominate the style. This tendency to explore and examine the less familiar aspects of man's relationships and environment might have made it inevitable that the more serious developments of metaphysical poetry should be in the field of devotional writing, both verse and prose. What the Cavalier poets took from Donne was used as a superficial adornment of their work, whose subject was generally love or courtly affairs. The successors of Donne who deserve to be described as metaphysical poets in a strict sense of the term left the imitation of his amorous manner to others, and followed—at a respectful distance—the example of his devotional verse.

Yet here too there is a marked disparity between the work of master and disciple; and if we are to speak of a school of Donne we must be clear about the extent of the influence we are claiming for him. Donne's poetry, of whatever kind, is shaped on the anvil of an individual temperament which changes very little between the relentless arguments of the *Songs and Sonets* and the tortured rhetoric of the *Holy Sonnets*. It is intensely personal writing, and no follower could have hoped to produce poetry of any value by imitating the idiosyncrasies of style which reflect Donne's turbulent feelings, and his straining efforts to secure himself against spiritual doubt. A true successor of Donne would find just as personal a manner of expression. He might not share the anxiety which impels much of Donne's finest devotional poetry; and writing which reflected a calmer and more assured mind might not readily be recognized as metaphysical at all. In respect of George Herbert, who has some clear right to be acknowledged as Donne's pupil, this is just the case. The quality of his work is most readily appreciated from a comparison with Donne. The opening lines of *Holy Sonnet IX* are immediately typical of the dramatizing of personal alarm which sounds so frequently in Donne's restless colloquies with God:

> If poisonous minerals, and if that tree
> Whose fruit threw death on else immortal us,
> If lecherous goats, if serpents envious
> Cannot be damned, alas, why should I be?

The lines are clamorous with ill-concealed terror, which accumulates through a series of jarring phrases until it bursts in the climactic 'Alas' and the rebellious protest, 'Why should I be?' The uneven rhythms of the passage reflect Donne's disturbed spirit, which has twisted language into the painfully knotted phrase 'else immortal us'. There are no concessions to musical effect, but an outspoken bluntness of reference which supplements the impression of a passionate outburst of feeling. No poem of Herbert's matches this roughness and violence of expression, and *The Collar* is perhaps the only work of his which recalls, even distantly, the mood of angry protest so typical of Donne. Herbert too can challenge God to reveal his purposes, which seem designed to frustrate and disappoint those who serve him:

> Shall I be still in suit?
> Have I no harvest but a thorn
> To let me blood, and not restore
> What I have lost with cordial fruit?
> Sure there was wine
> Before my sighs did dry it: there was corn
> Before my tears did drown it.
> Is the year only lost to me?
> Have I no bays to crown it?
> No flowers, no garlands gay? all blasted,
> All wasted?

This extract from *The Collar* (lines 6–16) resembles the opening lines of *Holy Sonnet IX* in its questioning of God's purposes, but the likeness goes no further. Where Donne is clamorous, Herbert is plaintive and a little wistful; and both the finer craftsmanship and the quieter movement of his poem suggest that his feelings allow him to present a more considered piece of writing than Donne's passionate urgency makes possible. Perhaps because *The Collar* does not convey such an impression of a sudden outburst of raw feeling we are less easily convinced that Herbert's complaints have any comparable basis: when he admits

> Sure there was wine
> Before my sighs did dry it

we know that there will be wine again. Even in this unusually troubled poem, Herbert's verse retains the characteristically dulcet quality which makes it difficult to believe that his spiritual misgivings trouble him very deeply. His language may have an artless simplicity, but we cannot feel—as we so often do with Donne—that he is speaking out of the experience itself, without reflecting about the terms he uses. Herbert picks his words with care, and with a very clear conception of the literary effect which he intends to produce. Unlike Donne, he habitually writes in the past tense, setting his crises of faith at some distance, and bringing the reader to safe ground at the end of the poem. We can suppose that he enjoyed a far greater sense of inward security throughout his life than did Donne, for his family circumstances protected him against many of the strains which Donne suffered; and we should not expect his poetry to reflect any comparable distress of spirit. But the difference between the two men does not lie in the degree of spiritual disturbance expressed by each so much as in the kind of poetry which each wills himself to produce. Herbert's is the writing of a meticulous literary artist; and in this respect he owes more to Jonson than to Donne.

This quality in Herbert's work is most readily seen in its use of emblematic images. The bare terms of metaphysical argument are uncongenial to him, and his poems commonly develop through an account of some private experience. He prefers to express himself picturesquely, through figures which are partly emblems to be 'read' in the way that allegorical characters are interpreted. His question in *The Collar*,

> Have I no harvest but a thorn
> To let me blood?

involves an essentially pictorial mode of expression. The terms which Herbert has unexpectedly linked together—harvest, thorn, blood—derive most of their force from their function as religious emblems, 'thorn' and 'blood' having imaginative associations with the Agony which transform their everyday character. The reader is not made to think or to follow a connected argument, but to respond to the unspoken meaning behind these pictorial figures. What seems at first reading to be uncontrived and almost naively expressed is in fact written with a good deal of sensitive artistry. Its simpleness of feeling and vocabulary reflect Herbert's literary purpose, and not his private background, which before he became a country priest had been a mixture of university and court. The cultivated pietism of his writing is in effect a courtly mode, appealing to the heart rather than to the mind, and seeking to move tender feelings by the note of wistful regret or wan bravery which Herbert strikes so frequently:

> I gave to Hope a watch of mine; but he
>   An anchor gave to me.
> Then an old prayer-book I did present;
>   And he an optic sent.   [magnifying-glass]
> With that I gave a vial full of tears;
>   But he a few green ears.
> Ah, loiterer! I'll no more, no more I'll bring:
>   I did expect a ring.

This concise, highly characteristic poem exemplifies Herbert's style and manner in many ways. It is charming and a little inconsequential, but put together with a craftsman's skill and delicacy. Its emblems of watch, anchor, prayer-book and the others are homely and picturesque, and present only a mild intellectual puzzle: it does not need much mental effort to realize that the watch represents impatience, the anchor constancy and the ring a state of union with God. The emblems have a pleasant oddity which give the poem some metaphysical likeness, but their pictorial function asserts itself more strongly: Herbert is again thinking in visual images rather than in intellectual terms, and the poem makes its point by its appeal to feeling. Its short lines represent the poet's repeated disappointment, and the two closing lines bring the poem to a climax of emotional frustration which is also its natural conclusion. We do not take this very seriously: his angry 'no more, no more I'll bring' suggests the hurt indignation of a child who will soon forget his disappointment and this hasty resolution. Herbert knows this, and has fashioned a carefully wrought poem about an engagingly minor experience; addressing himself to an audience who will appreciate its sensitive workmanship and respond to its wistful simplicity. Herbert may have cut himself off from the world of sophisticated affairs, but his literary standards and outlook remain those of a cultured society for whom stylistic grace is instinctive.

He is not always so distant from the forceful metaphysics of Donne. Occasionally he shows himself capable of producing the 'strong lines' which typify Donne's wrestling with ideas, and of forging analogies that are as farfetched yet persuasive as we expect of good metaphysical poetry. The second stanza of *The Agony* (lines 7–12) reveals this more powerful aspect of Herbert:

> Who would know Sin, let him repair
> Unto Mount Olivet: there shall he see
> A man so wrung with pains that all his hair,
>> His skin, his garments, bloody be.
> Sin is that press and vice which forceth pain
> To hunt his cruel food through every vein.

But despite the energy of the two last lines, this is not writing in the tradition of Donne. In *Good Friday, riding Westward*, Donne makes himself a spectator of the Crucifixion and makes us feel the horror of seeing the dying Christ. Herbert holds the Agony at a distance, and offers a picture of Christ's suffering which evokes pathos by its sensitively mannered account of pain. In the next stanza Herbert's references to the Crucifixion show a still greater tendency to soften the reality of torment and death, to the extent that bloodshed is made to seem attractive (lines 13–18):

> Who knows not Love, let him assay
> And taste that juice which on the Cross a pike
> Did set again abroach: then let him say
>> If ever he did taste the like.
> Love is that liquour sweet and most divine,
> Which my God feels as blood, but I as wine.

The ideas of this stanza can be justified by the doctrine of transubstantiation; but in expressing them Herbert prompts a response which not every reader will find agreeable. The communicant, Herbert implies, is not drinking consecrated wine but the blood which runs down Christ's body, and relishing it like a connoisseur. As a metaphysical conceit, this suggestion anticipates some of the more extreme parallels of Crashaw's religious verse; and like them indicates how seriously the intellectual force and forthrightness of Donne's metaphysics have been weakened by yielding to a courtly taste for bizarre elegance and touching sentiment. Metaphysical poetry may have gained other attractions in this process, and whether Herbert is preferable to Donne is a matter of personal choice. The more important critical issue is whether even Herbert is to be judged 'metaphysical' in his poetic style, or whether his writing is impelled mainly by purposes to which the familiar features of Donne's style are subservient.

A particular style, we have seen, can only be entirely valid for the writer whose personality it reflects: for him it is not a way of writing but the only means of shaping a literary equivalent of himself. Something similar is true of a literary period. A mode of writing goes out of fashion when it ceases to represent current sensibility and outlook. As the transformation of architectural style suggests, between Elizabeth and Charles the temper of English life changed too radically for a single idiom to continue in force. Although we may be encouraged to regard Donne's metaphysical style as foreshadowing a 'new' scientific outlook, it is in fact highly characteristic of its period. However unlike Shakespeare in lesser respects, Donne declares himself with a rhetorical grandeur which identifies him as a poet of the same age. Even when he is most aware of man's sinful and corrupt state, he remembers that man is also God's last and most splendid piece of handiwork, and the centre about which the whole universal fabric moves. This position gives an importance to human experience which justifies Donne's intense intellectual curiosity about himself, and which demands language appropriate to man's giant stature. The Donne of the *Holy Sonnets* speaks with such an accent of greatness, as though the whole of cosmos were involved in his struggle with the demons of spiritual doubt. Herbert makes no attempt to echo this heroic voice. He speaks out of a smaller and more homely world on which the twilight seems to be falling; mildly reproachful in the face of treatment which he does not understand, and seldom allowing his protest to ruffle the composure of his writing:

> I got me flowers to straw thy way,
>   I got me boughs off many a tree;
> But thou wast up by break of day,
>   And brought'st thy sweets along with thee.
>
> *Easter*, 1–4.

The flowers and sweets of this poem characterize the element of courtly grace in Herbert which belongs as much to his age as Donne's flamboyance to his. If, as Grierson suggested, metaphysical poetry was

Good Hopes, *we best accomplish may,*
By lab'ring *in a* constant Way.

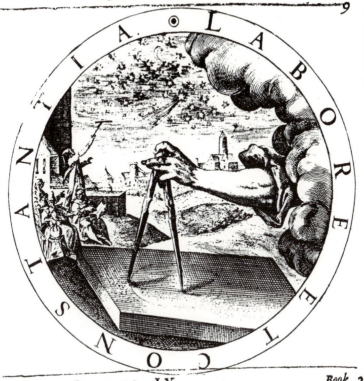

ILLVSTR. IX.   *Book.* 3

SOme Folkes there are, (and many men suppose,
That I my selfe, may passe for one of those)
Who many likely Businesses intend,
Yet, bring but very few, unto an end.
Which folly to prevent, this *Emblem,* here,
Did in a luckie houre, perhaps, appeare.
For, as to draw a *Circle,* with our hand,
We cause the brazen *Compasses* to stand
With one foot firmely fixed one the ground ;
And move the other in a *Constant-round* :
Right so, when we shall purpose to proceed
In any just, and profitable deed,
We first, should by a *constant-resolution,*
Stand firme, to what we put in execution :

An emblem, from George Wither's Collection of Emblems, *1635.*

inspired by a philosophical conception of 'the role assigned to the human spirit in the great drama of existence', it would be unreasonable to expect poets of the Caroline period to produce such writing. The poetry of Herbert and Vaughan crystallizes a sense of lonely bewilderment and helplessness that cannot be associated with any great drama. They wrote when the age of heroic individualism was past, and in a language tempered to their quieter experience. What they took from Donne was limited to figures of style; for like the still greater poet of his age, Donne forged a means of expression which was both unmistakably characteristic of its times and an intimate reflection of himself.

Part Two
Critical Survey

To the Noblest knight
Sr Edward Herbert.

Sr

I make account that thys Booke hath enough per=
formd wch yt undrtooke, both by Argument and
Example. Itt shall therfor the lesse neede to bee
ytsselfe another Example of ye Doctrine. Itt shal
not therfore kyll ytsselfe, that ys, not bury it self
for if ytt should do so, those reasons by wch that
Act should bee defended or excusd, were also lost
wt ytt. Since ytt ys content to liue, ytt cannot
chuse a wholsomer ayre then yor Library, where
Autors of all complexions are preserud. If any
of them grudge thys Booke a roome, and Sus=
pect ytt of new or dangerous doctrine, yon, who
know us all, can best Moderate. To those Reasons
wch I know yor Loue to mee wyll make in my fauer
and dischardge, yon may add thys, That though
thys Doctrine hath not beene tought nor defen-
ded by writers, yet they, most of any sorte of M
in the world, haue practisd ytt. — — —

yor uery true and earnest
frinde and Seruant
and Louer

J DONNE

Sample of Donne's writing

5 A critical examination of some poetry and prose

Songs and Sonets

Woman's Constancy

Now thou hast loved me one whole day,
Tomorrow when thou leav'st, what wilt thou say?
Wilt thou then antedate some new-made vow,
   Or say that now
We are not just those persons which we were?
Or that oaths made in reverential fear
Of Love and his wrath any may forswear?
Or, as true deaths true marriages untie,
So lovers' contracts, images of those,
10 Bind but till sleep, death's image, them unloose?
   Or, your own end to justify
For having purposed change and falsehood, you
Can have no way but falsehood to be true?
Vain lunatic, against these scapes I could   [evasions]
   Dispute and conquer, if I would;
   Which I abstain to do:
For by tomorrow I may think so too.

Donne's love poetry might be spoken by two entirely different charac-
ters. One is a lover almost oblivious of the outside world, assured by
the knowledge of love returned by a woman—perhaps his wife—
whose identity he feels himself to share. The other is a *roué* who scorns
the Petrarchan poets' attempts to deify woman, and exposes the
shameless motives of her behaviour with the acid wisdom of wide
experience. Many readers like to assume that the most profoundly felt
of the lover's poems were addressed to Ann More, either before or
after marriage; and that the scandalously outspoken and cynical on-
slaughts upon woman reflect the young man-about-town whom
Donne had been previously. But there is no need to suppose that either
of these figures mirrors Donne himself; and good reason to regard the
audacious cynic who speaks *Woman's Constancy* and *The Apparition* as a
persona which Donne adopts in order to heighten the shock effect of
his strikingly unconventional attitude.
   These two poems serve as showcase for the brilliantly inventive wit
of a young poet bent upon proving his originality and intransigeance;
which he does by addressing the mistress in blunt and unromantic

terms, and by showing a practised understanding of her insincerity. She has loved him for a whole day—in itself a miracle—and must obviously soon find an excuse for dropping him. How will she justify her fickleness? By back-dating a promise to some new lover, or by explaining that she is no longer the person who swore fidelity yesterday? Or will she declare that oaths made under compulsion—of love—have no binding force: or again, will she argue that just as death dissolves marriage, so sleep—a seeming form of death—dissolves yesterday's contract of eternal love? Or finally, will she represent her falseness as truth, in that she never intended to be faithful, and so is being true to her original intention? At this point the poet thrusts her excuses aside with a contemptuous phrase: 'Vain lunatic!' If he thought it worth the trouble he would take up her arguments and disprove them all; but it would be labour wasted, for by tomorrow he may be ready to echo them.

It seems safe to assume that Donne was the first English poet to call his mistress a lunatic. By using this abusive term in the context of love poetry he shows how far he is prepared to challenge accepted ideas and practices. The mistress is not to be treated as a remote goddess: she is not even a convincing liar, and the lover dismisses her hypocritical excuses with a scornful insult. Instead of following tradition by begging her favours or extolling her beauty, he invents for her the kind of insincere apology which he knows she will presently offer him as she breaks her vows. These ingenious excuses are the most 'metaphysical' part of the poem, crediting the mistress with a very unlikely ability to justify her behaviour by a series of sophisms which in fact prove Donne's wit. But in suggesting that the mistress might herself concoct such utterly specious arguments, Donne is portraying woman in a guise which no Renaissance poet would normally have considered. Speaking as a cynical realist, he depicts her as fickle and calculating; using her cunning to wriggle out of an unwelcome situation, by arguing that yesterday's oath is no longer binding. In exposing her hypocrisy, the poet seems to be making a protest against such moral casuistry; but the poem has a sting in its tail. By tomorrow, he will himself be ready to echo these empty excuses, and just as relieved to part company with this mistress of a night. He has expected nothing better of her; and to deny the mistress any satisfaction he admits finally that it suits his purposes that she should prove such a plausible liar.

Although our first impression may be that Donne is making a vituperative attack upon woman, it would probably be more correct to see the poem as an impudently witty assault on a prevailing convention, in which Donne stands accepted manners and attitudes on their heads. The drily realistic assumption that, having loved him 'one whole day', the mistress must be on the point of leaving him, establishes at the outset how emphatically Donne rejects the current fashion in love poetry. There is to be no highminded idealism, no unsatisfied longing, no heartbroken despair, but a down-to-earth appreciation of deceitful motives and rapid disillusioning on both sides. This lover is no helpless victim of a fascinating mistress whose coldness or hauteur drives him out of his mind, but a cynically knowing analyst able to predict exactly how she will disengage herself from a contract that has quickly become wearisome. He exposes her without indignation or protest: his own love has been just as transient, and he is glad to be rid of her. For once she has met her intellectual match, a lover able to out-do her in fabricating elaborate excuses; and so for once the mistress and not the lover is worsted. Here again Donne asserts his aggressive originality.

In point of style, *Woman's Constancy* has many characteristic features of metaphysical poetry. It begins abruptly, without preparation or setting: the lover addresses the mistress and the reader is left to imagine the circumstances for himself. The language is unromantically plain and straightforward, mixing colloquial expressions such as 'one whole day' with a few legal terms—'antedate' and 'contract'—but excluding literary decoration. The tone is strenuous and unrelaxed. After the briefest of preliminaries, the speaker begins to fire a series of pointed questions which hammer upon the mistress, and give her no chance of recovering her shattered composure. Obviously he does not intend her to answer, if there were any way of throwing back his accusations. As though the opening words of the poem turn on an electric current or open a floodgate, we feel ourselves dazed like the lady by a bombardment of questions, which stops only so that Donne can deliver his *coup-de-grâce* by remarking that he too is ready to see their liaison dissolve. In this way the poem develops not the kind of lyrical atmosphere common to most love poetry, but a sense of controlled power whose masculine force proves itself in this devastating exposure and mockery of the woman's attempt to disguise her fickleness. This energy, bursting upon the reader with an effect almost like that of physical violence, is a vital feature of Donne's style.

The Apparition

When by thy scorn, O murd'ress, I am dead,
And that thou think'st thee free
From all solicitation from me,
Then shall my ghost come to thy bed,
And thee, feigned vestal, in worse arms shall see.
Then thy sick taper will begin to wink,
And he whose thou art then, being tired before,
Will, if thou stir or pinch to wake him, think
    Thou call'st for more,
10 And in false sleep will from thee shrink.

And then, poor aspen wretch, neglected thou
Bathed in a cold quicksilver sweat wilt lie,
   A verier ghost than I.
What I will say, I will not tell thee now
Lest that preserve thee; and since my love is spent,
I'd rather thou should'st painfully repent
Than by my threat'nings rest still innocent.*

The Apparition, another poem of seventeen lines, shows Donne making a still more pungent attack upon the conventions of romantic love. The vitriolic opening line, 'When by thy scorn, O murd'ress, I am dead,' respects Petrarchan tradition to the extent of accepting that the lover will die of unrequited love; but the stinging accusation, 'O murd'ress', carries a charge of contemptuous feeling that is wholly alien to the self-pitying mood of the hopeless Petrarchan lover. This is very much a live man's poem, and if he contemplates his death it is for the malicious pleasure of planning how he will torment the woman whose unkindness killed him. His promise of how he will haunt her involves some revelations far more damaging to the lady than the simple accusation of murder. 'Then shall my ghost come to thy bed,' the poet declares, 'And thee, feigned vestal, in worse arms shall see.' The phrase 'feigned vestal', set parenthetically so that it gathers emphasis, blots the lady's reputation by a single, exactly calculated stroke. She has refused herself to the poet as though prizing her virginity above everything, but at her bedside the ghost will see the truth: the professed chastity that is a mask for sexual looseness. If there could be any more damning accusation than this—or any suggestion further from the elevated spirit of Renaissance love poetry—it is that the lady is not very fussy about whom she chooses as her sexual partner; and this Donne asserts. This blunt reference to her actual taste and habits prepares the reader for the still more outspoken comments by which the poet compounds his defamation:

And he whose thou art then, being tired before,
Will, if thou stir or pinch to wake him, think
   Thou call'st for more,
And in false sleep will from thee shrink.

This unsparingly realistic satire strips sex of all romantic glamour, and presents the lady as a ridiculous figure. She is to be branded as a libertine, but denied the satisfaction of appearing in a rhapsodic account of sexual fruition: instead, she is set down squarely in the exhausted aftermath of love-making, with a lover now limp and mulishly unresponsive to what he mistakes for further demands. These unaccommo-

---

*The lover would prefer her to sin and be haunted rather than take his warning and remain constant and chaste.

dating references are not intended only to humiliate the lady, for clearly part of Donne's purpose is to startle his readers by treating a subject normally wrapped in richly evocative ideas with a down-to-earth detachment which sees things in their banal actuality. He remains firmly anchored to the real world, and both the lady and romantic convention suffer by being brought down to the level of commonplace experience.

Ignored by her sleepy and unchivalrous lover, the lady will have to face her terror alone, running with sweat and shaking like a leaf. If we took the poem literally, we should say that here Donne was finding compensation for his wounded feelings through a wild fantasy of revenge; but the wit and controlled venom of *The Apparition* do little to encourage this reading. With the line, 'A verier ghost than I,' Donne establishes his complete mastery of the situation, in a manner very similar to that of the previous poem, where he leaves the woman without a leg to stand on. Having broken her resistance, as before he now adopts a quieter tone, though the sense of his remarks remains maliciously cruel; and to complete her demoralization he declares that he has, in any case, already ceased to love her. We might object that, if this is so, the lover will not die of a broken heart and so he will have no occasion to haunt his mistress; but the notion of romantic death has served its purpose of setting in motion a poem designed to ridicule such conceptions. Here again there can be no question of believing that a lover who expressed his feelings with such energy and concentrated purpose could be in much danger of succumbing to blighted hopes. The driving power displayed in this poem and in *Woman's Constancy* underlies Donne's confidence as a literary revolutionary, overturning the established attitudes of his day. To this extent only we may regard these iconoclastic poems as parts of his autobiography. The simple dramatic situations which he invents, here a discarded lover burning with angry contempt against woman's guile, allow Donne to liberate his creative energy through a passage of invective; gratingly uncouth in idiom but designed with great intellectual subtlety.

Donne's subtlety does not strike us immediately, for the impact of his vigorously colloquial language distracts attention from other aspects of the poem. Later we find it easier to notice how unobtrusively the free-speaking commentary of the first five lines is organized into a sentence, to form a compact section of the story. The next five lines, from 'Then thy sick taper' to 'from thee shrink', make up a second sentence and the middle section of the story; so that while Donne appears to be writing informally and upon impulse, using the vocabulary and expressions of spoken English—'thou think'st thee free', 'being tired before', 'pinch to wake him'—he is in fact giving his poem the ordered shape that goes with craftsmanship. Unlike *Woman's Constancy*, this poem does not involve metaphysical argument or moral casuistry, but is a relatively straightforward piece of story-telling in advance; arranged upon the simple basis of 'When . . . then . . . and then', and culminating in the frightening prospect of what the ghost will say, which the speaker conceals. This development provides a framework firm enough to contain the explosive parentheses through which the lover gives relief to his overcharged feelings: 'O murd'ress', 'feigned vestal', and 'poor aspen wretch', and braces the poem against the malice which cuts and twists through it. Except in these inter-jections, the speaker does not show his suppressed anger and indigna-tion, but adopts a silkily deliberate manner which hangs over words and phrases with a lingering enjoyment of the lady's rising panic. In the line, 'From all solicitation from me', the voice is made to pick out every syllable of the self-contemptuous term 'solicitation', which represents the lady's disparagement of his wooing. As he approaches the climax of his story the poet's pace does not quicken; and his pointing of the lines shows how unhurriedly he moves forward, savouring the sweetness of his revenge:

And in false sleep will from thee shrink.

This culminating line is uninterrupted but heavily accented; the spon-dee 'false sleep' being followed by three stressed words, 'from thee shrink', which give the promise a sense of absolute certainty. Donne is causing the event to happen through the power of his description, not to the lady but to the reader. The four lines ending in 'shrink' illustrate his remarkable ability to evoke a strong imaginative response through the use of entirely prosaic terms—here, monosyllabic words taken from common speech.

Elsewhere in *The Apparition* we find some characteristic use of images, where although Donne concedes something to metaphorical expression he does not lose his grasp upon literal facts. The line, 'Then thy sick taper will begin to wink,' calls up a visual impression of a dwindling flame; 'wink' having the sense of closing both eyes, and not only one. 'Sick taper' is a typically metaphysical image in its juxta-posing of seemingly unrelated ideas, though in fact an Elizabethan reader would have recognized a closer connection between 'sick' and 'taper' than would appear to us. The vital spirit of life was conceived to be a small flame within the body, and thus a guttering candle might indeed resemble a sick man approaching death. But the image is only half metaphorical, for while the adjective suggests other asso-ciations, the noun maintains the literal sense of Donne's reference. This is true of the two images which follow, 'poor aspen wretch' and 'cold quicksilver sweat'. The nouns are used literally, and each is qualified by an equally literal adjective—'poor', 'cold'—and by a figurative one. 'Aspen' involves an allusion to the natural world, rare in Donne; while 'quicksilver' has the typical unexpectedness of a meta-physical image, though its associations of beady, glistening and quick-moving droplets are splendidly matched to the notion of sweat breaking out all over the lady's body. The effect of this compromise between literal and figurative terms is to limit the scope of Donne's metaphor. He brings imagination into play, but does not allow it to distract attention from the actual object—the taper or the sweat—which he is referring to. In this way the intellectual element of his poem is made to dominate over its impulses towards imaginative impressionism, and the actuality of his subject is held firmly in view.

The Flea

Mark but this flea, and mark in this
How little that which thou deny'st me is:
It sucked me first, and now sucks thee,
And in this flea our two bloods mingled be.
Thou know'st that this cannot be said
A sin, nor shame, nor loss of maidenhead;
   Yet this enjoys before it woo,
   And pampered, swells with one blood made of two;
   And this, alas, is more than we would do.

10 O stay, three lives in one flea spare,
Where we almost, yea, more than married are!
This flea is you and I, and this
Our marriage-bed and marriage-temple is.
Though parents grudge, and you, we're met
And cloistered in these living walls of jet.
   Though use make you apt to kill me,
   Let not to that self-murder added be,
   And sacrilege, three sins in killing three.

Cruel and sudden, hast thou since
20 Purpled thy nail in blood of innocence?
Wherein could this flea guilty be
Except in that drop which it sucked from thee?
Yet thou triumph'st, and say'st that thou
Find'st not thyself nor me the weaker now.
   'Tis true: then learn how false fears be;
   Just so much honour, when thou yield'st to me,
   Will waste, as this flea's death took life from thee.

In *The Flea* this intellectual concentration is unremitting, and no side-issues offer even momentary relief from Donne's closely followed argument. Again his purpose is to establish his moral and intellectual mastery by refuting the mistress's reasons for keeping her virginity, and by proving the emptiness of her fears. His demonstration, argued over twenty-seven lines of sustained reasoning and outrageous sophistry, rolls inexorably over all her protests and finally reaches its irresistible conclusion that the loss of maidenhood is nothing more than a fleabite. The lady's case has been demolished as much by the sheer weight and resourcefulness of Donne's argument as by the reasons which he offers; and in the face of this defeat we must suppose that she can only surrender. There are of course no grounds for reading the poem as an indication of Donne's private morals, much less for supposing that it represents an argument used in some actual attempt at seduction. The witty point of *The Flea* lies in its preposterousness, not merely in the argument itself but in the tacit suggestion that the lady's resistance could be worn down by such means. Again Donne is proving his originality by turning convention upside down; making it seem that women are won not by gifts, faithful service and loving speeches but by metaphysical proof that virginity is worthless.

The argument of the poem begins and ends with a fleabite. The insect has bitten the lover and the mistress in turn, and now contains a mixture of their bloods. Thus the flea has brought about the kind of union which the lover desires, yet without raising any moral protest from the mistress; enjoying them both with no longwinded preliminaries, and growing into a compound being as they might if the lady would yield to him. When she threatens to kill the flea, he restrains her: the insect is now them, filled with their two bloods. It is also the marriage-bed in which they were physically united, and the church in which their marriage was celebrated. Despite hostile parents and the lady's own reluctance, they have become a single being within the flea's body. Although, hardened by custom, she might think nothing of murdering part of him by killing the flea, that crime would involve suicide and sacrilege; for she would also kill part of herself and destroy the marriage-temple in which they were united. But she persists in her triple crime; and having 'purpled her nail' in the flea's blood she refutes his argument about murder and suicide by showing that neither of them is any weaker for having lost the particle of life supposedly sucked from them. In this momentary triumph she gives the lover the means of crushing her in a final, unanswerable demonstration by turning her own point against her. She is right, he admits; and just as she lost nothing of consequence to the flea, so in surrendering to him her honour will suffer no more than a fleabite.

The poem is a *tour-de-force* of irreverent wit, taking a trivial and utterly unromantic incident as the occasion of an exercise in fantastic ingenuity. Donne's suggestion that the flea represents both the united lovers, their marriage-bed and a marriage-temple, and that by squashing it the lady commits three grave crimes, is perhaps the most astonishingly contrived of all metaphysical conceits. The poem was no doubt partly impelled by a current fashion for writing elaborately learned treatises on things of no importance, which in 1579 had pro-

duced a book proving 'that baldness is much better than bushy hair'.*
The close-knit structure of apparently serious argument which Donne
erects on so minute a basis sets an example of witty nonsense which
other Elizabethan writers might have despaired of rivalling. Yet how-
ever ludicrous his metaphysical disquisition on the flea and its mul-
tiple significance, Donne's argument succeeds in its purpose: the lady
leaps in to point out the fault in his analogy, and so plays into his
hands. Once again an inexorable process of reasoning, whose logical
flaws contribute to the final triumph, has enabled this very unconven-
tional lover to outwit the lady and to force his own terms upon her.

His disregard for convention appears most obviously in his frank
desire for sexual intercourse. In poetry of the polite tradition which
Donne pointedly rejects, the lover might approach the mistress as a
suppliant, but if he hoped to be granted this ultimate favour he did
not hint that she might yield to him physically. Her chastity and good
name were virtues which he was expected to honour, and his faithful
service was to be impelled by respect for her beauty of mind and
spirit, not by her attractive sexuality. Through his mistress's celestial
beauty the lover received a moral education, which led his thoughts
away from bodily desires. So Spenser tells his lady in Sonnet VIII of
the *Amoretti*:

> Through your bright beams doth not the blinded guest†
> Shoot out his darts to base affections wound;
> But angels come to lead frail minds to rest
> In chaste desires, on heavenly beauty bound.

Donne does not entirely reject this neoplatonic conception of love,
for in some of the poems which read as though addressed to Ann
More—in *The Relic*, for instance—he describes a mistress with whom
only spiritual union is possible. In *The Ecstasy*, making a more
balanced judgement between the opposing claims of body and spirit in
love, he speaks of the lovers' mutual understanding through a union
of souls and acknowledges that 'it was not sex' which brought them
together; but he also enters a passionate plea for the body to be
allowed its part in their union; 'Else a great prince in prison lies'.
But in *The Flea*, almost certainly with the intention of scandalizing his
readers, he writes as though seduction and physical satisfaction were
all that concerned the lover. This downright attitude is accompanied
by a matching toughness of mind towards the mistress. He does not
appeal for pity, or beg her to save him from heartbroken death by
giving up her virginity; but with the peremptory command, 'Mark

---

*Donne himself wrote a number of prose paradoxes with such titles as 'A Defence
of Women's Constancy', 'That Women ought to Paint', and 'That a wise man is known
by much Laughing'.

†i.e., Cupid

but this flea', he embarks upon a strenuous intellectual demonstration proving that she has no grounds for resisting him. It is a game he plays to win, and whose outcome is never seriously in doubt. If the poem has any deeper significance beneath Donne's witty outraging of convention, it would seem to lie in the wrestling with ideas by which Donne subdues an opposing argument, and makes himself master of an imaginary situation.

The Sun Rising

> Busy old fool, unruly sun,
> Why dost thou thus
> Through windows and through curtains call on us?
> Must to thy motions lovers' seasons run?
> Saucy pedantic wretch, go chide
> Late schoolboys and sour prentices;
> Go tell court huntsmen that the king will ride;
> Call country ants to harvest offices.
> Love, all alike, no season knows nor clime,
> 10   Nor hours, days, months, which are the rags of time.
>
> Thy beams so reverend and strong
> Why shouldst thou think?
> I could eclipse and cloud them with a wink,
> But that I would not lose her sight so long.
> If her eyes have not blinded thine,
> Look, and tomorrow late tell me
> Whether both the Indias of spice and mine   [gold]
> Be where thou left'st them, or lie here with me.
> Ask for those kings whom thou saw'st yesterday,
> 20   And thou shalt hear, all here in one bed lay.
>
> She is all states, and all princes I,
> Nothing else is.
> Princes do but play us; compared to this,
> All honour's mimic, all wealth alchemy.
> Thou, sun, art half as happy as we
> In that the world's contracted thus;
> Thine age asks ease, and since thy duties be
> To warm the world, that's done in warming us.
> Shine here to us, and thou art everywhere;
> 30   This bed thy centre is, these walls thy sphere.

The Sun Rising is another poem with a victorious outcome, though here Donne does not set himself the task of outwitting and overcoming his mistress. In point of the poet's relationship with the lady, this poem conforms more closely with Petrarchan convention; though not in making its setting a bedroom where the lovers lie in bed together. Sexual achievement has not disillusioned the poet, for he refers to his mistress with pride and boastful admiration; making hyperbolic claims for her beauty beside which the conventional lover's praises seem modest. The satirical attitude towards woman found in the three previous poems is transformed into the rhapsodic happiness of a lover who knows himself so closely integrated with his mistress that they form their own world:

> She is all states, and all princes I:
> Nothing else is.

Where before the poet's confidence springs from his awareness of his intellectual and rhetorical superiority over the woman, it is now based upon the deeper emotional assurance of love returned. Yet even with this settled assurance, Donne seems unable to abandon his habit of attacking and subduing a force which resists him. So, despite his happiness as a lover in *The Sun Rising*, this poem is not addressed to the mistress but to the sun who has disturbed their enjoyment, and whose busybody behaviour the lover resents as much as his fussy punctuality. The poem begins with an outburst of insulting phrases, 'Busy old fool, unruly sun . . . Saucy pedantic wretch', which directly parallel the terms of abuse applied to the cruel or deceitful mistress in other poems: 'vain lunatic', 'murderess', 'feigned vestal'. As the poem develops we recognize that it has a double purpose; in part to make a triumphant proclamation of the poet's good fortune as a lover, but more perhaps to answer the sun's challenge by rebuking his impudence and petty-minded concern with time, and by correcting his mistaken sense of duty. By the end of the poem Donne seems to have persuaded the sun to adopt his own point of view, and to regard the lovers not merely as the centre-point of the universe, but as the earth itself.

This double purpose gives *The Sun Rising* a special poetic interest, for as the speaker's attention shifts from the sun to his mistress, his tone varies from angry protest and scorn to lazy content; and the emotional texture of the poem thus changes repeatedly. The opening is indignant and irascible; the lover demanding an explanation of the sun's ill-mannered intrusion:

> Busy old fool, unruly sun,
> Why dost thou thus
> Through windows and through curtains call on us?
> Must to thy motions lovers' seasons run?

Then, as though the initial shock of displeasure has been absorbed, the lover opens a second phase of attack consisting of more pointed personal insult, jeering at the humble duties which the sun must perform in the world that is ruled by his movements:

> Saucy pedantic wretch, go chide
> Late schoolboys and sour prentices;
> Go tell court huntsmen that the king will ride;
> Call country ants to harvest offices.

In this last line the pace of the poem, so angrily impetuous a little before, has slackened perceptibly, as though to represent the sluggishness of harvesters turning out of bed. Their sleepy reluctance brings the lover back to his own deep comfort of mind and body; and as he contemplates his shared happiness the lines stretch out and become almost immobilized by the weight of stressed syllables, their movement checked like the flow of time within the lovers' room:

> Love, all alike, no season knows, nor clime,
> Nor hours, days, months, which are the rags of time.

The language is commonplace, almost drab; it includes no images and no explicit reference to feeling, and yet the whole statement is richly sensuous in its suggestion of relaxed and contented wellbeing. It is a mark of Donne's poetic strength that without inviting help from figurative or romantic terms he can make such worn colloquial language carry a potent emotional charge. His secret lies in the close matching of verse rhythms to the current of feeling which underlies the speaker's words, so that the reader seems to hear his emotional experience as the verse picks its way forward, now checked and now with a rush of eloquence. After the suggested luxury and ease of lines 9 and 10, the second stanza opens with another burst of scornful arrogance:

> Thy beams so reverend and strong
> Why shouldst thou think?

By stressing all four syllables of the short line, Donne gives the question a ring of personal assurance which makes what follows—the lover's boast that he could himself eclipse the sun, if he were willing to lose sight of his mistress for a moment—seem more than conceited swagger. When he goes on to the hyperbolic challenge of the next four lines, we are consequently not disposed to ridicule his suggestion; for we have been made to sense the deep emotional conviction which it represents. The experience of such absolute love can only be conveyed in subjective terms, and however exaggerated the idea itself, the measured emphasis of Donne's statement makes us feel—or again, hear—his unshakeable assurance:

> If her eyes have not blinded thine,
> Look, and tomorrow late, tell me
> Whether both the Indias of spice and mine
> Be where thou left'st them, or lie here with me.

As in the first stanza, he has now lost the angry impatience of his rebuke to the sun, and is again relaxing into the warm emotional serenity which makes his grand assertions seem like calm statements of fact:

> Ask for those kings whom thou saw'st yesterday,
> And thou shalt hear, all here in one bed lay.

By loading the last phrase—of its six monosyllabic words, only one is unstressed—Donne again creates an impression of solid conviction and truth. If the poet's remark seemed excited and impulsive, we should see its hyperbole as a lover's exaggeration and laugh at his romantic idea. In fact, it sounds like a soberly considered judgment, expressed in the plainest and most unpretentious language. Drawing upon no sensuous terms, and making 'kings' supply all the imaginative suggestions of splendour which he requires, Donne evokes a sense of fulfilment so complete that nothing less than the simplest form of words can represent it.

The idea of 'those kings' leads to the opening statement of the third stanza, in which the lover's hyperbole goes beyond all its previous limits of daring.

> She is all states, and all princes I;
> Nothing else is.

Again the weight and sober pace of the remark help to transform what might be an extravagant boast into a simple, entirely credible declaration. The lover's claim that, apart from themselves, nothing exists—'Nothing else is'—reduces hyperbole to the level of plain fact by words so stark and basic that no other sense can be read into them. We might expect a lover so ecstatically happy to make himself a little ridiculous by overpraising his mistress's beauty or by swearing eternal constancy, but Donne ignores these familiar gambits of love poetry. He describes his mistress in geographical terms, 'both the Indias of spice and mine', 'all states', and not by comparing her with precious stones and mythological figures; and he represents his rapture directly, as though by allowing the reader to take his pulse, and not by painting the lady's portrait. A lover might be mistaken in his judgment of the mistress's beauty, but the experience which he undergoes as he contemplates her cannot be either true or false; and it is this actuality of sensation which Donne sets himself to represent. The statement that 'princes do but play us' has no validity outside the poem, but it is not offered as a view of objective fact: it represents the sense of sovereignty and vital importance which springs from the lover's assured knowledge of his shared happiness. The terms 'mimic' and 'alchemy' applied to other kinds of distinction imply that they are worthless in comparison. This claims a good deal less than the opening remark of the same stanza, and yet is unconvincing; probably because the comparison implies that the lover is no longer absorbed in his personal situation, but looking beyond it.

If this is a weakness, the poem immediately recovers. The last four lines consist of a metaphysical argument—more exactly, of a proof by sophistry—showing that by shining upon the lovers the sun will be carrying out its appointed duty:

> Shine here to us, and thou art everywhere:
> This bed thy centre is, these walls thy sphere.*

The emphatic tone of the statement, and the uncompromising bareness of its language, reaffirm the speaker's absolute assurance; not merely as a lover but as an aggressive individualist who has challenged a greater force, and by sheer energy and determination bent him to his will. However successful as a love poem, *The Sun Rising* takes its dynamism from the poet's conflict with an authority whom he refuses to acknowledge, and who is forced to accept the poet's mastery. The sense of angry conflict is deeply alien to the lyrical mood which had seemed most natural to love poetry hitherto; but Donne seems to have found conflict an essential condition of his imaginative activity.

The Relic

When my grave is broke up again,
Some second guest to entertain—
For graves have learnt that womanhead,
To be to more than one a bed—
    And he that digs it spies
A bracelet of bright hair about the bone,
    Will he not let's alone,
And think that there a loving couple lies,
Who thought that this device might be some way
10 To make their souls, at the last busy day,
Meet at this grave and make a little stay?

    If this fall in a time or land
    Where misdevotion doth command,
    Then he that digs us up will bring
    Us to the bishop and the king,
        To make us relics: then
Thou shalt be a Mary Magdalen, and I
      A something else thereby.
All women shall adore us, and some men;

*In the context of Elizabethan astronomy, the term 'centre' signifies the earth, which stands at the centre of the universe. 'Sphere' has roughly the same sense as 'orbit' in modern English. Donne is thinking like a Ptolemaic astronomer, and not like a Copernican.

And since at such time miracles are sought,
I would have that age by this paper taught
What miracles we harmless lovers wrought.

First, we loved well and faithfully,
Yet knew not what we loved, nor why;
Difference of sex no more we knew
Than our guardian angels do:
    Coming and going, we
Perchance might kiss, but not between those meals:
    Our hands ne'er touched the seals
30 Which nature, injured by late law, sets free.
These miracles we did; but now, alas,
All measure and all language I should pass,
Should I tell what a miracle she was.

This characteristic of his writing is less evident in *The Relic*, which like *The Sun Rising* is addressed to his partner in a true love-match. It is much unlike the previous poem in its sombre subject matter, for here Donne contemplates a point of time after his death, when his grave will be opened and his bones thrown out to make room for another occupant. If *The Sun Rising* was strikingly unconventional, at least the lovers' situation was realistically appropriate; but the opening words of *The Relic*,

When my grave is broke up again,
Some second guest to entertain,

seem to have no conceivable application to a love poem. By making such an idea his starting-point, Donne shows how unpredictably his mind works; here finding a path from the macabre idea of being disinterred to the notion of holy relics, and then to an account of his loving relationship with his mistress. But the conceit which brings these ideas together is unforced, and the whole poem represents a steady and persistent growth of thought from the unexpected opening concept to the rueful admission with which it ends. Although the associations of idea are odd in themselves, within the working-out of Donne's curiously involved argument they are seen to happen naturally and spontaneously. The complete poem allows us to trace the form of an elaborate mental experience as it occurred—or rather, as it was thought into being—within Donne's creative consciousness.

Unlike the other poems we have considered, *The Relic* opens quietly. When his grave is reopened, Donne says, and the gravedigger comes across a bone encircled with a bracelet of his mistress' hair,* perhaps he will suppose that 'a loving couple' lie there, hoping to be reunited

*For a second poem on this love-token, 'that subtle wreath of hair which crowns my arm', see *The Funeral*.

on Judgment Day, and will leave them undisturbed. If this should happen during a period of 'misdevotion' or false religion, the grave-digger will carry these relics to the bishop, to be venerated as holy things: her hair as though it had belonged to another Mary Magdalen, the bone as though it came from one of her lovers. Together they will be adored; and as miracles will be expected of them, this poem sets down for future ages what wonderful things they have already performed. The great miracle lay in the virtuousness of their behaviour as lovers whose relationship ignored sex, who kissed only at meeting and parting, and who never challenged the moral law which restrains natural impulse. This miracle he can describe, but to give any proper account of her miraculous self lies beyond the power of poetry. Presumably the poet speaks of his mistress in the past tense here because he is imagining a time when she will be long dead, and not because he has already lost her. The tone of regret in this final statement helps to subdue the speaker's feelings, and to maintain the unusual reserve which Donne imposes upon his volatile temperament throughout this almost wistful poem.

Despite its macabre opening theme, *The Relic* has some flashes of comic wit which show Donne's readiness to joke even when his subject is generally serious. The notion of his grave being emptied, 'some second guest to entertain', is expressed in wrily ironic terms, and without any of the horror or indignation which such a prospect might arouse. There follows a remark about graves learning from women how 'to be to more than one a bed', which although not very complimentary to the mistress, proves that Donne's mood is less sombre than his subject. This playful spirit continues as he suggests that the gravedigger may think the relic a device contrived by the lovers to ensure a meeting on Judgment Day: as the resurrected souls reassume their bodies, the mistress must come to the lover's grave to claim the lock of hair woven into the bracelet. The idea itself is comic in its ingenuity, and becomes more amusing when Donne suggests that the gravedigger may hit on this explanation of the relic. There is another touch of levity in the reference to Judgment Day, where 'busy' seems to imply a homely occasion, such as a market-day, with no awesome solemnity but a good deal of haste and agitation.

In the second stanza Donne's humour takes a sly and possibly daring turn. When the relics have been accepted by the Church—not, of course, the Anglican faith, which did not admit them—then, Donne supposes,

> Thou shalt be a Mary Magdalen, and I
> A something else thereby.

This does not flatter the mistress, for before her conversion Mary Magdalen was a prostitute; but perhaps Donne would answer her protest by arguing that the mistake proved the blindness of the 'misdevotion' which he leaves us to identify. The comment about himself, who will be judged 'a something else thereby'—that is, through his association with Mary Magdalen—is mischievously comic. He may mean that he will be regarded as one of her customers, redeemed by his association with the saint whom she became: a reading encouraged by the reluctant pause after 'I', where the line-unit breaks the sentence. Alternatively, Donne may be hinting that his bone will be venerated as a relic of Christ, 'thereby' alluding to this more decorous aspect of the Magdalen's life. If this suggestion seems profane, Donne is still protected by the terms of his story; for it is not he but the idolatrous worshippers who will make the assumption. Whichever reading we prefer, Donne is bringing his comic wit to bear upon himself. It may be merely a private impression that the tone of 'a something else' is rueful, and that the speaker's unwillingness to be explicit is explained by the ignominious name to be put upon him. The line which follows, 'All women shall adore us, and some men', appears to support this reading. Donne is still showing some playful disrespect for woman in her romantic credulity: man is generally above such folly, though 'some men' admits that his sex too may succumb. The possibility that he will be mistaken for one of the Magdalen's clients is more in keeping with this ironically disparaging manner than with a profane sugges- tion that he will be mistaken for Christ.*

In the third stanza Donne drops his playful mood and speaks alto- gether seriously. He has been prepared to joke about the disturbance of his grave and the preposterous likelihood of becoming a holy relic; but when he begins to describe the virtuous love between himself and his mistress the tone of the poem changes. Where previously he has been definite and factual, even though writing about future events, he now admits uncertainty and vagueness: as lovers (lines 23, 24),

> we loved well and faithfully,
> Yet knew not what we loved, nor why.

The main sense of this remark is repeated in the next two lines (25, 26), which in idiom and idea suggest the innocence and simplicity of child- ren:

> Difference of sex no more we knew
> Than our guardian angels do.

The image is doubly appropriate: angels are sexless, and the simile suggests their watchful presence protecting the lovers against sin. These are not the 'strong lines' of metaphysical writing, but in their quietness an evocation of almost tender feeling. Donne has changed

---

* One might add that the slur implicit in 'some men' seems to be aimed at woman's romantic disposition to sentimentalize over a lover, and not at man's tendency to agnosticism.

his viewpoint, no longer predicting the future as a mocking realist but looking back—seemingly over a long span of time —to the period of this miraculous love, when his mistress was still alive. As we see from the legal image of breaking a seal in line 29, he makes no outward concession to romantic feeling, but follows his habitual practice of describing passionate experience—here, making love—in intellectual terms. None the less, the last stanza leaves an impression of wistfulness and nostalgia that is difficult to reconcile with its characteristically plain language and analytic detachment. This impression seems to derive chiefly from the changed manner of the last stanza. After the levity and fantastic wit of the two opening stanzas, Donne reaches the inner subject of the poem; and in his change of voice we recognize the deep emotion which has allowed him to play with ideas of gravedigging and the Last Judgment in so light-hearted a spirit.

The five poems so far considered are all markedly individual in form. *The Flea* has three nine-line stanzas, rhyming in couplets for six lines and concluding in a triple rhyme. *Woman's Constancy* has a more complicated structure. Its seventeen lines vary in length between five and two feet, and do not make a symmetrical pattern; and its rhyme scheme is no less complex. Lines 1–4 and 12–17 rhyme in couplets, but the seven lines which make up the middle of the poem present a problem which Donne solves by rhyming *cccdeed*; so that altogether its form is unpredictable. *The Sun Rising* consists of three ten-line stanzas, but the rhythm which they impose upon the poem is again a complicated one. The rhyme scheme is part of this complexity, *abba*, *cdcd*, *ee*, varying throughout the stanza as do the line-units, whose length fluctuates from two to five feet. These three examples characterize Donne's ingenuity in contriving the stanza form that will both contain his ideas and become part of their sense. The shape of each poem is, as it were, tailormade to suit the experience which Donne represents, and could not be used for any other purpose. But the *Valediction forbidding Mourning* is atypical of Donne's practice. It is set in the simplest of quatrains, with lines of even length rhyming alternately; and at first sight does not look like a metaphysical poem at all. However, Donne has chosen this unpretentious form with a purpose.

A Valediction forbidding Mourning

As virtuous men pass mildly away,
  And whisper to their souls to go,
Whilst some of their sad friends do say
    The breath goes now, and some say no;

So let us melt and make no noise,
    No tear-floods nor sigh-tempests move;
'Twere profanation of our joys
    To tell the laity our love.

Moving of th'earth brings harms and fears,
10   Men reckon what it did and meant;
But trepidation of the spheres,
       Though greater far, is innocent.

Dull sublunary lovers' love,
    Whose soul is sense, cannot admit
Absence, because it doth remove
       Those things which elemented it.

But we, by a love so much refined
    That ourselves know not what it is,
Interassured of the mind,
20   Care less eyes, lips and hands to miss.

Our two souls, therefore, which are one,
    Though I must go, endure not yet
A breach, but an expansion,
       Like gold to airy thinness beat.

If they be two, they are two so
    As stiff twin compasses are two;
Thy soul, the fixed foot, makes no show
    To move, but doth if th'other do:

And though it in the centre sit,
30   Yet when the other far doth roam
It leans and hearkens after it,
       And grows erect as that comes home.

Such wilt thou be to me, who must
    Like the other foot, obliquely run;
Thy firmness makes my circle just,
    And makes me end where I begun.

   This *Valediction* is one of several poems addressed to a woman by a
lover about to leave on a journey or voyage which must separate them
for some considerable while. Whether any of them were written for
Donne's wife does not immediately concern us, for they would not be
intrinsically better poems simply because that were so. Most readers
would agree that, whatever the circumstances, this poem is one of the
finest of the *Songs and Sonets*, for despite its out-of-the-way allusions
and images, a sense of firm and deeply-based emotion is evoked from
the first and consistently maintained. T. S. Eliot's phrase about the
'direct sensuous apprehension of thought' would be misapplied here,
for it is rather feeling which is given expression through intellectual
concepts. The central concern of this poem is to define the relation-
ship between the lovers which makes separation unimportant, or even
impossible; and to this end Donne works out equivalents for the force

which binds and unifies the lovers, drawing analogies from the impersonal field of science and craftsmanship.

The poem begins with an analogy which, although 'metaphysical' in its witty incongruity, includes a striking and entirely successful image of sensation. Their parting, the speaker is telling his mistress, must not involve a show of extravagant grief but a silent melting from one another; and as illustration he suggests a death so imperceptible that the watchers at the bedside cannot tell when the last breath is taken:

> Whilst some of their sad friends do say
> The breath goes now, and some say no.

The alliterated s-sounds in the first line make us hear the whispering about the dying man, and the assonance which links 'now . . . no' in the next line continues this sound effect, by representing the faint respiration which the friends are straining to hear. Thus while at first sight the analogy seems either strained or hackneyed—separation is death for all true lovers—its ideas are realized with such immediacy and conviction that we must accept it. However unlikely a parallel in its broad form, it contains an image of untroubled separation so apt that its incongruous details drop out of sight. In such passages the oddities of metaphysical style justify themselves completely in their imaginative effect.

In its inhibition of emotional display, this work is pointedly unlike another of Donne's valedictory poems, *Of Weeping*, where the lovers' tears and sighs become the subject of elaborate conceits designed to exhibit the speaker's ingenuity as much as his grief. In *A Valediction forbidding Mourning* Donne does not merely urge the lady to be reticent, but shows restraint himself by adopting a simple poetic form and a manner which invites none of his characteristic flamboyance. When he tells his mistress that it would profane their happiness 'to tell the laity our love'—meaning those who have not been admitted to its holy mysteries—we believe him, although the poem does broadcast the fact; for its tone is consistent with a wish to avoid making a show of private feeling. Their grief, Donne argues, is in any case too profound to be expressed by such means: earthquakes cause terror and perplexity, but the much greater movement of the spheres brought about by trepidation* is regarded as a natural occurrence, and upsets no one. The scientific parallel suggests that their parting, though far more momentous than any ordinary separation, must attract much less attention. Lovers of a 'dull sublunary' kind, Donne argues, know nothing beyond physical love; and cannot reconcile themselves to parting because, for them, bodily separation is absolute. All sub-

---

*An oscillating movement of the heavens, which makes the planets appear to go backwards—that is, from east to west—over part of their orbit. Its actual cause is a slight wobble in the earth's axis.

lunary beings are subject to change and decay, and in applying this term to other lovers Donne implies that he and she have the constancy and permanence found above the moon. For them, whose love has been purified to such a degree that they themselves cannot comprehend it, loss of physical contact is much less important. The phrase, 'interassured of the mind', seems openly to admit the need for unshakeable security which Donne so often represents, as much in the argumentative structure of his poems as in the passionate insistence of its working-out. The lovers form a single being, sharing a single soul; and their unity is not to be fractured by physical separation. Rather, their shared soul will extend itself as the gap between their bodies widens, 'Like gold to airy thinness beat' (line 24).

This delicate and richly suggestive analogy deserves closer attention than the more famous image of compasses which follows. In drawing a link between ideas as disparate as lovers' relationships and the goldsmith's craft, Donne makes a typically unexpected proposal, and again justifies himself imaginatively. Other metals—copper and lead, for instance—can be beaten into sheets, but none of them so impalpably thin as gold leaf; nor do other metals have the beauty, value and noble associations of gold. Donne's image gives the lovers' shared soul these splendid qualities, yet at the same time suggests its insubstantial nature through the evocative phrase 'airy thinness'. No other literary mode, one feels, could have enabled a poet to describe spiritual being in terms so concrete and yet so closely sympathetic to his argument.

Wisely perhaps, Donne does not develop this fine image, but shifts his ground to a further comparison which provides the theme of the three final stanzas. If the lovers do not share a common soul, Donne argues, then their individual souls are firmly joined together, like the legs of a pair of compasses: meaning the instrument which we now call dividers. Probably no other image is used so often to illustrate metaphysical poetry, and it might be well to point out that Donne has other interests than mathematics and navigation, and that his compasses do not necessarily involve a reference to some new science. What is more typical of metaphysical style is the way Donne extends and develops his initial idea, by arguing a series of parallels between the spiritually linked lovers and the joined legs of the compasses. 'Thy soul, the fixed foot' (line 27), he tells his partner, is not impelled to move until he does so, but then follows his example. In the same way, when the outer leg of the dividers describes a circle, its partner marking the centre turns about, as though watching. Again, when the outer leg describes an arc at the limit of its reach, its partner 'leans and hearkens after it' as though straining to keep in contact; and draws itself up straight when the outer leg completes its circular journey and 'comes home'. This corresponds with their own relationship, Donne tells the lady. Like the leg which describes the circle, he must trace out his traveller's course while she, the fixed foot, remains in one place.

His comment (line 34) 'Thy firmness makes my circle just,' is not easily paraphrased. The moving leg of the compasses describes a true circle only because the other holds its position throughout. This fixity represents the constancy and fidelity of the woman, and the assurance of her 'firmness' gives Donne the power to make his own circle true: both loving her with equal constancy, and throughout his journey moving along a line that must bring him back to his starting-point in her. The analogy is not exact, for when the outer leg of the compasses completes its circle it is at the same distance from the centre as during its movement; and obviously Donne means the closing of the circle to represent reunion at the end of the journey. This true circle has been drawn by their combined strengths, and its symbol of perfection stands for their flawless relationship and—perhaps not accidentally—for the rounded achievement of this poem.

The Elegies

It is irresistibly fascinating to speculate, and to try to establish from his poetry, what the author of both the *Songs and Sonets* and *The Holy Sonnets* was really like. However, it needs only a cursory reading of Donne's love poems to show that no single persona is involved; and that if Donne himself were the speaker in them all, the range of his emotional response must have been prodigious. This characteristic variety of attitude, tone and manner is most noticeable in the fifty-five *Songs and Sonets* which give Donne a greater opportunity of exploiting different situations and emotions; but the same variety is found in the *Elegies*, which contain some of Donne's most scandalously outspoken and unconventional love poems. We may be surprised at the title of these poems, which today suggests a lament or a funeral dirge rather than, as in Latin and Greek, the expression of erotic feeling, but this was the commoner Elizabethan sense of the term; when Donne took up the alternative meaning of the word in *An Anatomy of the World* (1611) he identified it as a 'funeral elegy'. In *As You Like It* the disguised Rosalind complains of a newcomer to the forest who 'hangs odes upon hawthorns, and elegies on brambles; all, forsooth, deifying the name of Rosalind'. When Marlowe translated Ovid's *Amores* they were published as the poet's *Elegies*: a point of wider relevance, for Ovid certainly supplied part of the stimulus of Donne's poems, which have the same impudence and extravagant wit.

We may suppose that when the younger John Donne protested against the unauthorized publication of his dead father's poems, 'very much to the grief of your petitioner and the discredit of the memory of his father', he had some of the love Elegies very much in mind. Although the earlier editions of Donne's work included neither *Elegy*

XVIII, Love's Progress, nor the equally scandalous *Elegy XIV, Going to Bed*, there were enough seeming disclosures of sexual irregularity in the remaining elegies to make the son feel that his father's reputation as dean of St Paul's was being irreparably harmed. But although all twenty of these poems are concerned with aspects of love or with women, not all of them were open to this kind of moral objection. Like the *Songs and Sonets* they involve a variety of attitudes, from constancy and respect towards the mistress to brazen indelicacy and wantonness. Two of them—*Elegy VI* and *Elegy XVI*—were conceivably written for his wife, as some of the *Songs and Sonets* may have been; and not only allude to circumstances like those which Donne and Anne More suffered before their marriage, but address the mistress with the kind of passionate sincerity which we might expect of Donne in this personal situation. But if we are critically honest we shall recognize that same dramatic intensity of feeling, the same sense of personal involvement, in other poems where there is no reason to suppose that Donne was writing out of private experience, and strong arguments to the contrary. It is part of Donne's power as a poet to convince us that the situation is actual, the emotions genuine, and that he is speaking out of his own immediate excitement. We may need to remember Touchstone's admission to Audrey that 'the truest poetry is the most feigning', because this ability to persuade readers that a fictional situation is actual is one of the hallmarks of a fine poet.

Of the twenty elegies, two fall outside the categories that can be imposed upon the rest. *Elegy IX, The Autumnal*, is a strangely paradoxical compliment to a middle-aged woman, which if we believe Walton was addressed to Donne's patroness Magdalen Herbert, the mother of George Herbert. The other, *Elegy XIV*, is unlike the other poems in taking narrative form, and is called *A Tale of a Citizen and his Wife*. In subject-matter it is akin to the other elegies, in showing the narrator mocking a bourgeois husband and coming to some kind of unspoken understanding with his pretty wife; but in style it hardly belongs with this group of poems, and internal allusions show that *Elegy XIV* must have been written about 1610, long after the main body of the *Elegies*.* If we set aside these two atypical examples we can characterize the others as declamatory poems or dramatic mono-logues, spoken by the poet, varying in length from twenty or thirty lines to a maximum of a hundred and fourteen, in rhymed couplets; and we may for convenience divide them into four groups or kinds. The first group depicts the poet as a passionate lover, sometimes involved in a liaison with a married woman, but dedicated and entirely sincere in his attachment, which the lady returns. Seven of the elegies explore this kind of situation, which in the *Songs and Sonets* has parallels in such poems as *The Sun Rising* and the *Valediction*

*Helen Gardner thinks it is not by Donne at all.

forbidding Mourning. Three of the seven are in fact valedictory poems. The second group comprised three elegies, addressed to a mistress who has proved faithless, and written in the cynically bitter style of *The Apparition* or *The Message*. Three more poems, forming the third group, are scathingly satirical about woman or particular women; and the remaining five elegies make up a group of scandalous or erotic poems spoken by a lover who boldly declares his interest in the mistress to be entirely physical and self-gratifying. There is nothing quite as shameless in the *Songs and Sonets*; for although in *Community* Donne argues that when the lover has found satisfaction he may take another woman—

> And when he hath the kernel eat,
> Who doth not fling away the shell?

—and although *The Flea* demonstrates that loss of maidenhead is no more than a fleabite, in the elegies the desire to shock and outrage convention carries Donne to a further extreme of impudence. Added to this the speaker of the elegies makes his improper proposals with a driving energy and explicitness which these other poems cannot match. The opening lines of *Going to Bed* are typical of this ruthless dynamism:

> Come, madam, come: all rest my powers defy;
> Until I labour, I in labour lie.

A further quality of the *Elegies* which makes them more striking than the *Songs and Sonets*, and which also gives them a sharper ring of truth, is their particularity of reference to environment and circumstances. In *The Sun Rising* we know that the poet and his mistress are in bed together, but that is all: whose bed they are in, whether they are married, how long they have known one another, what obstacles they have overcome, the speaker does not suggest. The lovers are isolated within a private world almost empty of material objects, and into which no other person can intrude.

But in the *Elegies* they enjoy no such immunity: they love as passionately, but in a setting which contains enemies, dangers and several kinds of obstacles which the poet speaks of in the course of his address to the mistress: not providing a detailed account of past events for the reader's benefit but reminding her of circumstances as familiar to her as to himself. The opening lines of *Elegy XVI* are a good example of the allusive technique by which Donne rapidly sketches in the background of the lovers' situation:

> By our first strange and fatal interview,
> By all desires which thereof did ensue;
> By our long starving hopes; by that remorse
> Which my words' masculine persuasive force

Begot in thee; and by the memory
Of hurts which spies and rivals threatened me,
I calmly beg: but by thy father's wrath,
By all pains which want and divorcement hath,
I conjure thee; and all the oaths which I
And thou have sworn to seal joint constancy.

These ten lines form the preamble to the lover's absolute refusal to allow his mistress to accompany him on his impending journey: they are not part of a story, a recollecting of their romantic past, but a means of impressing upon her the seriousness of his determination: yet of course they have the function of letting the reader overhear something of the trials and difficulties which the pair have endured. This is one of the poems which commentators have seen as a private utterance by Donne to Anne More, seemingly with some justification. The course of their relationship before marriage certainly involved some of the troubles mentioned by the poet, and the reference to 'thy father's wrath' and the pains of 'want and divorcement' seems to look directly at what followed Sir George More's discovery of his daughter's secret marriage. The allusion seems less certain when we find that although all the seventeenth-century editions of Donne's poetry follow the reading 'thy father's wrath', most of the manuscript collections read 'thy parents' wrath', which makes the other version seem to be an emendation by Donne's first editor, who wanted the poem to be recognized as a piece of autobiography. Even if 'thy father' is allowed to stand, *Elegy XVI* is incompatible with Donne's circumstances at that time. The lover of the poem is about to leave on a journey which will take him through France, Italy and Holland; and the lady will remain in charge of the nurse who may be startled by the lady's nightmares

crying out, 'O, O
Nurse, O my love is slain, I saw him go
O'er the white Alps alone; I saw him, I,
Assailed, fight, taken, stabbed, bleed, fall and die.'

Donne undertook no such journey at a time when Anne More was attended by a nurse, as a young and single gentlewoman might be; and had he done so, it seems highly unlikely that Anne would have proposed to accompany him disguised as a page. The autobiographical explanation fits only a few of the details, which taken together form the kind of background to love which recurs generally in those Elegies which describe a passionate attachment. The lover is beset by hazards and difficulties. He has managed to overcome the lady's reluctance by the 'masculine persuasive force' of his arguments—a phrase which neatly sums up the character of Donne's love poetry—but he is watched by household spies and threatened by rivals. His reference to 'our long starving hopes' suggests how close the lovers have been to despair at the continuing frustration of their desires: the oaths 'sworn to seal joint constancy' prove their determination not to be crushed by adversity. Their hopes have come nearest to disaster in the happenings which the poet alludes to indistinctly in the two lines which form the climax to his resolution:

> But by thy father's wrath,
> By all pains which want and divorcement hath,
> I conjure thee.

The enraged father, who discovers his daughter's unwelcome suitor and makes further meetings or correspondence impossible, figures more prominently in the quite different circumstances of *Elegy IV, The Perfume*. Again the opening lines of the poem present graphically and economically the desperate situation in which the lover finds himself:

> Once and but once found in thy company,
> All thy supposed escapes are laid on me;   [escapades]
> And as a thief at bar is questioned there
> By all the men that have been robbed that year,
> So am I—by this traitorous means surprised—
> By thy hydroptic father catechised.

Up to this point the lover has successfully evaded the lady's father despite constant vigilance and threats, and has carried on a love affair under the father's nose in complete secrecy:

> Though he hath oft sworn that he would remove
> Thy beauty's beauty, and food of our love—
> Hope of his goods—if I were with thee seen,
> Yet close and secret as our souls we've been.

The sardonic phrase 'hope of his goods' represents the father's cynical argument that the lover is interested only in the lady's dowry or her inheritance: it also suggests a rich family, and the deep suspicion and mistrust which such parents feel towards love that is merely romantic. The lady's bedridden mother keeps her under close watch despite this disability, and under cover of caressing and embracing her daughter tries to discover what love-tokens she may be wearing, or if any telltale marks of pregnancy can be detected:

> And, when she takes thy hand and would seem kind,
> Doth search what rings and armlets she can find;
> And kissing, notes the colour of thy face,
> And fearing lest thou'rt swoll'n, doth thee embrace;
> To try if thou [do] long, doth name strange meats,
> And notes thy paleness, blushing, sighs, and sweats.

The junior members of the family, the lady's 'little brethren' are also employed in this espionage service, and after bursting into the room where the lovers spend 'those sweet nights' are bribed to report what they have seen. Once again the particularity of the writing, and the graphic liveliness of the picture makes us feel Donne's involvement in events; though we may notice that this quality is just as striking in the description of the boys' interrogation—which the lover certainly did not see—as in the earlier part of the passage:

> Thy little brethren, which like fairy sprites
> Oft skipped into our chamber those sweet nights;
> And, kissed and ingled on thy father's knee,
> Were bribed next day to tell what they did see.

Evidently they saw nothing, as did the most memorable figure of the *Elegies*, the 'grim eight-foot-high iron-bound servingman' who guards the door of the house, and whom the lady's father also sets to watch:

> Though by thy father he were hired to this,
> Could never witness any touch or kiss.

What he might have seen had the lovers been less cautious does not emerge, for the poet only hints at how far their lovemaking went. In a sense that is a side issue, for the central concern of *Elegy IV*, as the title suggests, is with the perfume which betrayed the lover's presence in the house. 'But O, too common ill', he exclaims,

> I brought with me
> That which betrayed me to my enemy:
> A loud perfume, which at my entrance cried
> Even at thy father's nose: so were we spied.

As the poet proceeds to mock and satirize the lady's father and the other members of her family household we may wonder whether she was expected to approve his very disrespectful comments. He certainly does not consider her feelings when he suggests that a less attractive scent would not have aroused her father's suspicions: he would have supposed that his own feet or his bad breath were responsible. Here at least, if not earlier in the poem, Donne appears to be more interested in describing the lover's daring achievements in the face of hazards and opposition than in reporting the trials of an actual love affair. Despite the misfortune of being detected by his own perfume, the lover can congratulate himself on his cunning and secrecy up to that point; and expect his readers to sympathize with him in what is clearly an illicit relationship. When he speaks of his efforts to steal about the house in complete silence—

> I taught my silks their whistling to forbear;
> Even my oppress'd shoes dumb and speechless were

—he makes us see and hear the breathless tiptoeing hush of his shadowy passage along corridors of an enemy house towards a forbidden association: the triumph of a romantic lover over bourgeois dullness and vulgarity. The poem requires us to be on his side: to share his amused mockery and libelling of the citizen whose house he invades, and to associate ourselves with his behaviour. The lady exists only as a silent audience: the other figures of the household exist only to be ridiculed by the lover's more agile wit and his contempt for their bourgeois standards; and although he is caught the poem bubbles with his enjoyment of the situation and of the intellectual impudence which his effortless satire demonstrates.

In *Elegy I* Donne develops the *persona* of arrogant intruding lover several steps further. The opening words, 'Fond woman, which wouldst have thy husband die' set the contemptuous tone of the poem, and establish the lover's brazen indifference towards conventional morality. Donne obviously intends to shock his readers; not only by boldly admitting his adulterous liaison, but by introducing a mistress who wishes her husband dead, and a lover who is almost as scornful of her as of the absurd cuckold whom he has been abusing. Rebuking her complaints about her husband's recently awakened suspicions, the lover goes on insultingly:

> If, swoll'n with poison, he lay in's last bed,
> His body with a sere-bark covered,
> Drawing his breath as thick and short as can
> The nimblest crocheting musician,
> Ready with loathsome vomiting to spew
> His soul out of one hell into a new,
> Made deaf with his poor kindred's howling cries,
> Begging with few feigned tears great legacies,
> Thou wouldst not weep, but jolly and frolic be.

If there were any doubt about Donne's ability to imagine scenes and situations into existence, this passage should remove them. The picture of the dying man, his body encrusted with eruptive sores, panting for breath, and about to die in a great spasm of vomiting, is realized as graphically as any actual experience: the power to communicate such vivid ideas depending not on such actual experience but on the poet's mastery of language. Here the violent energy of the writing shows characteristically how Donne's imagination is jolted and twisted by the satirical impulse to arouse disgust and revulsion: 'loathsome vomiting' and 'spew' put the husband beyond reach of sympathy, although the picture of his deathbed agonies is merely fanciful. So too of course is the idea of his last moments being distracted by the howling of his poor relations,

> Begging with few feigned tears great legacies.

This tense, compact line explodes with a contempt and mockery that should remind us of Jonson, into whose world of misers and grasping heirs Donne seems to have strayed, a full decade before *Volpone*. The mockery persists, and as the lover argues that instead of being upset by her husband's growing suspicions the lady should thank him for the warning, he admits how hitherto both of them have scorned and jeered at him at his own table, without his realizing who was being ridiculed. This game must now stop, the lover warns her:

> We must not, as we used, flout openly
> In scoffing riddles his deformity;
> Nor, at his board together being sat,
> With words nor touch scarce looks adulterate;
> Nor when he, swoll'n and pampered with great fare,
> Sits down and snorts, caged in his basket chair,
> Must we usurp his own bed any more,
> Nor kiss and play in his house, as before.

The lover refers to his adultery in the cuckold's own bed quite shamelessly, as though the physical grossness and dull-wittedness of the husband justified this sexual liberty as well as the mockery which his victim has not recognized. It is difficult for a modern reader to judge how outrageous this poem must have appeared to its Elizabethan readers, accustomed to love poetry which expressed virtuous feelings, awed respect for the lady, and the most loftily moral hopes and intentions. Here Donne writes as a confessed adulterer whose understanding with the wife he has seduced allows him to advise her quite calmly to abandon their private jokes, and not to risk any further meetings in her husband's bed. 'We'll play in another house,' he tells her;

> What should we fear?
> There we will scorn his household policies,
> His silly plots and pensionary spies.

The cuckold will easily be outwitted, and become more ridiculous in the process. Some of the first readers of the *Elegies* who saw them in manuscript may have realized that Donne had lifted some ideas and perhaps his basic situation from the *Amores* of Ovid, where the poet's mistress Corinna is a married woman, and the lovers have a private means of communication very much like the riddling talk mentioned in *Elegy I*. But even those Elizabethan readers who recognized Donne's borrowings from Ovid might have been startled by his boldness in this first elegy, and by the realistic immediacy of the situations which Donne creates with this prompting from the *Amores*. Although Ovid ridicules Corinna's husband, and even criticizes him for not being sufficiently suspicious and watchful, he does not go to the lengths of suggesting—as Donne does—that this rival is old, gouty and overfed; or as he puts it so graphically, 'swoll'n and pampered with great fare'.

Probably this is the deformity which the lovers mock behind their hands: an idea made dynamically alive by a line of devastating satire:

> Sits down and snorts, caged in his basket chair.

'Caged' suggests the impotence of a trapped animal whose snorting, or snoring, gives the lovers a new source of amusement; and it also suggests how the husband's grossly obese figure is enclosed and immobilized by his basket chair—that touch of particularity which makes the scene so convincing. By going beyond Ovid in his ridicule, and especially by making the husband old and physically repellent, Donne encourages his lover to be even more impudently disrespectful and shameless; and outrages conventional morality still further by implying that husbands are creatures of coarse habits and appetites who deserve to be out-manoeuvred and cuckolded. The lover of *Elegy I* seems to be acting as spokesman of a witty, amoral generation bent upon discrediting totally the ethical standards of their elders, and at the same time scandalizing established opinion.

In *Elegy XII* Donne returns to the *persona* of adulterous lover, but not to the easy superiority of his counterpart in *Elegy I*. Rather, like the secret lover of *Elegy IV* and *Elegy XVI* who runs foul of the lady's father, the speaker of *Elegy XII* has enjoyed the love of a married woman but now must be separated from her, evidently without hope of being reunited. The opening words of the poem, 'Since she must go, and I mourn', tell us all we are to know about the circumstances of their separation; though perhaps uncharacteristically of Donne, the poem gives us a sense of the lover's desolation at being deprived of his mistress. 'I saw the golden fruit, 'tis rapt away,' he comments;

> Or as I had watched one drop in a vast stream,
> And I left wealthy only in a dream.

But this mood of depression is dissipated as the lover begins to rebuke the god of love for permitting this calamity when he had already been responsible for their suffering so many previous trials and difficulties; and here again Donne sketches the background of the lovers' present situation by referring to past events which are known to both speaker and mistress:

> Was't not enough that thou didst hazard us
> To paths in love so dark, so dangerous?
> And those so ambushed round with household spies,
> And—over all—thy husband's towering eyes,
> That flamed with oily sweat of jealousy;
> Yet went we not still on with constancy?
> Have we not kept our guards, like spy on spy?
> Had correspondence whilst the foe stood by?
> Stol'n—more to sweeten them—our many blisses

Of meetings, conference, embracements, kisses;
Shadowed with negligence our most respects?

The passage outlines a rather different adulterous liaison; from
Donne's point of view perhaps a new variant on a favourite theme.
The lady too is another man's wife, watched by household spies and
a madly suspicious husband: the lover is in great danger, but is
apparently still admitted to the house, where he makes his feelings
known to the lady by secret signs which although seeming casual are
the expression of his deepest emotions. The next three lines describe
how the lovers have

Varied our language through all dialects
Of becks, winks, looks; and often, under-boards,
Spoke dialogues with our feet far from our words.

This passage runs very close to Ovid in the fourth of the *Amores*, where
the lover tells Corinna how to exchange secret messages with him
in her husband's presence. 'View me, my becks and speaking coun-
tenance', he instructs her in Marlowe's translation,

Take and receive each secret amorous glance.
Words without voice shall on my eyebrows sit;
Lines thou shalt read in wine by my hand writ.
When our lascivious toys come in thy mind,
Thy rosy cheeks be to thy thumb inclined:
If aught of me thou speak'st in inward thought,
Let thy soft finger to thy ear be brought.

The instructions run on to some length, which Donne wisely com-
presses to a few lines: he is not, as we have seen, teaching his mistress
sign language, but running over the course of a liaison which has just
reached an impasse; and so for him these allusions to secret messages
are by the way. *Elegy XII* is also closer to Ovid in feeling than the other
poems of this group, where Donne exploits the situation for purposes of
satire and ridicule. Here the lover seems sincerely distressed by the
check to his hopes, and instead of shrugging off his disappointment and
beginning a new adventure he declares his constancy and his belief
that he and his mistress cannot truly be separated. 'Do thy great
worst', he tells Love,

my friend and I have arms,
Though not against thy strokes, against thy harms.
Rend us in sunder, thou canst not divide
Our bodies so but that our souls are tied;
And we can love by letters still and gifts,
And thoughts and dreams: love never wanteth shifts.

Unexpectedly the adulterous lover has been metamorphosed into a counterpart of the figure who threads his way through the *Songs and Sonets*, comforting himself and his mistress by the argument that for true lovers separation is impossible: an argument put most succinctly and with great tenderness in the *Valediction forbidding Mourning*. It is not easy to understand why Donne should have wished to combine these two elements in one poem, unless his purpose was again to startle and disconcert his readers by suggesting that an adulterer could be just as dedicated and nobly constant as the conventional lover who kept within the limits of sexual morality. When this lover exhorts his mistress to keep faith with him during their separation he demonstrates the unswerving fixity of mind which in a conventional love relationship could only evoke approval and administration. 'Declare yourself base fortune's enemy,' he advises,

No less by your contempt than constancy,
That I may grow enamoured on your mind
When my own thoughts I there reflected find;
For this to the comfort of my dear I vow:
My deeds shall still be what my words are now.

These are not the sentiments of a philanderer, and by asking his readers to associate them with adultery Donne seems to have been trying to shock established morality in a new way. But as we don't find in *Elegy XII* the raw violence of expression and idea which usually forms part of Donne's attack on conservative tradition, this reading of the poem is perhaps mistaken.

Elegy VII has such a violence of tone, and begins with an outburst of angry indignation against the mistress which is far from exhausted by the end of this comparatively short poem. The lover is deeply aggrieved that after he has shaped and educated a completely ignorant woman, teaching her sophistication in love when all she knew previously was naïve and childish, she should turn the tables on him by taking a husband who will then reap all the benefit of this education. 'Nature's lay idiot', he tells her, describing her absolute lack of experience in a contemptuous phrase,

I taught thee to love,
And in that sophistry O thou dost prove
Too subtle: fool, thou didst not understand
The mystic language of the eye nor hand...

It is no sentimental education that the lady has received: rather, she has been taught how to be knowing and sceptical, distinguishing between a true sigh of desperate love and a counterfeit, and between tears of burning passion and those of a passing infatuation. She has also been instructed in the fine arts of subterfuge and secret communication which other mistresses of the *Elegies* practise so easily. Looking back to her original naivety, the angry poet reminds her:

I had not taught thee then the alphabet
Of flowers, how they devisefully being set
And bound up, might with speechless secrecy
Deliver errands mutely, and mutually.

Once again Donne tells his story by making the speaker recall past
events familiar to the mistress, and by allowing the reader to overhear,
as through a half-open door, remarks not intended for him. The lover
again addresses the lady as if his behaviour were not open to moral
criticism, and as if by transforming a simple innocent into a woman of
worldly experience he had done something praiseworthy. As he recalls
her former lack of sophistication he mocks the bashful simplicity and
artlessness which, under his guidance, she has learnt to avoid:

Remember since all thy words used to be
To every suitor, 'Ay, if my friends agree':
Since household charms thy husband's name to teach
Were all the love-tricks that thy wit could reach.

Evidently her repertoire of love-tricks is now much enlarged, and the
lover claims full credit for the change without any suggestion that his
mockery of her catch-phrases and romantic games might be out of
place. The speaker assumes that the reader shares his own valuation of
sophisticated manners, and that uncorrupted innocence will seem as
laughable to us as to him. Again it may need an effort of imagination
to realize how outrageous this poem must have seemed to its
Elizabethan readers, not many of whom can have thought that the
lover might or should instruct his mistress in the practices of love. To
Berowne, if to no other Elizabethan lover, woman was in herself a
moral and liberal education through which he learnt the nature of
beauty, virtue and heavenly goodness. But here Donne is suggesting
that the man is the instructor, and when he claims that he has taught
the mistress to love he is not speaking of any morally uplifting
education, but of preparing her for sexual adventures in the wittily
dissolute society for which he speaks. Being his pupil she belongs
to him, he asserts, indignantly denying that the man she has now
married has any right. 'Thou art not by so many duties his', he argues,

That from the world's common having severed thee,
Inlaid thee, neither to be seen nor see,
As mine; who have with amorous delicacies
Refined thee into a blissful paradise.
Thy graces and good words my creatures be:
I planted knowledge and life's tree in thee,
Which O shall strangers taste?

In this context 'knowledge' has doubtful associations, and the re-
ference to planting 'life's tree' in the mistress is more openly equivocal.

The complaint that another man will now enjoy—legitimately—the fruit of the lover's course of instruction is morally as preposterous as his assertion that the lady remains his property: a point of view which would justify his continuing the close relationship which her marriage has interrupted.

Elegy V, His Picture, is the shortest of these poems and better known than most. It is another of the valedictions of which Donne seems to have been fond; and unlike the poems we have been considering it involves not a recapitulation of past events but a preview of the future. The lover is about to leave on a voyage, and gives the mistress a picture of himself—an Elizabethan miniature, perhaps—not merely as a keepsake but as a reminder of his former appearance if he should return physically transformed by the privations and exposure he will suffer. 'If weather-beaten I come back', he suggests,

> my hand
> Perhaps with rude oars torn, or sunbeams tanned,
> My face and breast of haircloth, and my head
> With care's rash sudden storms being o'erspread;
> My body a sack of bones, broken within,
> And powder's blue stains scattered on my skin,

how will she answer the scornful questions of his rivals, asking how she could love a man 'so foul and coarse' as he will then appear? The immediate interest of this passage lies in its suggestion of a military expedition overseas, in which the lover can expect to be exposed to a fierce sun, maimed and discoloured by gunfire and possibly shipwrecked. These hazards Donne himself accepted when he joined the Islands Expedition in 1597 after taking part in the raid on Cadiz a year earlier, though one does not suppose that he pitched his chances as low as this speaker suggests.

There is a secondary interest in the concern with physical transformation from youthful elegance into broken and disfigured deformity. Several of the *Songs and Sonets* display Donne's awareness of the grave and his own dissolution even when he is passionately addressing his mistress; and stylistically as well as in ideas his poetry has little to do with harmony and regularity. His picture of the lover crippled and prematurely aged, a laughing-stock to his rivals and a shocking contrast with the image of youth and gallantry in his portrait, is strongly characteristic of Donne's double consciousness, which barely allows him to contemplate beauty without imagining ugliness, truth without falsehood. The often brutal energy of his writing seems to derive some of its tormented dynamism from the unease of this divided awareness. In *Elegy V* the lover shows a much greater readiness to picture himself dead or horribly changed than to discuss his actual attractive appearance: the poem anticipates and tries to guard against the unbelievable physical transformation which may have occurred when next the mistress sees him. At such a time the portrait will remind her how he once looked, and prompt her to ask whether her own value is affected, and whether he now loves her less:

> This shall say what I was: and thou shalt say,
> 'Do his hurts reach me? Doth my worth decay?
> 'Or do they reach his judging mind, that he
> 'Should now love less what he did love to see?'

She will reassure herself by reflecting that the 'fair and delicate' qualities which the portrait depicts were merely the means of nourishing love at a juvenile stage of growth. Now, that love has

> grown strong enough
> To feed on that which to disused tastes seems tough.

The poem presents an odd mixture of conventional and unfamiliar. The lover's valediction is an established literary kind: an occasion to swear constancy and to promise to return unchanged in devotion to a mistress who does not always positively encourage such dedication. Donne's lover has the same dedicated feelings, but he may return radically altered in appearance: 'a sack of bones', weather-beaten and lined, his youthful vigour exhausted; and then the problem will be whether the mistress can retain any affection for the scarecrow figure who was once her lively and captivating lover. The unsentimental toughness of the argument which Donne puts into her mouth is indeed characteristic of him, but not of the conventional mistress, who would not have been required to face this testing situation. In the general context of Donne's love poetry the notion of a judgment 'grown strong enough' to accept food more intellectually demanding than Sidney or Spenser provided has a special aptness. Both in situation and expression this is a love poem as unconventionally stark and aggressive as the argument by which the lady persuades herself—or rather, is persuaded—to love the battered and unromantic figure who was once an Elizabethan gallant.

But if *Elegy V* takes an original line in this respect, at least it accepts the convention that love involves a deeply mutual relationship not of bodies but of inner personality. When the lover of *Elegy V* presents his picture he tells the mistress characteristically.

> Thine in my heart, where my soul dwells, shall dwell.

In all the Elegies we have so far considered, including those which deal with adulterous love and secret meetings, the lover maintains some contact with literary convention by expressing a passion which transcends an immediate sexual interest in the lady. But the *Elegies* also include some frankly erotic poems in which Donne throws this respectable convention overboard and makes his lover declare an unequivocal interest in the sheer physicality of sex. *Elegy XVIII, Love's*

Progress, wastes no time in stating its shameless premise that love has one 'right true' purpose: physical satisfaction:

> Whoever loves, if he do not propose
> The right true end of love, he's one that goes
> To sea for nothing but to make him sick.

This is the manner which still gives Donne his *succès de scandale*; aggressively unconventional, contemptuous of everything in woman except the 'centrique part' of their sex. Several of the elegies encourage us to adopt this simple picture of the young poet as the 'great visitor of ladies' which his acquaintance described. But the only thing which these poems tell us certainly about Donne is of his driving energy, his love of display, his delight in standing convention on its head. We should read the *Elegies* as outrageous *jeux d'esprit*, not as autobiograhy; perhaps with a regretful sense of how much that daringly inventive spirit was to be reduced by the years of frustration and lean emptiness which followed his romantic marriage to another of those jealously guarded daughters.

The Holy Sonnets

XIV

Batter my heart, three-personed God, for you
As yet but knock, breathe, shine and seek to mend;
That I may rise and stand, o'erthrow me and bend
Your force to break, blow, burn and make me new.
I, like an usurped town to another due,
Labour to admit you, but O to no end:
Reason, your viceroy in me, me should defend,
But is captived, and proves weak or untrue.
Yet dearly I love you, and would be loved fain,
10 But am betrothed unto your enemy:
Divorce me, untie or break that knot again;
Take me to you, imprison me, for I
Except you enthral me, never shall be free,
Nor ever chaste, except you ravish me.

The *Songs and Sonets* were written when Donne was a young man, and probably during the years immediately before and after his marriage in 1601. The nineteen *Holy Sonnets* belong to a later and darker period of his life, when the death of his wife in 1617 robbed him of his greatest comfort, and profoundly changed his personal outlook. These poems reflect a deep disturbance of spirit, and suggest that with his wife's death Donne lost the vital sense of security to which many of his love poems refer. He now looks to God for an assurance of love, but haunted by the recollection of his sins Donne seems unable to persuade himself either that he deserves or that he can expect divine forgiveness. His spiritual anxiety, sometimes rising to a climax of terror, as when he contemplates the possible imminence of God's judgment, 'What if this present were the world's last night?' (*XIII*. 1) is felt in the choked utterance of these poems, which wrench language and metre into strained phrases, to represent Donne's agitation directly.

The element of dialectic found in the love poems reappears in these sonnets, sharpened and given muscle by a more urgent need to prove—whether to himself or to God—that he can be saved from damnation. We may be incongruously reminded of the younger Donne's use of dialectic to silence a woman's resistance, or to justify inconstancy; for although the matter of the *Holy Sonnets* is utterly different, the poet's arguments are still forced to their conclusion without respect for a logical progression of ideas. Despite appearances they, like the love poems, are motivated by passionate impulse; and whether the argument hangs together matters much less than whether the poem resolves the alarm or disquiet which triggers Donne's attempt to reason himself into a state of spiritual calm.

The emotional explosiveness of the *Holy Sonnets* is countered by their structural formality. They have the usual fourteen lines of the Elizabethan sonnet, each of five feet; and they observe the usual division into octet and sestet. Their rhyme scheme is less familiar. Instead of rhyming in quatrains, *abab*, *cdcd*, Donne completes the octet with only two rhymes, which fall irregularly: *abba*, *abba*. This helps to unify the octet, but calls for a stricter discipline in shaping expression; and this demand upon the poet's craftsmanship acts as a brake on the vehement feeling which impels his poem. In *Sonnet XIV* this driving force manifests itself in an opening sentence as brutally violent as the treatment it appeals for:

> Batter my heart, three-personed God; for you
> As yet but knock, breathe, shine, and seek to mend.

The suddenness of the onslaught takes us unawares, and the strongly accented verbs 'knock, breathe, shine' ring like hammer-blows: fittingly, for Donne is making the lines act out the furious bombardment which will break his enslavement to sin and make him God's captive. He longs to be rescued from his sinfulness, but knows himself so hopelessly subjugated that gentle inducements cannot persuade him to reform; and he cries out to be overwhelmed by the power of God, which will shatter and then re-create him:

> That I may rise and stand, o'erthrow me and bend
> Your force to break, blow, burn and make me new.

After the check on 'stand' the voice leaps forward, telescoping the phrase 'o'erthrow me and bend' into a rush of sound; but in the next line the movement is again halted, and three more fiercely stressed words, 'break, blow, burn' hack into an almost obliterated metrical pattern. Within less than two lines, Donne has passed from rushing haste to something near immobility, first breaking down the natural stops in verse rhythm, and then setting harshly unnatural barriers across it. Altogether seven passages of this sonnet are elided, where Donne crushes words together to make them fit the decasyllabic line.* Nominally, he respects this verse form; for however he wrenches and compresses language, the line does not run to more than five feet; but as he rams words into blurred phrases, or dislocates the line unit with fiercely stressed monosyllables, Donne seems to be straining sonnet form to the point of breakdown. The impression that the lines can barely contain all that he crams into them is chiefly responsible for the explosive effect of this poem: through it we feel the speaker's desperation as he seeks to move God to take sterner measures with him.

The sense of violence is greatest in the opening four lines; a fact partly explained by the remarkable number of verbs which they include. The next four lines involve a change of tone, as Donne drops from the imperative to the apologetic and explains to God how powerless he is to resist sin unaided:

> I, like an usurped town to another due,
> Labour to admit you, but O to no end:
> Reason, your viceroy in me, me should defend,
> But is captived, and proves weak or untrue.

The suggestion of an armed conflict in Donne's simile might seen inappropriate to a man's relationship with God, but in the context of violent physical effort established by the opening lines of the sonnet, ideas of siege and warfare follow as though naturally. We might expect prayer to be respectful and submissive, but Donne shows as little regard for custom in his devotional writing as in his love poetry; and his image of a conquered city feebly trying to readmit its dispossessed prince seizes upon the reality of his spiritual state, ignoring polite convention. As a lover he disregards the usual forms of compliment, not troubling to describe his mistress's features but concentrating upon the vital subject of what unites her to him. In much the same way when he addresses God he goes straight to the crucial point, not attempting to praise God or to offer humble service but demanding to be told God's purposes towards him, or clamouring to be assured that he can be admitted to God's grace. The sonnet *Batter my heart* is typically of this aggressive and insistent approach, and

---

*The seven phrases are, 'me and bend', 'to another', 'to admit', 'dearly love', 'you and', 'me, untie', and 'you enthral'. In each of them two syllables are run together to form a single sound. Some editors indicate elision in Donne typographically, for instance, 't'another', 't'admit', and 'dearly'I love'.

of Donne's honesty in the moral self-appraisal which lies immediately behind his appeal. His innate inclination to sin is too strong a force to be reversed by his puny moral impulse; yet as he explains to God, he longs to be united with him. The voice which at the beginning of the poem is fiercely demanding now becomes muted and wistful:

> Yet dearly I love you, and would be loved fain,
> But am betrothed unto your enemy.

The idiom of the poem has changed radically, and so has Donne's metaphor. His relationship with God, seen in terms of physical conflict previously, is now presented as the unsatisfied yearning of a lover; and although this is a more familiar concept, Donne exploits his analogy with a particularity which transforms it. No longer in the thick of a spiritual battle, he speaks as a woman forced into a marriage contract against her will, who looks despairingly towards the man she loves, hoping that he may still claim her. This development of Donne's original idea seems to dislocate the poem by its unexpectedness, but in the closing four lines he brings the images of physical violence and passionate love together, as he renews his tormented appeal to be overwhelmed by God:

> Divorce me, untie or break that knot again;
> Take me to you, imprison me; for I
> Unless you enthrall me, never shall be free,
> Nor ever chaste except you ravish me.

The image of sexual violation might be thought grotesquely inappropriate to the relationship of God and man. But what we know of Donne's temperament through his style tells us how turbulent his feelings were, and we recognize that this startling analogy reflects a mode of apprehension natural to him, and not a deliberate attempt to be sensational. If he is to feel secure, God must take him with the sudden ferocity of possession which the metaphor implies; and thus although the image may be theologically doubtful, in terms of feeling it is amply justified. Moreover, by combining the concepts of love and violence which provide the poem's two main imaginative themes, the metaphor of rape ties together these diverse elements of Donne's argument in a firmly unified conclusion.

Despite the power of Donne's images in this sonnet, not they but his argument dominates the poem. As in several of the love poems, here too Donne's emotional energy is harnessed to an intellectual task; and by the end of the sonnet he has worked out an answer to his distracting spiritual problem, which he storms at God to accept. Significantly, his answer involves a double paradox: Donne can never be free until God has taken him prisoner, nor chaste until God has possessed him by force. These vary the form of a similar paradox earlier in the poem (line 3), 'That I may rise and stand, o'erthrow me', and together show how much of the poem is directed by intellectual wit. The intensely purposeful argument determines how the sonnet develops, and makes all other features of the poem subordinate to its driving needs. It is this feature of Donne's devotional poetry which distinguishes him most clearly from those who wrote in the later metaphysical manner. His poetry is essentially argument: a hard, stubbornly persistent core of dialectic whose purposes dictate the poem's general form and the particular nature of its images.

Prose writings

Although it is for his poetry that Donne is chiefly remembered, the greater part of his work is in prose; and it was in this capacity that he was best known to his own contemporaries. The two sides of his literary character belong roughly to different periods of his life, separated by the difficult years preceding his taking orders as an Anglican priest. The dashing and licentious love poems and elegies were probably written before Donne's marriage in 1601. The long years of domestic hardship and depression which followed are unlikely to have encouraged any further poetry of this kind; and we may fairly assume that his *Nocturnal upon St Lucy's Day*, written at the year's midnight, represents the profoundly depressed state into which he had collapsed from the excited bravado of his amorous and satirical writing. That sense of spiritual exhaustion and hopelessness is evident in the world-view of *The First Anniversary*, published in 1611; and the pessimistic outlook which Donne had by then adopted was to persist in almost everything he wrote thereafter. He continued to produce poetry, and in the *Good Friday* of 1613 and the *Holy Sonnets* displayed a creative power and passionate feeling at least matching the achievement of the youthful *Songs and Sonets*; but his devotional poetry is underlaid and often dominated by spiritual anxieties as forceful as the overbearing arguments of his erotic verse had been.

With Donne's acceptance of the priesthood, the private interests which we see him working out in his religious poems were diverted into the public expression of his sermons, several of which were published in his lifetime. The posthumous collection entitled *LXXX Sermons*, which came out in 1640, suggests how much of Donne's literary energies was absorbed by this part of his duty. Not unwillingly, we should think; for it seems clear that in preaching, Donne was not simply giving his congregation sound theological advice, but deliberating aloud over problems and issues—especially those concerning death and judgment—in which he was himself deeply involved. It would be difficult to read even a random passage from the sermons without feeling Donne's emotional and intellectual involvement in the argument which it pursues, and the appropriateness of his place in the pulpit. The strongly marked dramatic character of Donne's poetry is a natural concomitant of powerful emotion, which finds its fullest expression in the immediacy of speech rather than in a report of previous experience. The sermons allowed him to continue this enacting of private feeling and thought, as though in a dramatic monologue or soliloquy where the effect of the written word is heightened by gesture, facial expression and tone of voice.

Devotions upon Emergent Occasions

Of the prose works of Donne published in his lifetime, the most popular was the *Devotions upon Emergent* Occasions*, which first appeared in 1624. The little book was reprinted twice that year, with two further editions in 1626 and 1627. It followed Donne's recovery from a dangerous sickness during the previous year, and takes the twenty-three days of illness as the basis of private meditation and prayer about the spiritual condition of himself and the world, which Donne sees reflected in the diseased state of his body. Walton, not the most reliable of biographers, supposed that Donne had written the book on his sickbed; but he was probably deceived by the dramatic presentation of the sick man's experience as a continuing process, which conforms with Donne's habitual literary practice. As in the poems he repeatedly works out an argument under the reader's nose, reaching a conclusion as he writes the last line, so in the *Devotions* Donne describes the onset and development of the disease as though unable to tell how it will end, or whether indeed he will be alive to finish the book. His macabre interest in dissolution may have been great enough to have impelled him to keep a spiritual diary of his changing condition during the twenty-three days of a sickness which puzzled and alarmed his physicians; but it seems more likely that the *Devotions* was composed after his recovery, in the characteristically dramatic manner which gives his writing its sense of living immediacy. It may seem paradoxical that this ability should have been directed towards the subject which obviously fascinates Donne throughout—his steady progress towards death. But we have noticed in an earlier chapter of this book that death figures obsessively even in the love poems, whose irrepressible energy reveals Donne's youthful vitality. With the disappointment of his hopes in 1601 that obsession seems to have taken increasing hold on his mind. The three-week ordeal by sickness which brought him near to death in 1623 probably did not evoke day by day those particular thoughts and arguments which provide the matter of the *Devotions*. But the illness gave him opportunity and justification for writing an intensely introspective commentary on the subject of decay and death, which his own desperately sick state embodied.

However compulsive its thinking, the book is organized on an

*unexpectedly arising

unusually formal plan. The work is first divided into twenty-three sections or stations, each corresponding to a stage in Donne's sickness. The first section describes the premonitory signs of approaching illness; the second the failing of strength and loss of bodily faculties; in the third he takes to his bed, and in the fourth the physician is sent for. In the eighth section the king sends his own physician to help; and in the thirteenth—that is, thirteen days after the onset of the still undiagnosed complaint—'the sickness declares the infection and malignity thereof by spots'. Four days later, in section nineteen, the physicians are sufficiently satisfied with their patient's condition to administer a purge; and after another two days Donne is able to leave his bed. These divisions allow the reader to trace the course of the illness from its first manifestations to a period of crisis lasting three or four days after the appearance of spots, and to the point of recovery where the physcans leave Donne warning him of the danger of a relapse.

But although the changes in his bodily condition provide the design in which the book is organized, Donne is not greatly interested in the disease itself, except as it symbolizes or gives form to the spiritual condition of himself and mankind generally. To explore this concern he divides each of the twenty-three sections of *Devotions* into three parts: a meditation, an expostulation and a prayer, and makes his physical state or the treatment prescribed for each day supply the motif or text for a three-part disquisition upon the moral and theological truths which that theme calls to mind. The meditation is usually secular, sometimes involving scientific ideas. *Meditation IV*, on the theme 'The physician is sent for', argues its way towards this appreciation of man's helplessness compared with the ability of certain animals to cure themselves:

> We have the physician, but we are not the physician. Here we shrink in our proportion, sink in our dignity, in respect of very mean creatures who are physicians to themselves. The hart that is pursued and wounded, they say, knows an herb which being eaten throws off the arrow: a strange kind of vomit. The dog that pursues it, though he be subject to sickness, even proverbially knows his grass that recovers him.*... Man hath not that innate instinct to apply those natural medicines to his present danger as those inferior creatures have: he is not his own apothecary, his own physician, as they are.

In the Expostulation which follows Donne carries on a one-sided

---

*Apparently an unconscious recollection of Lyly's *Euphues*, published in 1578, which Donne could hardly have avoided reading. 'The dog having surfeited, to procure his vomit eateth grass, and findeth remedy: the hart being pierced with the dart runneth out of hand to the herb dictanum, and is healed. And can men by no herb...procure a remedy for the impatient disease of love?'—*The Descent of Euphues*, ed. James Winny, Cambridge 1957, p. 27.

dialogue with God, himself supplying answers to the enquiries which he addresses to his divine creator. 'Thou didst not make clothes before there was a shame of the nakedness of the body,' he tells God,

> but thou didst make physic before there was any grudging* of the sickness; for thou didst imprint a medicinal virtue in many simples,† even from the beginning. Didst thou mean that we should be sick when thou didst so, when thou madest them? No more than thou didst mean that we should sin when thou madest us: thou foresawest both, but causedst neither.

To complete the section, the Prayer takes up the same motif, drawing passages from the Bible which mention healing and curing to support its appeal for God's help. 'Thy Son went about healing all manner of sickness', Donne recalls, quoting a line from Matthew iv,

> no disease incurable, none difficult; he healed them all in passing. Virtue went out of him, and he healed all, all the multitude, no person incurable: he healed them every whit—as himself speaks‡— he left no relic of the disease; and will this universal physician pass by this hospital and not visit me? not heal me? not heal me wholly?

The task of maintaining this conceptual design, calling for variations on twenty-three themes in the different voices or attitudes of each three-part section, demanded two particular abilities of its author. The first was a well-stocked mind, able to form analogies and parallels between his physical condition and a wide diversity of learned topics and ideas. A close familiarity with the Bible formed part of this ability. The second was a linked imaginative power of pursuing such analogies, based on the sectional theme, along philosophical by-roads and into erudite corners of knowledge without losing track of a purposeful argument. More briefly, one might say that the task Donne proposed for himself in *Devotions* was the writing of a metaphysical prose work; for the intellectual and imaginative qualities just described are dominant characteristics of the literary style developed in his poetry. The thirty-odd years which separate the wild young poet from the sombre dean of St Paul's may have crushed Donne's vitality, but they could not substantially alter the configuration of his mind. It would be difficult to read the passage quoted below, taken from *Meditation IV*, without recognizing its author in the oddity of thought: an oddity produced not by random reflections or by day-dreaming, but by a thrust of intellectual energy which persists until it has fully explored and defined its idea:

> It is too little to call man a little world: except God, man is a

*symptom of approaching illness
†medicinal herb
‡John vii: 23

diminutive to nothing. Man consists of more pieces, more parts, than the world; than the world doth; nay, than the world is. And if those pieces were extended and stretched out in man as they are in the world, man would be the giant and the world the dwarf; the world but the map, and the man the world. If all the veins in our bodies were extended to rivers, and all the sinews to veins of mines, and all the muscles that lie upon one another to hills, and all the bones to quarries of stones, and all the other pieces to the proportion of those which correspond to them in the world, the air would be too little for this orb of man to move in, the firmament would be but enough for this star.

Beneath the strangely fanciful thinking, the passage vibrates with an imaginative excitement not easy to locate. We become spectators of the process which it represents, as a single challenging idea acts as trigger to a rapidly growing train of thought, which quickens as the mind warms and takes fire, rising and filling as though in sympathy with the concept of giant growth. The lengthening rhythms of Donne's sentences, like the strides of that growing giant, suggest how completely his feelings are engaged in the intellectual conceit which he is developing; and warn us not to assume that he is merely playing with ideas. The private depression which *Devotions* manifests so plainly is in part a consequence of the disappointment which Donne shared with many of his contemporaries as the impulse of Renaissance humanism waned. Hamlet's idealistic conception of man as 'the beauty of the world, the paragon of animals collapsed, into a disgusted acknowledgement that this noble creature was nothing more than the quintessence of dust; a beast destined to rot back into the base matter from which he was raised. This awareness overshadows much of Donne's thinking, but without completely obliterating the sense of man's greatness; as the opening of *Meditation IV* proves. The dualism of man was one of the great commonplaces of Elizabethan thought; and when Donne remarks in *Expostulation III* that he is 'not in heaven because an earthly body clogs me, and not in the earth because a heavenly soul sustains me', he might simply be expressing that commonplace in his own terms. But *Devotions* helps to show how sharply he felt the truth of this familiar idea. In his own single person, and on the limited stage of his sickbed, he enacts the humanist tragedy of the irreconcilably divided state of man, whose boundless aspirations are curtailed by a double susceptibility to disease and sin. Donne's consciousness of the splendid creature which he should and might have been, and the spiritually corrupted being he has become, pervades his account of the illness in which his fallen condition is reflected.

The curious mental associations and twists of thought which characterize Donne's habit of mind show themselves most plainly in the way he develops ideas that are implicit in the heading to each section of the *Devotions*. Some of these provide an obvious theme which he treats intensively, without substituting a related or neighbouring idea to vary the argument. The sixth day, for instance, has the title, 'The physician is afraid'; and *Meditation VI* seizes this theme as though with a sense of the patient's matching agitation:

> I observe the physician with the same diligence as he the disease; I see he fears, and I fear with him; I overtake him, I overrun him in his fear, and I go the faster because he makes his pace slow; I fear the more because he disguises his fear; and I see it with the more sharpness because he would not have me see it.

In the *Expostulation* the theme is not varied, but followed doggedly through a succession of worried questions which Donne himself answers reassuringly, calming the fears which break out afresh as soon as they have been checked. 'But for all this metaphorical bread, victory over enemies that thought to devour us', his doubtful self asks,

> may we not fear that we may lack bread literally? and fear famine, though we fear not enemies? 'Young lions do lack and suffer hunger, but they that seek the Lord shall not want any good thing.* Never? Though it be well with them at one time, may they not fear that it may be worse? 'Wherefore should I fear in the days of evil?' says thy servant David.† Though his own sin had made them evil, he feared them not. No? not if this evil determine in death? Not though in a death: not though in a death inflicted by violence, by malice, by our own desert: fear not the sentence of death, if thou fear God.

As these two extracts suggest, the constant repetition of a single term, used well over a hundred times in the whole section, has the effect of embedding the notion of fear in the reader's mind, and of making him share the sense of alarm felt by Donne's physician. But elsewhere in the *Devotions* the argument turns first upon one theme and then reaches another which replaces it, with an impression of natural development which may have been unplanned. A watchful reader will see this process taking place in the tenth and twelfth sections of the book.

On the tenth day of Donne's sickness his physicians 'find the disease to steal on insensibly, and endeavour to meet with it so'. Taking 'insensibly' as his theme, a term whose modern equivalent would be imperceptibly or unnoticed, Donne opens *Meditation X* with a cosmic observation which does not immediately reveal his purpose: 'This is nature's nest of boxes: the heavens contain the earth, the earth cities, cities men. And all these are concentric: the common centre to them all is decay, ruin'. That purpose comes into view after twenty or so lines of this rumination, when he comments that in each of these three

*Psalm xxxv: 70
†Numbers xiv: 9

spheres 'those are the greatest mischiefs which are least discerned'. The next stage in his argument is developed through references to the two great calamities which the earth must suffer: the Flood, and the apocalyptic fire which will consume it at the Second Coming. Man was forewarned of the Flood, and made preparations for it that saved Noah and his family; but the fire will descend without warning and destroy life completely. Next, Donne compares man's ability to protect himself against the 'pestilent breath' of the dog-star* with his exposure to the baleful influence of comets and blazing stars, which arrive unannounced. 'No almanac tells us when a blazing star will break out', he remarks, 'the matter is carried up in secret; no astrologer tells us when the effects will be accomplished, for that is a secret of a higher sphere than the other; and that which is most secret is most dangerous'. Here the Meditation reaches its stated theme; and having referred to secret activities in the heavens, the first of the concentric 'boxes' mentioned in the opening sentence, Donne can now apply his motif to the two remaining spheres: the body politic and individual man. 'It is so also here in the societies of men, in states and commonwealths', he begins;

> Twenty rebellious drums make not so dangerous a noise as a few whisperers and secret plotters in corners. The cannon doth not so much hurt against a wall as a mine under the wall; not a thousand enemies that threaten so much as a few that take an oath to say nothing.

The individual man in whom his analogy is completed proves to be himself: justifiably since, as he now discloses, his body seems determined to withhold all symptoms which might enable his physicians to diagnose the disease. 'The pulse, the urine, the sweat', he admits, listing three indications of bodily condition which Galenist practitioners consulted,

> all have sworn to say nothing, to give no indication of any dangerous sickness. My forces are not enfeebled, I find no decay in my strength; my provisions are not cut off, I find no abhorring in mine appetite; my counsels are not corrupted nor infatuated, I find no false apprehensions to work upon mine understanding: and yet they see that invisibly, and I feel that insensibly, the disease prevails.

By the end of *Meditation X* the theme of secrecy has been impressed on a commentary which moves in typically unpredictable manner from cosmic decay, the Flood and the final conflagration to comets and astrologers' almanacs, to political conspiracy and military siege, and the secret kingdom which disease has established within Donne's body:

---

*The star Sirius, in the constellation of the Great Dog; supposedly the precursor of great heat, and so of feverish illness.

the whole unlikely train of thought linked together by a central idea. But the *Expostulation* which follows gradually turns away from the theme of the *Meditation* to another motif, at first without rejecting the notion of secrecy. Recalling that St Augustine had wished that Adam had not sinned, Donne approaches God with a wish that the serpent who tempted Eve might still go upright, so that he would more easily be seen. 'He works upon us in secret, and we do not discern him', Donne explains, 'and one great work of his upon us is to make us so like himself as to sin in secret, that others may not see us; but his masterpiece is to make us sin in secret, so that we may not see ourselves sin'. The double theme of secret sins persists weakly to the end of the *Expostulation*, but is progressively overtaken by the simpler idea of sin itself. Remembering the psalmist's petition, 'Cleanse thou me from secret sins', Donne asks,

> Can any sin be secret? For a great part of our sins, though—says thy prophet—we conceive them in the dark, upon our bed, yet, says he, we do them in the light: there are many sins which we glory in doing, and would not do if nobody should know them.

In the Prayer the theme of secrecy is missing, and Donne's recollection of his own sins grows with the awesome rapidity of a tidal wave, threatening to engulf a soul clinging obstinately to belief in divine mercy. 'If I confess to thee the sins of my youth', he asks God,

> wilt thou ask me if I know what those sins were? I know them not so well as to name them all, nor am I sure to live hours enough to name them all—for I did them then faster than I can speak them now, when everything that I did conduced to some sin—but I know them so well as to know that nothing but thy mercy is so infinite as they.

Two days later Donne's physicians decided that the brain was being oppressed by poisonous vapours rising to the head from the stomach, and treated this condition by poulticing the feet with freshly killed pigeons, in the hope of drawing down the harmful gases. *Meditation XII* takes its theme from this purpose, and begins with a dramatic abruptness familiar from several of the love poems, 'What will not kill a man if a vapour will?' The developing argument matches the energy of this initial question, and runs through an association of ideas as bizarre and unexpected as any metaphysical conceit could bring together. 'To die by a bullet is the soldier's daily bread', he continues, 'but few men die by hail-shot'. Evidently Donne means by a hailstone, for what follows enlarges this point:

> If this were a violent shaking of the air by thunder or by cannon, in that case the air is condensed above the thickness of water, of water baked into ice, almost petrified, almost made stone; and no wonder that kills. But that that which is but a vapour, and a vapour not

forced but breathed, should kill; that our nurse should overlay us, and air that nourishes us should destroy us! But that it is a half atheism to murmur against Nature, who is God's immediate commissioner, who would not think himself miserable to be put into the hands of Nature, who does not only set him up for a mark for others to shoot at, but delights herself to blow him up like a glass, till she see him break even with her own breath?

The keyword 'vapour' is varied as air and breath in a half-page of rumination which links together subjects as diverse as elephants, bullets, daily bread, hailstones, thunder, cannon, suffocation, atheism, target practice and glass-blowing. The short opening sentences of the *Meditation* are replaced by much longer rhetorical periods as Donne's imagination quickens and takes fire, breaking out of confinement into bolder comparisons which combine scientific ideas with growing emotional excitement. 'Nay', he goes on, steadying himself for an intellectual leap,

if this infectious vapour were sought for, or travelled to, as Pliny hunted after the vapour of Aetna, and dared and challenged death in the form of a vapour to do his worst, and felt the worst, he died; or if this vapour were met withal in an ambush, and we surprised with it out of a long-shut well, or out of a new-opened mine, who would lament, who would accuse, when we had nothing to accuse, none to lament against but Fortune, who is less than a vapour? But when ourselves are the well that breathes out this exhalation, the oven that spits out this fiery smoke, the mine that spews out this suffocating and strangling damp, who can ever after this aggravate his sorrow by this circumstance; that it was his neighbour, his familiar friend, his brother that destroyed him; and destroyed him with a whispering and calumniating breath, when we do it to ourselves by the same means, kill ourselves with our own vapours?

With this rapid widening of the scope of the meditation, the theme too is extended to include volcanic gases, exhalations, fiery smoke and the poisonous damp given off in mines. The ideas which Donne's argument gathers together are heterogeneous enough, but their yoking is not violent, as this passage shows. His mind is in a state of excited activity, and snatching up ideas not upon any rational principle but as imagination recognizes occult similarities. Donne's violence, if the term is to be admitted, is seen not in any forced marriage of intellectual concepts but in the passionate eagerness of an argument which allows no room for protest or disagreement. The reader of *Devotions* is being treated in much the same way as the mistresses of the love poems, who are overwhelmed by an irresistible power of persuasion.

The thought that men may kill themselves with their own vapours leads Donne to the paradox that he may unintentionally become 'mine own executioner'; and then to a typically Elizabethan comparison of the individual with the body politic. 'That which is fume in us', he comments, 'is in a state, rumour; and these vapours in us which we consider here pestilent and infectious fumes are, in a state, infectious rumours, detracting and dishonourable calumnies, libels'. Just as the vapours most dangerous to personal health arise from our own bodies, he argues, as do the rumours most harmful to the state originate there.

> What ill air that I could have met in the street, what channel,* what shambles, what dunghill, what vault, could have hurt me so much as these homebred vapours? What fugitive, what almsman of any foreign state, can do so much harm as a detractor, a libeller, a scornful jester at home?

This demonstration that the state too may do execution upon itself through one of its rebellious members completes Donne's analogy, and brings *Meditation XII* to its final sentence. As these extracts indicate, a simple idea has been analysed and exploited with the thoroughness of a compulsive purpose which refuses to abandon its search until every conceivable potentiality of the theme has been explored. In the closing words of the *Meditation*, as though signalling his readiness to accept another motif, Donne introduces a second term from the heading to the section. Libellous and licentious jesters, he admits, will speak what venom they can, but 'sometimes virtue, and always power, be a good pigeon to draw this vapour from the head, and from doing any deadly harm there'.

Expostulation XII begins with this new theme in hand, though at first it continues to employ the previous one. Vapour is now recognized as 'the hieroglyphic' both of God's blessings and of his judgments, one expressed in the vapour which went up from the earth at the Creation, the other in the thick cloud of incense which God received from sacrifices. The second of these biblical references may have prompted Donne to vary the term a little later. 'Now all smokes begin in fire', he argues, 'and all these will end so too: the smoke of sin and of thy wrath will end in the fire of hell. But hast thou afforded us no means to evaporate these smokes, to withdraw these vapours'? The simple theological answer to this question can only be a reference to Christ's redemption of man, but Donne cannot offer any such direct reply. He prefers an involved answer, which although reaching the same terminus moves circuitously, and by means of allusions to ascending and descending whose figurative purpose is only gradually revealed. 'When thine angels fell from heaven', he begins, 'thou tookest into thy care the reparation of that place, and didst it by assuming, by drawing, us thither'; and then balances this comment against another shaped to the same design: "When we fell from thee here, in this world, thou

*gutter

tookest into thy care the reparation of this place too, and didst it by assuming us another way; by descending down to assume our nature in thy Son'.

By repeating the notion of rising and falling he has established a basis of argument, and can move from premise to inference, still using the figure he has constructed: 'So that though our last act be an ascending to glory—we shall ascend to the place of angels—yet our first act is to go the way of thy Son, descending; and the way of thy blessed Spirit, too, who descended in the dove'.

The allusion to Christ's baptism enables Donne to associate the spiritual dove with the pigeons which his physicians have applied to his feet; and now the significance of his references to ascending and descending is revealed. 'Therefore hast thou been pleased to afford us this remedy in nature', he concludes his demonstration,

> by this application of a dove to our lower parts, to make these vapours in our bodies to descend; and to make that a type* to us, that by the visitation of thy Spirit, the vapours of sin shall descend, and we tread them under our feet. At the baptism of thy Son the dove descended; and at the exalting of thine apostles to preach, the same spirit descended. Let us draw down the vapours of our own pride, our own wits, our own wills, our own inventions, to the simplicity of thy sacraments and the obedience of thy word; and these doves, thus applied, shall make us live.

The intricacy of Donne's thought in these two sections of his book provide all the proof we need that his metaphysical style is not contrived or assumed, but a natural if highly idiosyncratic mode of expression for an intensely active mind. Writing reflects not only the contents of the mind—the stored-up pieces of information and experience which constitute knowledge—but the form of the writer's consciousness: the way he assembles what he knows into a meaningful design, or imposes intelligible order upon experience. Seen from this point of view, the twenty-three sections of the *Devotions* and their three-part divisions represent a means of organizing Donne's incessant mental activity—a process which rummages tirelessly and purposefully through the contents of his mind—into a significant pattern.

But we may ask whether the deeper significance of the *Devotions* does not lie in the triumphant organization of ideas within the individual sections of the book, rather than in its detailed account of twenty-three days of illness. Unlike most of us, who are capable of dealing only with one idea at a time, Donne seems in moments of mixed intellectual and imaginative excitement to have apprehended ideas in family groups; seeing not just one central idea but a constellation of related concepts.

*symbol, emblem

Reader and critics who find these relationships strained and improbable are not perhaps allowing for the particularity of a mind strikingly unlike their own, which habitually disregards intellectual categories in its hectic search for similitude. The discovery of hidden likenesses or kinship, the pigeons at the sick man's feet, the descending dove of the Spirit, does not constitute an end in itself. Donne's major task is to demonstrate that the oddly assorted ideas enclosed by his metaphysical conceits are indeed related, and together comprise wholes. Whether the demonstration convinces his readers, who are invited to recognize a connection between Noah's Flood and the rising of the dog-star, is not immediately to the point. A writer's primary need is to give shape to his own imaginative awareness, by whatever means seems to him truest to that inner experience. The individual reader must then decide whether his work holds sufficient interest to justify the task of learning the private language—in Donne's case, the tortuously involved style, the constant mixing of religious, scientific and domestic ideas, the outlandish analogies—in which the work is written.

As suggested above, Donne seems to write not just to convey ideas but to represent the experience of intellectual apprehension, the finding of ideas and the exploring of their interconnections, together with the emotional excitement which accompanies this process. Partly in consequence of this excited pulse, partly because he continues to attack and worry particular notions until he has squeezed them dry, his writing gives the impression of being compulsive: an activity forced on him by an inward need which demands to be satisfied. Perhaps understandably, the *Devotions* is a deeply agitated work. As the record of an acutely sensitive man's approach to death by an unidentified disease, whose course is as obscure as its origins, the book could only reflect a certain fearfulness. The fact that several of the *Expostulations* show Donne arguing with his fear, assuming in one voice a spiritual confidence which his other self does not feel, emphasizes his nervous anxiety. But Donne's agitation is not contained by a fear of death. Many passages of his book show him writing in self-tortured awareness of the corrupted moral nature which his sickness symbolizes. 'The root and fuel of my sickness', he tells God in *Expostulation XXII*,

> is my sin, my actual sin; but even that sin hath another root, another fuel, original sin; and can I divest that? Wilt thou bid me to separate the leaven that a lump of dough hath received, or the salt that the water hath contracted from the sea?

He recoils from sin in disgust, yet knows that the weakness of man's moral nature condemns him against his will to live enslaved by what he hates. 'So long as I remain in this great hospital, the sick, this diseaseful world', he writes in *Expostulation XI*, 'so long as I remain in this leprous house, this flesh of mine, this heart—though thus prepared for thee, prepared by thee—will still be subject to the invasion of malign and pestilent vapours'. This revulsion from the body, diseased from its conception and repeatedly infected by sin, leads him a *Prayer XVIII* to describe himself as already dead; 'dead in an irremediable, in an irrecoverable state for bodily health'; a creature dead even in its birth.

Donne's morbid obsession with death may have grown out of the conviction that his destined life, and the fulfilment it promised, had been destroyed in the reversal which followed his marriage; and that the being who survived this death-blow to ambitious hopes was, as the letter to Wotton suggests, an unburied corpse. But that prolonged frustration did not change the intellectual habit already established in the early poems, where the same compulsive searching for relationships, the same eagerness to prove union or sympathy between things widely dissimilar in kind dominates his writing. This, and not fear of death, is the compelling force behind the *Devotions*: a need to secure himself against personal chaos by holding together as many of the elements of his consciousness as could be persuaded to unite. When T. S. Eliot remarked that in the mind of the poet fragments of experience as disparate as reading Spinoza and the smell of cooking 'are always forming new wholes', he was identifying one of the persistent motives of imaginative creation: the urge to remake reality in a form more agreeable to the artist. Although the literary model which Donne hammers together may contain too many joints to seem structurally sound, evidently it answered his private purposes by representing the unified and connected state of things which gave him assurance.

Although Donne's thinking and expression must attract more notice than the form of his work, his *Devotions* deserves special scrutiny as the most carefully structured of all his prose writings. As the twenty-three sections of the book carry the reader through the successive phases of Donne's sickness, the three parts of each section treat a relevant motif in three different modes, so that each motif is developed both conceptually and dramatically, or by different voices. But Donne's illness is not held firmly in view throughout the book. From the thirteenth day, when the patient breaks out in spots, until his physicians see signs of recovery on the nineteenth, the disease is evidently in its critical phase; but for the three days immediately preceding the improvement in Donne's condition we lose sight of him. *Devotions XVI, XVII* and *XVIII* take their theme from the tolling of a bell in an adjoining church, which makes Donne reflect upon the condition of a man worse afflicted than himself. 'Perchance he for whom this bell tolls', he begins *Meditation XVII*, 'may be so ill as that he knows not it tolls for him; and perchance I may think myself so much better than I am as that they who are about me, and see my state, may have caused it to toll for me; and I know not that.'

During the crucial phase of his own sickness, Donne transfers a large part of his attention from himself to this unknown companion in misfortune, feeling a kinship with him which deepens when the other succumbs. On the eighteenth day 'the bell rings out, and tells me in him that I am dead'; and despite Donne's ignorance of the circumstances he is strongly drawn to associate himself with this dead counterpart of himself. 'I was not there in his sickness, nor at his death', he admits,

> I saw not his way nor his end, nor can ask them who did thereby to
> conclude or argue whither he is gone: I know not. But yet I have one
> nearer me than all these, mine own charity: I ask that, and that tells
> me he is gone to everlasting rest and joy and glory.

It would be hard not to sense some special significance in the fact that Donne's recovery begins at this point. Another sick man, known to him only through the tolling of the bell, has died at the point where Donne himself might have yielded to his disease; and helped by Donne's prayers for his salvation, has reached the end which Donne himself hopes to attain. 'Lay hold upon his soul, O God', he asks in *Prayer XVIII*, 'till that soul have thoroughly considered his account';

> and how few minutes soever it have to remain in that body, let the
> power of thy Spirit recompense the shortness of time, and perfect his
> account before he pass away; present his sins so to him as that he
> may know what thou forgivest, and not doubt of thy
> forgiveness;...breathe inward comforts to his heart, and afford him
> the power of giving such outward testimonies thereof, as all that are
> about him may derive comforts from thence, and have this
> edification: that though the body be going the way of all flesh, yet
> the soul is going the way of all saints.

Donne would probably have been incapable of speaking such comforting and assuring words to himself, for the oppression of his own sin was too great to encourage any easy hope of salvation; but as priest he can pray for this unknown parishioner with a strong certainty that God will forgive and accept him. In performing this priestly task Donne seems to have brought himself spiritual comfort, and a measure of psychological release which helped or perhaps inititated the process of recovery. How this should have come about may be suggested by a comment in *Meditation XVI*, where Donne first acknowledges his relationship with those whose funerals take place during his sickness!

> There is a way of correcting the children of great persons, that other
> children are corrected in their behalf and in their names; and this
> works upon them who indeed had more deserved it. And when these
> bells tell me that now one and now another is buried, must not I

acknowledge that they have the correction due to me, and paid the debt that I owe?

The sentence of death, which here he describes as a form of correction, falls not on him but on a substitute or scapegoat; a person unseen and unknown, with whom Donne associates himself. Some of the force of his insistence that the reader should 'never send to know for whom the bell tolls; it tolls for thee', comes from his need to feel that his own confrontation with death is postponed by the passing of such a counterpart whose identity he shares. Knowing that another, in his words, has 'paid the debt that I owe', he experiences a sense of relief great enough to reverse the tide of depression which threatens to overwhelm him, and the crisis passes.

From the little Donne tells us about the disease which almost ended his life in 1623 it seems impossible to determine what he was suffering from. Evidently his physicians were baffled and unable to form a diagnosis; understandably, if as Donne asserts in the passage quoted earlier, his body continued to function as though nothing were wrong, keeping its distress a secret. The onset of the sickness was dramatically swift. 'In the same instant that I feel the first attempt* of the disease, I feel the victory', Donne tells us,

> in the twinkling of an eye I can scarce see; instantly the taste is insipid and fatuous;† instantly the appetite is dull and desireless; instantly the knees are sinking and strengthless;‡ and in an instant sleep—which is the picture, the copy of death—is taken away, that the original, death itself, may succeed; and that so I might have death to the life.

These are not recognizable symptoms of any specific physical complaint, but of a listless and defeated state of mind, and if we are to take Donne's comments seriously we might reasonably assume that he is describing the onset of an attack of depression severe enough to incapacitate him for three weeks. That would of course explain why his physicians —using the admittedly crude means at their disposal —can find nothing wrong with him; and why in their puzzlement they turn to an explanation of the sickness which may have some truth in it. 'They tell me it is my melancholy', Donne comments in a disgruntled passage of *Meditation XII*;

> Did I infuse, did I drink in melancholy into myself? It is my thoughtfulness: was I not made to think? It is my study: doth not my calling call for that? I have done nothing wilfully, perversely toward it, yet must suffer in it, die by it.

*assault
†tasteless
‡The symptoms described here are incompatible with the unchanged physical state which mystifies Donne's doctors in *Meditation X*.

Yet in the next sentence he reverts to an idea of men acting as their own executioners, which in a variety of forms recurs several times in the course of the book, as though realizing that he is not suffering from an infection from outside, but from a sickness self-inflicted. Of the possible causes of depression mentioned in the *Devotions* the likeliest is also the most recurrent; the crushing sense of guilt derived from an obviously exaggerated sense of personal sinfulness. 'Look therefore upon me, O Lord, in this distress', he begs in *Prayer IX*,

> and that will recall me from the borders of this bodily death; look upon me, and that will raise me again from that spiritual death in which my parents buried me when they begot me in sin, and in which I have pierced even to the jaws of hell by multiplying such heaps of actual sins upon that foundation, that root of original sin.

We need to remember that unless the *Devotions* was written during the period of Donne's illness, which is improbable, the book does not represent his thinking at that time: indeed, a victim of severe depression may be incapable of logical or purposeful thought. What may have been written after his recovery does not necessarily tell us what preoccupied his mind during those three weeks, when the tense dialectic that characterizes him may have collapsed into intellectual numbness and confusion. It is not impossible that the shock of Donne's great misfortune, when marriage swept away his secular ambitions forever, made him susceptible to attacks of depression which continued with increasing severity throughout his life; and that his neurotic obsession with his own diseased state—his corrupted soul, his dying body, and his unpardonably sinful record—embodies his attempt to rationalize the profoundly negative feelings, the sense of empty nothingness, which he suffered during such black periods. To say that this is not impossible does not imply that the hypothesis must be true, but a modern reader of the *Devotions*, uncomprehending of its pessimistic theology but better able to understand depression than Donne, may find the book easier to grasp if he reads it in this sense. As an autobiographical record of a dangerous illness and the spiritual reflections which occurred at each stage of the disease, the work explains itself. As an attempt to impose order and meaning retrospectively on a prolonged and debilitating attack of depression, by knitting together the dissociated fragments of Donne's private world, its significance is more obscure; but its interest justifies the task of puzzling it out.

Part Three
Reference Section

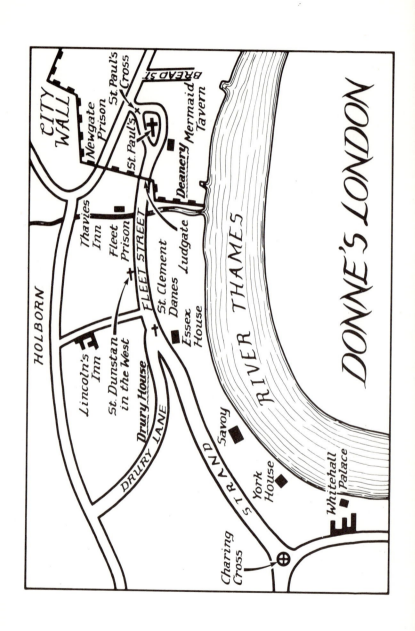

DONNE'S LONDON

Short Biographies

BACON, FRANCIS, BARON VERULAM, 1561–1626. Educated at Cambridge and Gray's Inn. Between 1607 and 1618 he was appointed successively solicitor-general, attorney-general and lord chancellor. In 1621 he was found guilty of bribery and deprived of office. He published his *Essays* in 1597, with an augmented edition in 1625; but the writing for which he is chiefly remembered consists of scientific and philosophical works in English and Latin, notably *The Advancement of Learning* 1605 and the *Novum Organum* 1620. These gave considerable impetus to the interests which led to a new scientific outlook later in the century.

BEDFORD, LUCY COUNTESS OF. Date of birth uncertain: she married Edward Russell, third earl of Bedford, in 1594, and died in 1627. She was Donne's friend and patroness from 1608 until her death. Many of his letters and at least eight of his poems are addressed to her. *A Nocturnal upon St Lucy's Day* may allude to her, and she is more certainly the woman to whom *Twickenham Garden* refers. Ben Jonson and Drayton were among those who addressed complimentary poems to her.

BROOKE, CHRISTOPHER, *c.* 1575–1627. As a young man he studied at Lincoln's Inn, where he shared a chamber with Donne, who addressed *The Storm* to him. Together with his brother Samuel, who acted as priest at Donne's wedding, he was imprisoned for his part in the ceremony. He became a bencher of his Inn, but kept up his connection with the literary world: he published elegies, an eclogue and a work called *The Ghost of Richard III*.

BROWNE, SIR THOMAS, 1605–82. Practised as a physician at Norwich after studying at Oxford and several continental universities. His *Religio Medici* was written in 1635 and published in 1643: *Vulgar Errors* appeared in 1646 and *Urn Burial* in 1658. He was knighted during a royal visit to Norwich in 1671.

CAREW, THOMAS, *c.* 1598–1639. Educated at Oxford, was secretary to the ambassador at Venice and then appointed to an office at Court by Charles I. One of the 'tribe of Ben' who wrote a masque and many songs and lyrics, published in 1640. His name is pronounced 'carey'.

CLEVELAND, JOHN, 1613–58. A Leicestershire man educated at Cambridge, where he attracted the attention of Charles I by his speech during a royal visit. A vehement royalist, he was ejected from his college fellowship by parliamentary visitors and joined the king's forces at Oxford. His political satires made a great impression, in particular his scathing attack on the Scots. His non-satirical writing includes an elegy on Milton's friend Edward King.

DANVERS, SIR JOHN, *c*. 1588–1655. The second husband of Magdalen Herbert, whom he married in 1608 when she was more than twice his age. Donne lived at their house in Chelsea in 1625 during a time of plague in London. In that year Danvers was elected M.P. for Oxford, and continued to sit in Parliament until the civil war. He sided with the parliamentary party, and became sufficiently prominent to be one of the signatories to Charles I's death-warrant.

DENHAM, SIR JOHN, 1615–69. Born in Dublin and educated at Oxford: a royalist who was compelled to surrender Farnham Castle to the parliamentary forces in 1642. In the same year he published *Cooper's Hill*, a topographical poem containing an address to the Thames whose terms were adopted as the critical standard of urbane writing later in the seventeenth century.

DRUMMOND OF HAWTHORNDEN, WILLIAM, 1585–1649. Born near Edinburgh, where he was educated. He was a friend of Drayton and an acquaintance of Ben Jonson, who visited him in 1619. He recorded Jonson's remarks about literature and contemporary poets; these *Conversations* hold more interest today than Drummond's original writing, which included poems and a history of Scotland.

DRURY, SIR ROBERT, 1577–1615. Educated at Cambridge for a time, then became a soldier and was knighted in the field at seventeen. He was again fighting in the Low Countries in 1597, and later served in Ireland. His hopes of a diplomatic career did not materialize, possibly because his hot temper stood against him. After the death of his daughter Elizabeth in December 1610 at their home at Hawstead in Suffolk he became friend and patron to Donne, who accompanied him on a journey abroad in 1611–12 and lived at his invitation in Drury House, Drury Lane, London, until his ordination.

EGERTON, SIR THOMAS, *c*. 1540–1617. After studying at Lincoln's Inn he rapidly acquired fame as a lawyer. In 1581 he was appointed solicitor-general, and in 1592 attorney-general. Francis Bacon, whom he was to succeed as lord chancellor, acknowledged his 'fatherly care' of young barristers. Egerton become lord keeper in 1596. A close friend of Essex, he was one of the officers of state locked up in Essex's house during the abortive uprising of 1601, and he took a prominent part in the trial which followed.

GOODYER, SIR HENRY, 1571–1628. One of Donne's closest friends, to whom he wrote very frequently. One of the *Letters to Several Personages* is addressed to him from Mitcham. Goodyer was elected M.P.

Tomb of Lady Magdalen Herbert in Montgomery church, Powys

for a Cornish constituency in 1603, and was knighted in the same year after being made one of the gentlemen of the king's privy chamber. He seems to have lived extravagantly after this, and to have run into difficulties which Donne eased by a gift of money.

HARVEY, WILLIAM, 1578–1657. Educated at Canterbury and Cambridge. He first revealed his discovery of the circulation of the blood in a lecture to the College of Physicians in 1616, but did not publish his treatise until 1628. As physician to Charles I, he was present with him at the battle of Edgehill in 1642.

HERBERT, GEORGE, 1593–1633. After his education at Westminster and Cambridge he followed the court, and was appointed public orator of his university. A few years before his death he withdrew from courtly life and entered the priesthood, living very simply as rector of Bemerton in Wiltshire, where he died. His religious poems were published in 1633 as *The Temple*. His elder brother Edward (HERBERT OF CHERBURY 1583–1648), distinguished himself as philosopher, historian, poet and diplomat. Their mother, Magdalen Herbert, was widowed in 1597 and in 1608 married Sir John Danvers. Donne's correspondence with her, and presumably his first acquaintance, dates from 1607. She died in 1627 and Donne preached a funeral sermon in Chelsea Old Church over her.

HEYWOOD, JOHN, C. 1497–1580. Donne's grandfather on his mother's side. At first a chorister and court musician, he was later a writer of interludes and entertainments, which included the comedy *The Four Ps*. He was a favourite of Mary I, who enjoyed his wit. At the accession of the protestant Elizabeth he went into exile. At least five editions of his *Epigrams* were published in the early years of her reign.

JONES, INIGO, 1573–1652. Architect who introduced classical style into England. He was responsible for several important London buildings, notably the Banqueting House in Whitehall and the Queen's House at Greenwich. He also designed costumes, decor and machines for court masques by Jonson, Heywood, D'Avenant and others.

JONSON, BEN, 1572–1637. Educated at Westminster, then followed his stepfather's trade as bricklayer and saw military service in Flanders. In 1597 he joined Shakespeare's company as an actor. His *Everyman in his Humour* was performed a year later. The first of his many masques was presented at court in 1605, with scenery by Inigo Jones. James I granted him a pension in 1616 after his major comedies *The Alchemist, Volpone* and *Bartholomew Fair* had been written and staged. A friend of Shakespeare, Bacon, Donne, Chapman and many other writers. His critical opinions, published in 1641 as *Discoveries*,

The chapel at Lincoln's Inn.

were taken up by the 'tribe' of young poets now called Cavaliers, and influenced the development of a lucid and impersonal poetic style.

KER, SIR ROBERT, 1578–1654. A courtier who accompanied James I to England in 1603. He was made personal attendant to Prince Henry, and under Charles I master of the privy purse. In 1639 he was awarded a pension of £2000 and given the title of Earl of Ancrum; but the civil war reduced him to poverty and he fled to Holland, where he died in debt. Donne gave him a copy of his *Biathanatos* and an MS collection of his poems before going to Germany in 1619, and wrote many letters to him.

KING, HENRY, 1592–1669. Educated at Westminster and Oxford. He took orders, and after being a prebendary of St. Paul's during Donne's years as dean, became bishop of Chichester. A personal friend of Donne, whose will he executed, and of Jonson and Walton. He wrote and published poems, of which the verses addressed to his dead wife are the most famous.

LOVELACE, RICHARD, 1618–58. Educated at Charterhouse and Oxford: a wealthy and handsome courtier who fought for the king after being imprisoned by parliament in 1642, when he presented the so-called Kentish petition. He was imprisoned again in 1648, and spent the time preparing his *Lucasta*—a collection of lyrics, songs and odes—for publication in 1649. He seems to have died in want.

LYLY, JOHN, *c.* 1554–1606. One of the 'university wits' of the English renaissance. After studying at Oxford he published the first part of *Euphues* in 1578, a prose tale whose preposterously mannered style impelled the literary fashion of 'euphuism'. Subsequently he wrote a series of urbanely witty comedies which were privately staged by boy actors; notably *Compasbe, Endymion* and *Mother Bombie*.

MARVELL, ANDREW, 1621–78. Educated at Hull and Cambridge. After spending four years on the continent, partly at Rome, in 1651 he became tutor to the daughter of Lord Fairfax, at whose country house near York he probably wrote his poems praising country life and retirement. These were not published until 1681. After the Restoration he was M.P. for Hull and a political satirist.

MORE, GEORGE, 1553–1632. Father of Ann More, Donne's wife. After studying at Oxford and the Inner Temple, he was elected M.P. for Guildford and knighted in 1597. A year later he became sheriff of Surrey and Sussex. James I appointed him a chamberlain and treasurer to Prince Henry; and in 1615 he became lieutenant of the Tower of London.

MORTON, THOMAS, 1564–1659. Educated at York, where he was at school with Guy Fawkes, and Cambridge. He took orders in 1592, and proceeded D.D. in 1606. From being a university lecturer in logic, he rose to be a chaplain to James I, dean of Winchester, and bishop successively of Chester, Lichfield and Durham. He published over twenty works, some in Latin, showing the fallaciousness of Catholic doctrine, always in temperate terms.

SIDNEY family. Chiefly remembered for Sir Philip Sidney, 1554–86, courtier, soldier and poet, whose *Arcadia*, *Apology for Poetry* and *Astrophel and Stella* characterize the spirit of the English renaissance. The family estate at Penshurst, which passed into other hands at the marriage of Sir Philip's niece, was the subject of two complimentary poems by Jonson.

VAUGHAN, HENRY, 1622–95. Educated at Oxford and London, where he studied law. After the civil war, in which he fought as a royalist, he practised as a physician at Brecknock. His best work as a poet was published in 1650 and 1655 as *Silex Scintillans* (sparkling flint); contemplative and half-mystical pieces rather than directly religious in the manner of Donne and Herbert.

WALTON, IZAAK, 1593–1683. London ironmonger, the friend of Donne, Henry King and Sir Henry Wotton. He is chiefly remembered for his *Compleat Angler*, 1653, and for the biographies of Donne, Herbert, Hooker and Wotton which were published together in 1670.

WEBSTER, JOHN, *c.* 1580–1625. The son of a London tailor who turned to the stage, and became one of the outstanding Jacobean dramatists. His first plays were comedies, but in *The White Devil* and *The Duchess of Malfi* he proved his power as a writer of sombre tragedy which mirrored the pessimism of his age.

Places to visit

London

Because of the Great Fire there is very little left of the London that Donne knew, for even St Paul's Cathedral was destroyed at that time. As the London map on page 182 shows, we can visit the modern transformations of a number of older places.

Lincoln's Inn, where Donne was in turn student, preacher and religious director, shows least alteration, and of the Whitehall he knew the Banqueting House remains as it was in the days of King James and his son.

Most impressive and appropriate is the one reminder of the Dean: the effigy still standing in Wren's St Paul's executed by the sculptor Nicholas Stone, who used the shrouded picture as on page 44 and supplemented that famous sketch with his personal knowledge of his subject. In Chelsea Old Church is to be found a smaller copy of it, also by Stone, in memory of Donne's association with the neighbourhood and the church from 1625.

Mitcham, Surrey

Originally a separate community in Surrey but now part of Greater London. Here Donne lived for years in a cottage which remained in Whitford Lane until the 1840s. Other parts of Surrey associated with Donne's life are to be found on the map on page 27.

Blunham, Bedfordshire

The church still uses a silver-gilt chalice and inscribed stand that Donne presented.

Montgomery, Powys

Montgomery Castle was the home of Magdalen Herbert and her sons, Edward and George, all well known to Donne. He wrote *The Primrose* there and it was while travelling from Polesworth, Warwickshire, to visit the Herbert family that he wrote his poem, *Good Friday 1613: Travelling Westward*.

Select bibliography

Biography

IZAAK WALTON, *Life of Donne*, 1640. Available in World's Classics, Oxford University Press, 1927

R. C. BALD, *John Donne: A Life*, Oxford University Press, 1970

Editions of Donne's work

Complete English Poems, ed. A. J. Smith, Penguin, 1971

Elegies and Songs and Sonets, ed. Helen Gardner, Oxford University Press, 1965

The Epithalamions, Anniversaries, and Epicedes, ed. W. Milgate, Oxford University Press, 1978

The Divine Poems, ed. Helen Gardner, Oxford University Press, 1953; second edition 1979

Songs and Sonets, ed. Theodore Redpath, Methuen, 1956

Satires, Epigrams and Verse Letters, ed. W. Milgate, Oxford University Press, 1967

Critical studies

BENNETT, JOAN, *Five Metaphysical Poets*, Cambridge University Press, 1964

GRANSDEN, K. W., *John Donne*, Longman, 1954

GRANT, P., *The Transformation of Sin*, McGill-Queen's University Press, Montreal, 1974

MARTZ, L., *Poetry of Meditation*, Yale University Press, 1954, revised 1962

LEISHMAN, J. B., *Donne: the Monarch of Wit*, Hutchinson University Library, fifth edition 1962

ROSTON, M., *The Soul of Wit*, Oxford University Press, 1974

SIMPSON, E. M., *A Study of the Prose Works of Donne*, Oxford University Press, 1924, revised 1948

SMITH, A. J., *John Donne: The Critical Heritage*, Routledge and Kegan Paul, 1975

SPENCER, T., and others, *A Garland for John Donne*, New York, 1932

STEIN, A., *John Donne's Lyrics*, Minnesota University Press, 1962

TUVE, ROSAMUND, *Elizabethan and Metaphysical Imagery*, Chicago University Press, 1947; Phoenix edition 1961

Anthologies

Metaphysical Lyrics and Poems, ed. H. J. C. Grierson, Oxford University Press, 1921

The Metaphysical Poets, ed. Helen Gardner, Penguin Poets, 1957

Dr Johnson's essay on metaphysical poetry appears under 'Abraham Cowley' in *Lives of the English Poets*, 1779–81, reprinted in Everyman's Library. The essay by T. S. Eliot is included in the *Collected Essays*, Faber and Faber, 1931

Index